BIBLICAL THEOLOGY

of the

NEW TESTAMENT

BIBLICAL THEOLOGY
of the
NEW TESTAMENT

By

CHARLES CALDWELL RYRIE,
Th.D., Ph.D.

MOODY PRESS
CHICAGO

Copyright ©, 1959, by
THE MOODY BIBLE INSTITUTE
OF CHICAGO

Library of Congress Catalogue Card Number 59-11468

ISBN: 0-8024-0712-9

Moody Paperback Edition, 1982

13 14 15 16 17 Printing/BB/Year 87 86 85 84 83

Printed in the United States of America

*In commemoration of ten years of teaching
this book is gratefully dedicated to
all my students
and particularly to that special group
who have contributed in various ways
to my own life and thinking
and ministry.*

Preface

THIS IS A BOOK which grew out of the necessity of preparing lectures in Biblical Theology. As they were developed the distinctive benefit of the Biblical Theology approach to the study of the Scriptures became more apparent. Then came the suggestion to write for publication. This has now been done with great personal profit to the author and with the prayer that the effort may prove of great benefit to others.

In a work of this sort one is indebted to many people. Some of this debt is acknowledged in the references in the text to the work of others. Dr. Howard F. Vos, textbook editor of Moody Press, gave many helpful suggestions along the way. The assistance of Mr. Henry A. Way, Jr., in typing the manuscript, proofreading, and preparing the indexes has been invaluable.

This is a book to be used with a Bible always and with commentaries frequently. It should assist any reader to have a new appreciation of the authors, circumstances, and writings of the New Testament, and in our day when we so desperately need more doctrinal preaching, Biblical Theology can be used to meet that need. May our Lord Himself, without whom we can do nothing, prosper this work for His own glory.

CHARLES C. RYRIE

Contents

Part V
THE THEOLOGY OF HEBREWS

Part VI
THE THEOLOGY OF PETER AND JUDE

Part VII
THE THEOLOGY OF JOHN

Introduction

WHAT IS BIBLICAL THEOLOGY?

THE APPROACH OF BIBLICAL THEOLOGY to the Scriptures is unique. Biblical Theology is not Systematic Theology nor exegesis, nor is it merely a different arranging of the same material. Rather it is a combination which is partly historical, partly exegetical, partly critical, partly theological, and thereby totally distinctive. Biblical Theology is concerned with the reason why something was written as well as with the content of what was written. It not only examines the product but investigates the procedures and presuppositions that went into the writing of the Scriptures.

It is a rewarding study. The Word of God is seen in the manner in which it was revealed—progressively. The whole is traced in the way God gave the Bible—part by part. The perspective is that of the historical setting in which the truth came. The theology of the Bible emerges out of the thought of the writers as seen in their writings; it is never superimposed on those writings. Indeed, the approach of Biblical Theology furnishes the best way to preach and teach doctrine to people; for through it they will realize that theology is a part of the very fabric of the Bible itself and not something that has been forced upon it or read into it. The reward of studying the progress of revelation part by part will be to see the Scriptures in a detailed naturalness of beauty which Biblical Theology alone can bring out.

11

The term *Biblical Theology*, then, must have a very specific meaning since it stands for such a distinctive method of Bible study. However, the term is not always so understood, for it can also be used in a general way. It could indicate any theology that is based on the Bible. Yet, if what has been said above is true, it must have a more particular meaning than that. Thus our first task is to formulate an exact definition and clearly to understand the concepts involved in that definition of Biblical Theology.

I. THE DEFINITION OF BIBLICAL THEOLOGY

Biblical Theology is that branch of theological science which deals systematically with the historically conditioned progress of the self-revelation of God as deposited in the Bible. Biblical Theology is not always defined thus, nor has it always been applied to the same branch of theological science. In Pietistic circles it denoted a more popular (as opposed to scholastic or ecclesiastical) presentation of the doctrines of Christianity. By others the term is taken to mean the early creed of apostolic Christianity in contrast to the later development of doctrine in the history of the Church.[1] More recently with the rise of evangelical Bible schools, Biblical Theology has come to stand for any theology which claims to be based solely on the Bible. In other words, this popular notion makes Biblical Theology that which emphasizes the revelational nature of Christianity while minimizing or ignoring rational or philosophical aspects. Though such a theology may be Biblical, it is not necessarily Biblical Theology.

If Biblical Theology is that branch of theological science which deals systematically with the historically conditioned progress of revelation as deposited in the Bible, it has four major characteristics. First, the results of its investigations must be presented in a systematic form. In this Biblical

[1] Cf. H. Schultz, *Old Testament Theology* (Edinburgh: T. & T. Clark, 1895), I, 1.

Theology is like any other branch of theological science. However, to say that Biblical Theology must be systematized is not to identify it with Systematic Theology, but it is to say that whatever it is, it is not formulated in an unsystematic manner. This first characteristic, though a necessary one, is not a distinguishing one.

The second feature of Biblical Theology does distinguish it from other Biblical studies. Biblical Theology pays careful attention to the fact that revelation was embodied in history. It is not, however, merely a historical science nor are its investigations only of historical circumstances.[2] Neither is this historical emphasis, major as it is in Biblical Theology, a minimizing of the fact that although revelation may have been conditioned by historical circumstances, it is given in words (cf. I Cor. 2:13). Nevertheless, investigation into the lives of the various writers of Scripture, into the circumstances which compelled them to write, and into the historic situation of the recipients of their letters will aid immeasurably our understanding of the doctrine revealed in the words they wrote. This study of the historic conditioning of doctrine is a major emphasis of Biblical Theology.

The third feature of Biblical Theology is also a distinguishing one, for it concerns the progressiveness of revelation. Biblical Theology investigates the progress of doctrine not only as it was revealed by various writers of the Bible but also in its different stages of development. It is obvious but too little recognized that what we now call the completed revelation of the Bible was not given all at once. Neither was it given uniformly, for God chose to give differing amounts to different men in various periods of human history. Revelation was not completed in one act but was unfolded in a long series of successive acts and through the minds and hands of many men of varying backgrounds. This characteristic of Biblical Theology of presenting the progress of doc-

[2] As R. F. Weidner, *Biblical Theology of the New Testament* (New York: Revell, 1891), I, 13.

trine represents, so to speak, a theistic view of revelation as contrasted with a deistic view; for it recognizes the fact that God's work of revelation was not completed all at once and then left to run its own course. Biblical Theology, then, is a very profitable method of studying the Word of God, for it views the text in the same way in which it was written. Years ago Bernard in his most valuable work, *The Progress of Doctrine in the New Testament,* emphasized the importance of this approach of Biblical Theology to the Scriptures. He said:

> Into all our parishes and all our missions the thousands of evangelists, pastors, and teachers are sent forth with the Bible placed in their hands, and with solemn charges to draw from its pages the Gospel which they preach. But when those pages are opened, they present, not the exposition of a revelation completed, but the records of a revelation in progress. Its parts and features are seen, not as arranged after their development, but as arranging themselves in the course of their development, and growing, through stages which can be marked, and by accessions which can be measured, into the perfect form which they attain at last.[3]

The last characteristic of Biblical Theology is that its source of doctrine is the Bible. This is not to rule out the use of historical facts which may come from other sources, but it is to affirm that the doctrine to be systematized is found in the words of the Bible. Not all writers on this subject accept the verbal, plenary inspiration of the Scriptures as well as their authority, as does the author of this book, but all do recognize that Biblical Theology is not concerned with any other means of revelation than that which is found in the Bible.

II. The Relation of Biblical Theology to Other Biblical Studies

The validity of the definition above is further substanti-

[3]p. 20.

ated by comparing Biblical Theology with the other branches of theological science.

A. *Its Relation to Apologetics*

Biblical Theology assumes the results of the discipline of apologetics and builds upon them. Obviously the kind of results which are assumed will make a great deal of difference. As far as the present writer is concerned, he believes that apologetics has confirmed, among other things, the case for theism, supernatural miracles, and verbal, plenary inspiration of the Scriptures.[4] It is on that foundation that this work builds.

B. *Its Relation to New Testament Introduction*

As with apologetics, the results of the investigations of New Testament introduction are for the most part merely assumed and not reiterated in a work on Biblical Theology. However, since Biblical Theology cannot do without the critical investigations of introduction, the latter must precede the former, and to some extent must be included in it. Matters of authorship, date of writing, and destination are of utmost importance to the historical perspective of Biblical Theology, and in most instances these matters can be stated in summary fashion on the basis of the results of New Testament introduction. Occasionally, New Testament scholars are in such disagreement concerning certain of these critical matters that the Biblical theologian must concern himself in greater detail with them in order to lay a solid foundation on which to build his theology. For instance, it is deemed necessary to deal in detail with the matter of the authorship of the Pastorals before proceeding with Pauline theology, for New Testament scholars are sharply divided on this question, which has to be settled conclusively in order to determine the amount of source material which rightfully

[4]Cf. E. J. Carnell, *An Introduction to Christian Apologetics* (Grand Rapids: Eerdmans, 1948).

belongs to Pauline theology. But, in general, Biblical Theology does not enter into detailed critical investigations, for
as Weiss correctly points out, "it is only a historico-descrip-
tive, not a historico-critical, science."[5]

C. *Its Relation to Exegesis*

Biblical Theology stands in the closest connection to exegesis, for it builds directly upon it. Exegesis must be grammatical (it must tell us exactly what the author said) and it
must be historical (it must tell us what the writer said in his
own time), and this historico-grammatical interpretation is
the basis of all Biblical Theology. The careful, thorough
Biblical theologian will have included in the preparation for
his task an exegesis of all the Biblical material under consideration. It makes some difference to a proper conception of
Pauline theology, for instance, whether in Ephesians 5:26
the writer is speaking of sanctification or the rite of baptism
or both; therefore, a careful exegesis of such a verse is an
absolute necessity for accurate theology. The solution of
textual problems, which is a part of the task of exegesis, is also
foundational to the science of Biblical Theology. One cannot be a theologian without being an exegete, though one
can be an exegete without being a theologian. Biblical Theology goes beyond exegesis, for it not only presents what the
writer said but seeks to discover the theological pattern in
his mind, of which the writing was a reflection.

D. *Its Relation to the History of Christian Doctrine*

Biblical Theology has a close connection with certain aspects of historical theology, but it is certainly different from
the history of Christian doctrine. The latter science is the
study of what the readers of the Bible thought about the
Word either individually or collectively in Church councils.
Biblical Theology is the study of what the writers of the

[5]B. Weiss, *Biblical Theology of the New Testament* (Edinburgh: T. & T. Clark, 1882), I, 9.

Bible thought and said. It studies revelation at its human source, while the history of Christian doctrine studies the interpretation of the Church.

E. *Its Relation to Systematic Theology*

There is undoubtedly widespread confusion or vagueness concerning the distinction between Biblical Theology and Systematic Theology. This may be due largely to the fact that there are many similarities between the two sciences. For example, both are (or should be) based on the Bible (although Systematic Theology may include other sources of knowledge). Both are Biblical. Both are systematic. It is farthest from the truth to think of Systematic Theology as unbiblical or Biblical Theology as unsystematic. Nevertheless, there are some basic differences which distinguish these two areas of learning.

1. *As to precedence.* Strictly speaking Biblical Theology is foundational to Systematic Theology. In practice in our educational institutions Systematic Theology courses are usually prescribed, while Biblical Theology courses are generally elective. This would give the false appearance that Biblical Theology logically follows the study of Systematic Theology. Logically and chronologically Biblical Theology should take precedence over Systematic Theology, for the order of study ought to be introduction, exegesis, historical backgrounds, Biblical Theology, and finally Systematic Theology. That is, such an order ought to be followed if we were going to start from scratch, but since we do not, we teach Systematic Theology in the prescribed courses. Actually this is as it should be, for in the limited scope and time of a theological curriculum students should reap the benefit of the thought and work of others as they do in Systematic Theology courses. Later they can study the method and results of Biblical Theology.

2. *As to purpose.* The purpose of Biblical Theology is to discover what the writers of Scripture themselves regarded as truth not only from what they wrote but from that which their writings reflect of their theological thinking. The purpose of Systematic Theology is to set forth not only the truth but the reasons why it is truth. In this contrasting frame of reference, then, the former is purely historical, and the latter is historico-philosophical. By so much it may be said that Biblical Theology has no need of Systematic, but Systematic has every need of Biblical.

3. *As to perspective.* Systematic Theology displays Christian thought in one harmonious whole from today's viewpoint. Biblical Theology, on the other hand, presents the thought of the leaders of Judaism and Christianity from the historical standpoint of the particular period in which they labored. The perspective of the one is that of today; of the other, that of the Biblical writer.

4. *As to content.* Systematic Theology, of course, as far as its Biblical sources are concerned, is based on all of the Bible as a whole. Biblical Theology investigates particular parts of the Bible, and although the sum of all these parts will be the entire Scriptures, the investigations are divided so that the contents of each particular period or the thought of each particular writer is surveyed separately. Systematic Theology is as a blossom, each petal of which Biblical Theology has examined separately and in detail.

In conclusion, then, it is apparent that although Biblical Theology sustains relationships to other branches of Biblical study, it nonetheless is a distinct science of its own. The Biblical theologian must know something of the conclusions of apologetics and introduction, he must be a thoroughly qualified exegete, and he must be a competent historian. He is then ready to investigate and systematically set forth the historically conditioned progress of the self-revelation of God as deposited in the Bible, and the results of his impartial historical inquiry into the original founts of truth will not be a Systematic Theology but a Biblical Theology.[6]

III. METHODOLOGY IN BIBLICAL THEOLOGY

The method of Systematic Theology is to systematize all the truth revealed on any given subject under the generally accepted and humanly devised categories of Theology Proper, Anthropology, Soteriology, etc. The method of Biblical Theology is to systematize the truth revealed during a given period or through a given author. Generally speaking, Biblical Theology of the Old Testament presents the truth as it was progressively revealed in various periods, while Biblical Theology of the New Testament systematizes the truth as it was progressively revealed through the various writers of the New Testament. The reason for this is apparent. The doctrine of the Old Testament was revealed throughout many centuries, while that of the New was confined to less than one century. Therefore, New Testament Biblical Theology, while not unaware of the progression of time involved in the writing of the New Testament, is chiefly concerned with the progress of doctrine as revealed through the various human authors. Thus the plan of this book is to present in order the theology of the Synoptics, the theology of Acts, the theology of James, Pauline theology, the theology of Hebrews, the theology of Peter and Jude, and Johannine theology. Such an arrangement emphasizes the writers involved while also recognizing in a secondary manner and as much as possible chronological progression.

Having decided that New Testament Biblical Theology should be concerned mainly with development through men rather than periods, the student is faced with another decision of methodology. He must decide what sort of outline to use in his development of the thought of these men. A few have

[6]For a survey of the history of Biblical Theology as a science see James Lindsay, "Biblical Theology," *International Standard Bible Encyclopaedia* (Grand Rapids: Eerdmans, 1943), I, 469-72.

chosen to follow the same outline which is generally used in Systematic Theology. In other words, all the teaching of an author is merely catalogued under the usual categories. This does show at a glance what the writer taught on each subject, but it tends to be little more than a subdividing of the science of Systematic Theology, and it certainly does nothing toward revealing the theological bent of the mind of the author involved. Therefore, it seems highly preferable to develop Biblical Theology according to the outstanding areas of the thinking of the writer involved or according to the particular distinctiveness of revelation to and through that man or during that period. This, then, will be the approach followed so that the student of Biblical Theology will remember that Pauline theology is outstanding for such-and-such doctrines or that the theology of James centers around certain central categories of thought. This historical rather than dogmatic approach will also help give to the student an insight into why, for instance, the theology of James has certain doctrines at its core, and it will do this in a way that no mere systematizing of the record into standard categories can possibly do. Occasionally it will be helpful to summarize certain aspects of a man's theology for the sake of completeness, but in the main the purpose will be to accentuate his emphases and to try to account for those principal theological patterns of his mind as revealed in his writings.

IV. Value of the Study of Biblical Theology

It should be clear by now that Biblical Theology is not a miniature Systematic Theology subdivided into periods or persons, for it is not the mere repetition of dogmas under the accepted systematic outline as those dogmas were stated by a particular writer of Scripture or during a particular period. It is a fresh approach to the Word of God which is neither entirely exegetical, nor historical, nor theological, nor expository, but a combination of all these approaches. What, then, in particular is the value of this approach?

A. *Biblical Theology Views Doctrine in Its Historical Context*

Failure to view doctrine in its historical context is often a serious weakness of Systematic Theology, for frequently the theological system is that which determines the meaning of a verse or passage rather than the passage molding the system. Viewing doctrine in its historical context is the best preventive against this misuse of a theological system. For instance, a student of mine once concluded that since he could not find sin specifically mentioned in Acts 2, Peter did not preach about sin on the Day of Pentecost. His error was simply that he failed to understand the doctrine of repentance (Acts 2:38) in its historical setting in the sermon and against the background of the recent crime of the crucifixion of Christ. The Biblical Theology viewpoint guards one against such mistakes.

B. *Biblical Theology Emphasizes Theological Substructure*

Biblical Theology relieves the situation wherein fundamental doctrines of the faith seem to depend mainly on the testimony of isolated proof-texts.[7] It is not that they do, but it is often true that the usual presentation of certain doctrines in Systematic Theology gives the impression that those doctrines depend on one or two Biblical texts. The doctrine of inspiration is a good example. Usually two texts are set forth as the New Testament proof of the doctrine (II Tim. 3:16 and II Pet. 1:21). The impression is sometimes left with the student that these are the only two texts which can be used to demonstrate the inspiration of the Scriptures. There is no better corrective of such a misconception than the study of James from the viewpoint of Biblical Theology. Although

[7] G. Vos, *Biblical Theology* (Grand Rapids: Eerdmans, 1954), p. 27.

James does not make any direct statements concerning inspiration, the investigation of the doctrine of the Word in his Epistle reveals beyond any shadow of doubt that there was in his mind a definite substructure of the doctrines of the inspiration and authority of the Word. Theological substructure is just as valid proof of any doctrine as explicit statements, and no discipline in all the realm of theological studies reveals theological substructure as Biblical Theology does.

C. *Biblical Theology Helps Balance the Doctrine of Inspiration*

Inspiration may be defined as God's superintending human authors so that using their own individual personalities they composed and recorded without error His revelation to man in the words of the original autographs. Such a definition, of course, includes the ideas of God's superintendence (not dictation) of the entire Bible, verbal inerrancy, and the proper place of the human instrument. In recent times the doctrine of inspiration has suffered at the hands of both friend and foe. Liberal scholarship has virtually denied any divine element in inspiration by its redefining of inspiration in terms of author instead of the writing. Insofar as the Bible was true it was inspired, but it became the task of the liberal critic to determine at what points the Bible was true. In combatting this religious-historical approach, conservatives have had to emphasize the divine authorship of the Scriptures. The result of this emphasis has been the accusation by liberals and more recently by neo-orthodox theologians that dictation is the conservative doctrine of inspiration. This is done in spite of the fact that the conservative disavowal has been widely publicized for many years.[8] Nevertheless, it must be admitted that there has been an underemphasis of the human factors in inspiration. This lack of emphasis Biblical Theology corrects, for its historical approach looks

[8] J. G. Machen, *Christianity and Liberalism* (New York: Macmillan, 1923), pp. 73-74.

behind the words of the writings and points up the individual backgrounds, interests, and styles of the authors. Biblical Theology emphasizes the part that the writers had in the composition of the Word of God, while, of course, building on the divine superintendence of the writings.

D. *Biblical Theology Fosters a Deep Appreciation of the Grace of God*

The benefit of Biblical Theology as stated in the preceding section is realized when the approach is mainly from the viewpoint of the variety of authors. The one before us now is realized when the approach is made from the viewpoint of the different periods in revelation. When one studies, for instance, the theology of the Pentateuch and then Pauline theology he cannot help being impressed with the sharp contrast in the content of revelation. This is true, of course, only if in the study of the theology of the Pentateuch one is careful not to read the New Testament back into the Old; but if that is not done, one can only stand in amazement at the fullness of the revelation of the grace of God in Jesus Christ in contrast to that which was revealed in the shadows of the Old Testament. Such a contrast can only bring thankfulness and humility to the heart of the one who lives today in the blazing glory of the fullness of revelation, and that contrast is one of the certain products of the study of Biblical Theology.

This, then, is the subject which we investigate in this book. But the individual pursuit of that investigation can be done in several ways. Some who use this book may want only to scan it in order to trace the central thoughts in the progress of revelation. Others, and we trust this will be the larger group, will want to study it thoroughly. This should be done with an open Bible, used (1) to read several times the books involved in each theological division and (2) to look up each reference mentioned as this text is studied page by page.

The author has endeavored to hit some sort of balance between tracing the overall movement of thought and the specific development of individual doctrines. This has not always been easy to do, for the temptations to go overboard in both directions have presented themselves many times. The result could undoubtedly be improved upon, but any deficiencies in this matter are not due to a lack of sincere desire to maintain a balance within the work and a reasonable limit to the total work. This has required condensation and outlining in many places which can be compensated for only by the reader's faithful use of his Bible along with this book. Differences of interpretations of some Biblical texts have had to be passed by without much discussion. In such cases the reader should avail himself of commentaries on those passages.

Biblical Theology is one approach to the Scriptures. Distinctive as it may be, and fruitful as its benefits are, profit and blessing cannot be guaranteed the reader or student apart from the ministry of the Holy Spirit. It is He who takes of the things of Christ and shows them to us (John 16:13-15), and unless that ministry is operative in the heart there can be no benefit from the study. To reap the fullness of His ministry should be the constant concern of every student of the Word of God. May God grant it for all who read this book.

Part I

THE SYNOPTIC THEOLOGY

Chapter 1

INTRODUCTORY MATTERS

"THE SYNOPTIC THEOLOGY" is not quite synonymous with
"The theology of Jesus," for the former includes and is
larger than the latter. It would be simpler to consider only
the teachings of Jesus in this division of the book, for then
one would be free from any of the considerations relative to
the different authors who recorded the words of Jesus.[1] However, if Biblical Theology concerns the progress of the revelation of God as deposited in the Bible, matters relative to
the depositing, i.e., the emphases and viewpoints of the various writers, must be given consideration even in the Synoptic
Theology. The reasons behind the selectivity of Matthew,
Mark, and Luke are of importance to the Biblical theologian
and must be given consideration in a Biblical Theology.

This is not to say, however, that in this division we seek
only to notice the emphasis of the writers. Synoptic Theology
incorporates the theology of Jesus; therefore, a section on
the teachings of our Lord must be included. It is obvious to
any reader of the Gospels that Matthew is the most theological
Gospel, that Mark is the most chronological, and that Luke
is the most personal. Therefore, the plan of this division
(after considering introductory matters) will include the
principal theological themes of Matthew, the teachings of
Christ, and the personal additions of Luke. This will be done

[1]As John M. King, *The Theology of Christ's Teaching* (London: Hodder
& Stoughton, 1902).

by interweaving the teachings of Christ and the personal additions of Luke into the doctrinal framework of Matthew, the theological Gospel.

I. INTRODUCTORY MATTERS ABOUT MATTHEW

A. *Its Position in the Canon*

Beyond all question, the Gospel of Matthew exerts a greater influence simply because it stands first in the New Testament. A reason for its position is that it was thought to have been written first. Whether that be true or not, its primary position is of inestimable help in bridging the gap between the Old Testament hope of the Messianic kingdom and the New Testament Church. Without Matthew we would be overwhelmed in a theological morass.

B. *Authorship*

The Gospel does not actually claim to have been written by Matthew though the Early Church Fathers uniformly ascribed it to him.[2] That is not to imply, however, that the matter of authorship is based solely on tradition, for although the book does not expressly claim to have been written by Matthew it clearly testifies to that fact. For instance, the feast in the house (Matt. 9:10) is said by the other Gospel writers to have been in Matthew's house (Mark 2:15; Luke 5:29) — the silence of Matthew's account thus pointing to the Matthean authorship. Furthermore, it has often been pointed out that since Matthew was an obscure apostle there would be no reason for assigning the first Gospel to him unless he truly were the author. A forger would have chosen a more prominent name under which to publish the Gospel.

Little is known directly of the man, whose name means "gift of God," but certain facts can be gleaned from the record. He must have been a Hebrew of the Hebrews and not a Hellenist, for he was well taught in the prophecies of the

[2]Eusebius, *Ecclesiastical History*, III, xxxix, 16, quoting Papias; Irenaeus, *Against Heresies*, III, i, 1.

Old Testament. We know that he was a tax-collector, an occupation which caused him to be despised by his fellow Jews, but an occupation which brought him some degree of wealth. No special incident in the life of Christ is connected with his name, and after the listing of his name among those in the upper room awaiting Pentecost (Acts 1:13) he disappears entirely from the Biblical record. Tradition says that he preached for fifteen years in Palestine and then to Ethiopians, Macedonians, Syrians, and Persians. Eastern Church tradition says that he died peacefully, while Western Church tradition asserts that he was executed.[3]

Obscurity and lack of prominence, however, does not make Matthew any the less great. "Still water runs deep," and so it was with Matthew, for to the man of whom both sacred and secular history says so little we are indebted for some of the most profound theology in all the Bible.

> We may picture Matthew to ourselves as a silent, unobtrusive, contemplative man, "swift to hear and slow to speak," . . . with a mind teeming with the associations of his nation and deeply conscious of the momentous drama which was being enacted before him of which he felt himself called upon to be the chronicler and interpreter to his own people.[4]

In reading the Gospel one is conscious only of the regal person of Jesus Christ; in studying the Gospel one also becomes aware of the reverent scholarship of the theologian, whose God-given task was to interpret this person to his readers.

C. *Date and Place*

Liberals place the date of Matthew after A.D. 70 for two reasons.[5] First, they say that the presence of the Trinitarian

---

[3] For a summary see A. Carr, *The Gospel According to St. Matthew, Cambridge Greek Testament* (Cambridge: Cambridge University Press, 1887), pp. xv-xvi.

[4] *Ibid.*, p. xvi.

[5] A current tendency among liberals is toward an earlier dating of Matthew.

baptismal formula in the last chapter could not be accounted for otherwise, and second, they assert that the record of chapters 24 and 25 reflect the destruction of Jerusalem. This, of course, is based on their absolute disallowance of the possibility of prophetic utterance.

Conservatives are divided on the question of the primacy of Matthew. Some believe that this was the first Gospel written, which would date it around A.D. 50, while those who hold that Mark was written first date Matthew shortly before the year 70. This problem is discussed below more fully.

Probably the best suggestion as to the place of writing is Antioch in Syria.

D. *Original Language of Matthew*

Papias, in the reference from Eusebius already cited, is reported to have said that Matthew's Gospel was written originally in Aramaic. Some authorities reject the testimony of Papias since no trace of an Aramaic original has survived. Others hold that although there was originally an Aramaic Gospel, it was Matthew himself who because of the demand of ever-increasing numbers of Greek churches composed a Greek edition of the Gospel.

E. *The Theological Purpose of Matthew*

If none of the Gospels gives us a complete picture of the life of Christ, and if the emphasis of Matthew is theological, then it may well be asked what is the particular purpose distinctive to Matthew. The Gospel answers four questions: (1) Is Jesus of Nazareth the Messiah of the Old Testament? (2) Why did Jesus fail to bring in the promised Messianic kingdom? (3) Will that kingdom ever be brought in? (4) What is God's purpose today? In other words, Matthew is concerned with the King and His kingdom and with the Founder and His Church. Questions one through three above relate to the primary emphasis concerning the kingdom and question four to the decidedly secondary emphasis on the Church. This twofold emphasis is introduced in the very first verse: "The book of the generation of Jesus Christ, the son of David, the son of Abraham." That is, the Gospel concerns Jesus Messiah, the son of David (which relates Him directly to the kingdom promises included in the Davidic Covenant of II Samuel 7), and Jesus Messiah, the son of Abraham (which links Him to the Abrahamic Covenant of Genesis 12, which included the whole world).

II. Introductory Matters About Mark

A. *The Emphasis of Mark*

It has already been pointed out that Mark is the chronological Gospel. More than forty times the writer uses the word *straightway*, which shows both action and chronological relationship. The readers were mostly Gentile Christians, not Jewish believers. For this reason the genealogy of Christ is not included (for it would have meant little to Gentiles), the Sermon on the Mount is not reported (for it concerned kingdom life in which Jews, not Gentiles, would be primarily interested), and the condemnations of the Jews and their sects receive little attention. This attention to the needs of his Gentile, and doubtless primarily Roman, readers also accounts for the interpretation of Aramaic words in the Gospel (cf. 3:17; 5:41; 7:34; 9:43; 10:46; 14:36; 15:22, 34).

> The Gospel . . . must present the character and career of Jesus from the Roman side, or point of view, as answering to the idea of Divine power, work, law, conquest, and universal sway. To the Roman these are the credentials of Jesus, no less essential than prophecy to the Jew. . . .[6]

[6]W. G. Scroggie, *Guide to the Gospels* (London: Pickering & Inglis, 1948), p. 169.

B. *The Author*

The Gospel of Mark stands as a perpetual testimony to the fact that failure does not necessarily mean the end of usefulness. The author was the son of a woman of some means and position in Jerusalem (Acts 12:12), and his friendship with Peter was close (I Pet. 5:13).[7] As a young man Mark had the rare privilege of serving Paul and Barnabas on the first missionary journey (Acts 13:5), though he failed to stay with them through the entire journey. The reason for this is not stated but Paul evidently thought that it was not a valid one (Acts 15:39). Twelve years later, however, Paul acknowledges Mark as a fellow-laborer (Col. 4:10-11), and by the time of Paul's second imprisonment Mark had evidently entirely erased the unfavorable impression left by his earlier desertion (II Tim. 4:11). He apparently ministered in Rome (I Pet. 5:13; II Tim. 4:11), and tradition adds that he founded the church at Alexandria, Egypt, where he died a martyr's death.[8]

C. *Date and Place of Writing*

The matter of the date of Mark depends entirely on one's conclusions relative to the Synoptic problem. If Mark was written first it may be dated as early as A.D. 50; if not, it may be dated later, though not later than 70. The place of writing is usually said to be Rome, a fact which would seem to be true according to references in Eusebius.[9] It was evidently Peter, the close friend of his mother Mary, who took Mark under his wing, rescuing him from uselessness after the incident at Perga, and who supplied Mark with the facts of the life of Christ (note the comparison of the outline of Mark with Peter's message recorded in Acts 10:34-43).

[7]Mark's companionship with Peter is mentioned by the Church Fathers; cf. Eusebius, *op. cit.* III, xxxix.
[8]Legend says that Mark's body was removed from Alexandria to Venice in 827 where it lies buried today.
[9]*Op. cit.*, II, xv; III, xxxix; VI, xxv.

D. *A Note on the Synoptic Problem*

In a word the Synoptic problem is, How can we account for the similarities between the Gospels and at the same time preserve the independent character of their witness? In dealing with the problem there are two errors to be avoided. Though it is necessary not to ignore the problem, it is equally essential not to become so occupied with it as to miss the message of the writings. The facts of the matter are: (1) only 50-55 verses of Mark are not found in either Matthew or Luke (since 500 of Matthew's 1,068 verses are similar to those found in Mark and 320 of Luke's 1,149 are found in Mark); and (2) there are about 250 verses in Matthew and Luke which show close parallelism and which are not found at all in Mark. Fact (1) seems to point to the conclusion that Mark was written first and Matthew and Luke had access to it when they wrote. Fact (2) seems to suggest that there existed another source which Matthew and Luke used but which Mark did not.

Some have solved the Synoptic problem by suggesting that the similarities between the Gospels can be accounted for by realizing that a great deal of precise and accurate oral tradition about the life and teachings of Christ was common knowledge among the early Christians, and since Matthew, Mark, and Luke would have known this tradition they would have drawn upon it in their writings, thus accounting for the similarities even though the writings were published independently and possibly even simultaneously.[10]

Others (liberals and some conservatives[11]) admit that the two facts above do point definitely to the conclusions suggested; namely, that Mark was written first and was used by Matthew and Luke, and that Matthew and Luke used another source which is generally called Q because Q is the first letter

---

[10]M. C. Tenney, *The New Testament, An Historical and Analytical Survey* (Grand Rapids: Eerdmans, 1953), pp. 169, 215.

[11]Scroggie, *op. cit.*, pp. 83-94.

of the German word for source.[12] Whichever solution is preferred is of no great moment to the Biblical Theology of the Synoptics; only let it be realized that the evangelical doctrine of inspiration is in no way jeopardized if one accepts the idea that Mark was written first and that such a document as Q existed at one time. Sources are no more a problem to the student of the Synoptics than the quotations from the Book of Enoch are in Jude or the sources of all of Moses' information as recorded in the Pentateuch. Inspiration concerns the record, not the sources.

III. INTRODUCTORY MATTERS ABOUT LUKE

Matters concerning Luke himself and his method of research are to be discussed under the division on Acts. However, a few items must necessarily be included here.

A. *Luke's Sources*

From the brief discussion of the Synoptic problem it has been shown that some conclude that about one-third of Luke was either related to oral tradition or to Mark. Further, it was seen that about one-sixth of the Gospel has no relationship to anything in Mark but is similar to material in Matthew, suggesting to some that Luke used a source which has been tagged Q. However one accounts for these parts of Luke, there remain other portions which are peculiar to this writer. The material in 9:51—18:14 is distinctive to Luke, the facts of which may have been gleaned from one or more of the seventy who were sent out by Christ and whose mission is reported in that section. The so-called doublets which are found in that section (expressions and stories similar to

[12]A weighty argument against this evidence for an early date of Mark is the testimony of Irenaeus (*Against Heresies*, III, i, 1), in which he says, "And after their [Peter and Paul] exodus Mark, the disciple and interpreter of Peter, having committed to writing the things that Peter used to preach, delivered them to us." However, two questions must be answered in order to evaluate properly this testimony: (1) Does "exodus" refer to the apostles' death or a departure from Rome? (2) Were the writing and delivering at the same time?

ones found in Matthew and Mark but under different circumstances) are easily accounted for by remembering that a teacher often uses the same or similar material under different circumstances.

Another major section which is peculiar to Luke is 1:5—2:52, the infancy stories. Some say that it is pure invention (but how could a Greek invent the Hebraistic hymns of Elizabeth and Mary?). Others see it as something added later by an editor. Such views must be rejected. The most likely suggestion as to the source of the information contained in those chapters was made by Ramsay, who submits that Mary herself told Luke of these intimate matters in the manner in which a woman would be apt to tell a physician.[13]

B. *Date and Place of Writing*

As in the case of Matthew, liberal writers generally place the date of Luke after the year 70 because of their disregard of the prophetic element in the Bible.[14] If, however, the possibility of prediction is not shunned (cf. especially Luke 21:20-24) the idea of a pre-70 date can be entertained. Nevertheless, the possibility of prophecy is not the only argument for an early date; actually, the early date for Luke is related to the question of the date of Acts, which will be discussed later. If it may be assumed for the moment that Acts must be dated during the lifetime of Paul, then of course the Gospel of Luke must have been written around 60.

Suggestions as to the place of writing are in reality little more than guesses. Caesarea seems to be as likely a candidate as any place, or possibly Luke wrote the Gospel in Rome. It might even be that he began it in one place, say Caesarea, and finished it in Rome.

[13]W. M. Ramsay, *Was Christ Born at Bethlehem?* (London: Hodder & Stoughton, 1898), pp. 78-83.
[14]A. H. McNeile, *An Introduction to the Study of the New Testament* (Oxford: Oxford University Press, 1953), p. 33.

C. *The Distinctivenesses of the Gospel*

1. *The medical matters.* The Gospel of Luke is distinctive in a number of ways. First, and most obvious, of course, is the interest which Dr. Luke displays in medical matters.[15] This interest is reflected not only in the use of medical terms (cf. Luke 4:38; 7:15; 14:2; 18:25) but also in the unusual interest displayed in the accounts of healing and the details of diagnoses and cures in those accounts which are not recorded by the other Gospel writers (cf. Luke 4:38; 5:12; 8: 55; 22:50). These matters show the professional interest of a physician, not merely the normal vocabulary and concern of an educated Greek.

2. *The infancy narratives.* Closely connected to the medical interest in the Gospel is Luke's recounting of the events surrounding the birth of Christ. He alone records those inner thoughts which, as has already been suggested, he may have learned from Mary herself simply because he was a physician. Only Luke records the annunciation to Zacharias and Mary, the songs of Elizabeth and Mary, the birth and childhood of John the Baptist, the birth of Jesus and the visit of the shepherds, the circumcision of Jesus and His presentation in the temple, and the only details we have about the childhood of the Lord. Beyond any doubt this is a significant emphasis.

3. *The interest in individuals.* Luke also displays an uncommon interest in individuals. Nineteen of Christ's parables are reported by Luke only and many of these concern individuals. For instance, it is Luke who preserves the parables of the good Samaritan (10:30-37), the rich fool (12:16-21), the rich man and Lazarus (16:19-31), the Pharisee and the publican (18:9-14), and the classic parables of the lost sheep, the lost silver, and the lost son in chapter 15.

4. *The emphasis on prayer.*

[15]Cf. W. K. Hobart, *Medical Language of St. Luke* (London: Longmans, Green and Co., 1882), and A. T. Robertson, *Luke the Historian in the Light of Research* (Edinburgh: T. & T. Clark, 1920), pp. 90-102.

5. *The teaching concerning the place and work of women.*
6. *The interest in poverty and wealth.*

All of these topics will be dealt with in detail later.

Chapter 2

THE CHRISTOLOGY OF THE SYNOPTICS

A THEOLOGY OF THE SYNOPTICS, we have said, must include the principal theological themes of Matthew, the teachings of Christ, and the particular emphases of Luke. If it is true that Matthew's Gospel is the theological Gospel, and if it is recognized that the Holy Spirit's superintendence of the writings caused it to be so, then the content of this section ought to interweave the contributions of Mark and Luke into the theological framework of Matthew.

That framework is very simple. It concerns the King and His kingdom. In other words, it concerns Christology and eschatology. Many other doctrines are involved, but they can all be related to those two basic areas of theology, which then become the basic outline for all the Synoptic Theology.

I. THE PRESENTATION OF THE KING

A. *The Genealogy of the King* (Matt. 1:1-17; Luke 3:23-38)

1. *The divisions of the genealogy.* If the King and the kingdom are the prominent themes of the Synoptics, it is not surprising to find a genealogy at the opening of the record. The genealogy which Matthew presents is not an ordinary one as is Luke's. It is very obviously adjusted to the author's purpose of arranging the genealogy in three divisions. This

arbitrary division requires that there be some omissions (cf. I Chron. 3:11-12). What is the explanation for this? Lightfoot says it is to be found in the usual Jewish procedure in these matters of genealogies. They often adjusted the genealogy so as to suit their purposes of neatness of arrangement. "They do so very much delight in such kind of contents, that they oftentimes screw up the strings beyond the due measure and stretch them till they crack."[1] Although there is much truth in this statement, it is not the whole explanation. The solution is really to be found in the theological purpose of the Holy Spirit through the human instrument, Matthew. His purpose is to emphasize Jesus as the Son of David and therefore the King of Israel. To do this the first division of the genealogy ends with David and the second begins with his name. Thus the reader's attention is immediately focused on David, who alone in the genealogy is called the king. This is in line with the writer's purpose, for his Gospel concerns "Jesus Messiah, son of David." The second division ends with the Babylonian captivity, which would be a stinging reminder to the Jews that they were far from realizing the fulfillment of the promises concerning their Messianic kingdom. Thus the divisions of the genealogy emphasize the two aspects of the theological framework of the Gospels— the King and the kingdom.

2. *The distinctiveness of the genealogy.* It has already been noted that the content of Matthew's genealogy is different from that of Luke; the first contains only forty-one names while the second contains seventy-four names. Luke's arrangement is not artificial as Matthew's is, and Luke goes back to Adam, while Matthew traces the King to Abraham. Of course, the fact that Matthew uses the word *begat* does not mean that he is giving the immediate offspring, for the word *begat* is used even when generations are skipped (cf. Matt. 1:1; II Chron. 22:9).

[1]A. Carr, *The Gospel According to St. Matthew, Cambridge Bible*, p. 31, quoting Lightfoot.

Endless discussion has been made as to whether or not the two genealogies are distinctive as to the parent of Jesus. Many today say that Matthew's genealogy is through Joseph while Luke's is through Mary. Plummer voices the major objection to this view; for, he says,

> it is probable that so obvious a solution, as that one was the pedigree of Joseph and the other the pedigree of Mary, would have been very soon advocated, if there had been any reason (excepting the difficulty) for adopting it. But this solution is not suggested by anyone until Annius of Viterbo propounded it, *c.* A.D. 1490.[2]

However, Godet argues effectively for Mary's lineage in Luke on the basis of the absence of the article before Joseph (3:23) which links Jesus directly with Heli and seemingly puts Joseph out of the genealogy altogether.[3] Many, on the other hand, hold that both genealogies are Joseph's. Various explanations are given for this possibility, one of which is that Matthan and Matthat are the same person, making Jacob and Heli brothers and Joseph the son of Heli and nephew of Jacob. If Jacob died without heirs his nephew Joseph would have become the heir, or possibly Joseph became the heir of Jacob because Heli (assuming that his own wife was dead) married Jacob's widow according to the custom of levirate marriage.[4]

Whatever be the correct solution to this problem, one thing is quite clear. Both genealogies demonstrate Jesus' right as heir of David. Matthew lays stress on Joseph's being the husband of Mary in order to show that since Joseph recognized his wife's son in a legal sense as his own, Jesus was legally the heir of David. Luke entirely omits Mary's name,

[2]A. Plummer, *A Critical and Exegetical Commentary on the Gospel According to Luke, International Critical Commentary* (Edinburgh: T. & T. Clark, 1910), p. 103.

[3]F. Godet, *A Commentary on the Gospel of St. Luke* (Edinburgh: T. and T. Clark, 1890), I, 195-204.

[4]J. G. Machen, *The Virgin Birth of Christ* (New York: Harper, 1930), pp. 207-9.

and while he is careful to avoid the impression that Jesus might be the natural son of Joseph, he nonetheless disallows the possibility of slighting Jesus' kingly claims by avoiding to link Him solely to His mother.[5] Thus the right of the King is carefully guarded and clearly presented, and that right to the throne was never contested during His lifetime on the ground that His descent from David was doubtful (cf. Matt. 12:23; 15:22; 20:30-31; 21:9, 15).

3. *The doctrine of the genealogy.*

a. The doctrine of kingship. As mentioned before, the highlighting of David the king and the legality substantiated by the genealogies emphasize the kingly aspect of the genealogy.

b. The doctrine of Gentile salvation. The secondary theme of the Synoptics, that of salvation for Gentiles, is implicit in both genealogies. In Matthew it is seen in the linking of Jesus with Abraham and the Abrahamic covenant, which promised blessings to all nations in the Seed. In Luke it is seen in the tracing of the genealogy back to Adam.

4. *The doctrine of grace.* It has often been pointed out that Matthew's artificial arrangement of names includes those of four women. Two of them were Gentiles, Rahab and Ruth, and Ruth, being a Moabitess, was expressly cursed (Deut. 23:3). Three of the four women were wicked sinners —Tamar's fornication, Rahab's harlotry, and Bathsheba's sin being well-known. Yet their inclusion in the genealogy of the Messiah is a display of the triumph of the grace of God.

B. *The Birth of the King* (Matt. 1:18—2:23; Luke 1:26—2:38)

1. *The doctrine of the virgin birth.*

a. The meaning of the virgin birth. The virgin birth

---

[5]This is true no matter whether one understands the genealogy to be that of Joseph or of Mary. If the former, Jesus is then linked to Joseph and the case is the same as in Matthew; if the latter, Jesus is linked to his grandfather Heli through Mary, but without mentioning her name, for the Jews said, "*Genus matris non vocatur genus*" (*Baba Bathra,* 110 a).

means that the conception of Christ was without a human father and thus contrary to the course of nature. It was not the opening of Mary's womb, as in the case of Elizabeth, but the activating of it apart from a human male being, and after the conception took place the course of pregnancy and birth were normal.

b. The importance of the virgin birth. Some say that this doctrine is not necessary for saving faith. Perhaps that could be granted, but it cannot be granted that it is irrelevant to the facts upon which faith rests. One doubtless can be saved without consciously including the virgin birth in the facts which he believes, but it is incredible to think that one can be saved while knowingly denying the doctrine, for it is vital to the facts of faith. Without the virgin birth there is only a sinful Saviour, and such a Saviour can provide no real salvation.

c. The testimony to the virgin birth. Both Matthew and Luke attest to the fact and manner of the virgin birth. Luke speaks of the manner by simply saying that the Holy Spirit overshadowed Mary (Luke 1:34-38). Ultimately a miracle has to be admitted, the result of which was the birth of the sinless Son of God. Matthew attests to the fact of it by his precise use of the feminine singular relative pronoun in 1:16. Had he used a plural it would have indicated that both Joseph and Mary were the parents of Jesus, but the strict use of the feminine singular attests to the fact that Mary alone was the human parent of Jesus. Matthew's only comment concerning the method of the virgin birth is his use of *ek* with a genitive of source in 1:18 (indicating that the Holy Spirit was the originating source).

2. *The announcement of the King.*

a. The announcement to Mary (Luke 1:31-33). The announcement of the birth of Messiah was made to Mary in great detail. Gabriel told her that (1) the Incarnation would be in a man (cf. Jer. 31:22), (2) His name would be Jesus (a common Jewish name meaning Jehovah is Saviour), (3) He would be great in His essential nature, (4) He was the Son of God, and (5) this One would be the fulfiller of the Davidic covenant.

b. The announcement to Joseph (Matt. 1:18-25). When Joseph discovered that his betrothed was with child he had two courses of action. He could have made a public example of Mary; i.e., he could have summoned her before the court and had her condemned and stoned as an adulteress. Or he could divorce ("put away" in v. 19 is the usual word for divorce) her privily, i.e., without assigning a cause. This action would have been a real divorce even though they were not yet married, because the entire year before the marriage was considered a binding period of betrothal, and, although the betrothed lived in her own home, she in her relationship to the man was considered as if married and thus subject to the divorce law. Joseph's dilemma was solved by the angelic announcement to him concerning what God was doing.

c. The announcement to the shepherds (Luke 2:8-14). At the time of the birth further angelic announcement was made to the shepherds in the fields. Their message contained three elements: (1) the shepherds need not fear (showing that human nature is not on good terms with Heaven), (2) the Saviour would not favor only one nation but all nations, and (3) He would bring forgiveness of sins.

3. *The adoration of the King.*

a. By the shepherds.

b. By Simeon and Anna (Luke 2:22-38), Forty days after the birth Mary presented herself for purification and the baby Jesus received further adoration from Simeon and Anna in the temple. Their words show recognition of the Messiah in the person of Jesus, and their pious characters must have been typical of at least some in Israel at the time of our Lord.

c. By the wise men (Matt. 2:1-12).[6] The adoration of the

_____

[6]In spite of all the arguments to the contrary it has not been proved to the mind of the author that the wise men did not come at the time Jesus was

wise men reveals certain points of theological interest. (1) It shows the religious condition of Israel. Even though the shepherds had spread abroad the news, evidently few Jews had paid any attention to it, else the wise men would not have had to inquire so diligently. Even when members of the Sanhedrin repeated the prophecy of Micah, they paid no attention to those who might have led them to the fulfillment of it. (2) It shows the depravity of the human heart as epitomized in Herod and his actions. (3) It shows the religious condition of some Gentiles, for the wise men exhibited great faith in following the star and great perception in acknowledging the baby Jesus as God. (4) It shows God's providential care. The theological import of the gifts they brought is simply in their being concrete recognition of the worth of the King to whom they were brought. Their practical import is that they were likely used by Joseph to transport and sustain his family in Egypt. They may have been the provision of God for that purpose.

C. *The Boyhood of the King* (Matt. 2:13-23; Luke 2:39-52)

Very little is said concerning this period of the King's life apart from the sojourn in Egypt and the Passover visit to Jerusalem at the age of twelve. However, certain relevant facts can be gleaned from the record which we have.

1. *The environment of our Lord.* The Lord Jesus was reared in a godly family. We know that they went to Jerusalem every year—a journey which must have put a severe strain on the finances of a carpenter. Furthermore, Mary went along, and since it was not required by the Law that women go, that shows something of the extreme piety of the

born. Trench (*The Star of the Wise Men* [Philadelphia: H. Hooker, 1850]) suggests very plausibly that the star may have appeared first at the time of the conception, thus causing the arrival of the wise men in Bethlehem to coincide with the birth. The fact that Matthew uses *paidion*, little child, to describe the baby (2:11) does not prove anything, for the word is used of a newborn child as well as an older one (cf. John 16:21). The fact that they found Him in a house is only reasonable, for one cannot imagine the family staying in the stable any longer than absolutely necessary.

family. The Lord's family was also endowed with great initiative, for in spite of the fact that they were poor and had to work hard for everything, they saw to it that the children were educated. Since we know that the Lord never attended the schools (Mark 6:2; John 7:15) this education must have taken place in the home, and we know that it included the ability to read (Luke 4:16) and write (John 8:6). The Lord Jesus was reared in a wicked city; for Nazareth, being on the crossroads of trade routes, had nothing but a bad reputation (John 1:46). And yet the boy lived a sinless life in the midst of such surroundings.

2. *The example of our Lord.* Those years of maturing still stand as an example for all (Heb. 5:8). He faithfully obeyed the Law (cf. Deut. 16:1-3); He obeyed His parents (Luke 2:51; this included the time when He was alone in the big city of Jerusalem for three days); He worshiped God (Luke 2:49); and His development during those years was a complete one (physical, mental, social, and spiritual; Luke 2:52).

D. *The Baptism of the King* (Matt. 3:13-17; Mark 1:9-11; Luke 3:21-22)

1. *The method of His baptism.* Christ was baptized by another man, and it is hard for us to appreciate what this means. We are accustomed to seeing baptism performed by one man upon another person, but such was not the case in the time of our Lord. Up to that time all baptisms into Judaism were self-administered.[7] A proselyte into Judaism had to be circumcised, offer a sacrifice, and baptize himself in the presence of the rabbis before he was entitled to the privileges of Judaism. Thus baptism was well-known, but it was a self-imposed rite. When John came asking men to be baptized by him it was the most startling way he could

[7]A. Edersheim, *The Life and Times of Jesus the Messiah* (Grand Rapids: Eerdmans, 1943), II, 745-47; and C. H. Kraeling, *John the Baptist* (New York: Charles Scribner's Sons, 1951), pp. 99-101.

ask them to identify themselves with what he was preaching. He was not asking them to become Jews (they already were) ; the Church had not yet been founded so he was not asking them to join that; he himself was starting no new organization; he, though of the tribe of Levi (Luke 1:5), was evidently not consecrated a priest; therefore, submitting to baptism at his hand was indisputable testimony to one's identification with John's ministry and message. The method of being baptized by another person, new with John the Baptizer, was the method of Christ's baptism.

2. *The meaning of His baptism.* Sufficient has been said above to make it clear that the meaning of the Lord's baptism was identification. This is the meaning of all baptism. The Jewish proselyte identified himself with Judaism when he baptized himself. The Christian identifies himself with Christianity (the message and the group) when he is baptized. Our Lord identified himself with *righteousness* and the *kingdom* when He was baptized by the one who preached, "*Repent* for the *kingdom* of heaven is at hand." Here was the fulfiller of all righteousness and the King of the kingdom identifying Himself thus.

Other views of the meaning of Christ's baptism are frequently advanced. Some conservatives feel that it was the rite of entrance into his priesthood.[8] However, our Lord was never a priest after the order of Aaron, for He was disqualified by tribe. Into what, then, could the One who was eternally a priest after the order of Melchizedec be initiated?

Liberals often regard the Lord's baptism as an identification with sinners, and they mean by this that Christ was declaring in His baptism that He was a sinner. Other views are generally little more than variations of these three basic ones.

[8]L. S. Chafer, *Systematic Theology* (Dallas: Dallas Seminary Press, 1947), V, 61-63.

E. *The Temptation of the King* (Matt. 4:1-11; Mark 1:12-13;
　　Luke 4:1-13)

There remains one final act in the drama of the presentation of the King—His temptation. Mark reports that this occurred immediately after the baptism, and tradition says that it took place in the wilderness near Jericho.

1. *The instigator of the temptation.* All three accounts of the temptation expressly state that the Holy Spirit was the One who led the Lord into the test. This, of course, was not a solicitation to evil (for God does not do that), but it was a testing to prove that He was the divine King. The tests were not directed toward evil ends but toward accomplishing legitimate ends by evil means—means which, if they had been used by the Lord, would not only have proved Him to be sinful but also would have proved Him to be the wrong kind of king for Israel—a king of power only and not a suffering servant. To prove Jesus as the rightful king was the purpose behind the instigation of the Spirit of God.

2. *The instrument of the temptation.* Satan was, of course, the instrument used to accomplish God's purpose in this matter. When the light is the brightest the shadows are the darkest; thus we find intense activity on the part of Satan during the entire life and ministry of Christ.

3. *The intent of the temptation.*

a. On Satan's part. Satan's intent in the temptation was to make Christ sin by taking shortcuts to the accomplishments of His Messianic purposes; i.e., by offering Him legitimate ends by illegitimate means. This Satan attempted to do by appealing to the flesh, the pride of life, and the eye. It is obvious that there is nothing wrong with Christ's commanding stones to become bread in order to feed Himself, nor with Christ's proving Himself to be supernatural by casting Himself off the pinnacle of the temple, nor with His having the kingdoms of this world, which He *will* have some day. The evil, then, was not in the ends to which Christ was tempted to go, but it was in the means of accomplishing those ends, for they were means which did not include the suffering with the glory.

b. On God's part. If the Holy Spirit led our Lord into the testing, then God must have had some purpose in it, and that purpose was to demonstrate the sinlessness of His Son through His complete obedience to the full will of God.

This, then, was the proof of the fact that Jesus could not sin. It was not merely that He was able not to sin, but He was unable to sin. Objections are always raised to this doctrine of the impeccability of Christ, for such a doctrine is supposed to deny the reality of temptation and remove all possibility of genuine sympathy (Heb. 4:15). It does neither. The reality of any testing does not lie in the moral nature of the one tested, and the possibility of sympathizing does not depend on one-to-one correspondence in the problems which call forth the sympathy. The test was real, for although the Lord could not have sinned as far as natural ability is concerned (I John 3:5b), He did have the power to turn stones into bread, cast Himself off the pinnacle of the temple unharmed, and take the reins of world government but to have done so under the circumstances of the test would have been sin; therefore, He could not have done these things on that occasion. The realm of testing was different from anything known to human beings, but the reality of testing was actual and sufficient basis for our complete assurance of His sympathizing interest.

II. THE AUTHENTICATION OF THE KING

A. *The King Authenticated by His Names and Titles*

The names and titles ascribed to the Lord Jesus Christ by those who followed Him comprise the first line of proof for the authentication of His kingship. The proof is built upon the investigation of the various Gospel writers' use of such names as "Jesus," "Lord," "Christ," and such titles as "Lord,"

"Saviour," "Prophet," "King," "Son of God," and "Son of Man."[9] Mark's contribution to the investigation is very minor, for Mark includes no names or titles that do not appear in some other Gospel, and his use of them is the least theological.

The name *Jesus* is almost without exception simply the narrative name for our Lord; i.e., the name used in the narration. This is to be expected, for the terminology of our Gospels would largely follow the terminology of the oral and/or written sources which lie behind them, and the description of our Lord in the accounts of His ministry would have been under the simple designation *Jesus*. However, there are a few outstanding exceptions which show that the writers themselves conceived the name *Jesus* as a title meaning "Jehovah is salvation." The clearest examples of this fuller conception are in Luke (1:31; 3:21, 23; Matt. 1:21). It is also Luke who uses the simple designation *Jesus* frequently in combinations which exhibit clear Messianic connotations (cf. Luke 8:28; 17:13; 18:38; Matt. 1:1; 16:21). It would be expected that Luke would take the lead in this because of his personal exposure to Paul's teaching; and it is normal, too, to discover similar, though less frequent, usage in Matthew (Mark's use of combinations is limited to 1:1). Thus "Jesus" was used by the Gospel writers not merely as a name of a person but as a title which signified the work of that person as Saviour.

"Lord" is an honorific title of especially high connotation. It was used by those who were outside the circle of Christ's followers in ways that were both sincere and insincere and to mean sometimes no more than "teacher" but sometimes much more (Mark 7:28; Luke 5:8; 6:46; 7:6; 10:17). Although it was a common form of address, it was also clearly used as a synonym for *Adonai* (Mark 2:28; 12:37). Further-

[9] Cf. B. B. Warfield, *The Lord of Glory* (London: Hodder & Stoughton, 1907), for detailed usage of all the names and titles of Christ by all the New Testament writers.

more, the fact that "Lord" is used by Luke as an alternative narrative designation to "Jesus" shows Luke's lofty conception of Jesus as deity (cf. 7:13, 19; 10:1, 41; 11:39; 12:42; 13:15; 17:5-6; 18:6; 22:61). Therefore, we may conclude that, although the word may have a very ordinary significance, it was used of Jesus of Nazareth in a way which authenticated His claims as King.

All the Gospel writers record titles of the Lord which are definitely Messianic. He is the Prophet (Matt. 13:57; 16:14; 21:11, 46; Mark 6:15; 8:28; Luke 7:16, 39; 9:8, 19; 13:33-34; 24:19). The designation *Saviour* as Luke uses it is linked with the Messianic prophecies (1:47; 2:30; 3:6; 24:46). The use of "Christ" also substantiates His Messianic claims (Matt. 1:17; 11:2; Mark 8:29; 12:35; 13:21; 14:61; 15:32; Luke 2: 26; 22:67; 23:39; 24:26, 46). Other Messianic titles include "King" (Matt. 2:2; 27:11; Mark 15:2, 26; Luke 23:2), "Shepherd" (Matt. 26:31; Mark 14:27), "God's elect" (Luke 9:35, R.V.; 23:35), and "Son of David" (Matt. 12:23; 15:22; 20: 31). All of these titles, of course, help authenticate His claims.

Two other important titles remain to be discussed—"Son of God" and "Son of Man." The title *Son of God* is not a subsequent Pauline addition to the claims of Christ. That He was very God was revealed by this title at the beginning of His ministry; viz., at His baptism (Matt. 3:17; Mark 1:11; Luke 3:22). He did not become the Son of God at that moment, nor was He merely conscious of it from that time on; rather, the voice of the Father was a confirmation of His deity. This is also affirmed not only by the Father at the baptism but also by the Devil at the temptation, for Satan said, "If thou be the Son of God" (Luke 4:3, 9). The Greek phrase is a first-class condition which shows that the Devil's method was not to throw doubt on the fact of Christ's being the Son of God but to incite Him to prove the reality of it by exercising the power of God. It may well be translated, "Since thou art the Son of God." By parable the Lord also Him-

self taught that He was the Son of God (Luke 20:13-14).
At His trial all who witnessed understood that He was clearly
claiming to be divine (Mark 14:61; Luke 22:67). Thus the
Synoptics are filled with proofs of His claims to be God.

The Lord's own favorite designation of Himself was the
title *Son of Man*. It is found thirty times in Matthew, four-
teen times in Mark, and twenty-five times in Luke, and is
used only by the Lord of Himself. This frequent use must
have turned the minds of the people back to the prophecy of
Daniel (7:13-14), and in so doing it connected Jesus with
the setting up of the kingdom. But the Lord's frequent use
of this title also had another purpose, for it emphasized the
lowliness and humanity of His person. In this way He endeavored to unite in the minds of the Jews the Saviour with
the kingdom; i.e., He tried to get across the idea that the
kingdom was to be built on a suffering and humiliated Saviour. Thus the title has both a soteriological and eschatological meaning (cf. Matt. 24:27, 30, 37, 39, 44; 25:31; 26:2, 24,
45, 64; Mark 8:31; Luke 19:10). In all these passages the
clear emphasis is on the fact that the human person who was
to suffer and die was the same one who would come in great
glory to set up the kingdom. Uniformly, too, the title *Son of
Man* is somehow linked to the earth, whether it be in reference to the suffering Saviour or the reigning King. As the
suffering of the Son of Man was on earth, so also His kingdom
will be on the earth.

His names and titles, therefore, show our Lord to have
been a real man but not a mere man, for the names and titles
are filled with the highest implications. They show that
Jesus of Nazareth was an authoritative teacher, the Son of
God, the Redeemer, and the Messiah of Israel.

B. *The King Authenticated by His Miracles*

A miracle is an extraordinary act in the physical realm,
perceptible by the senses, caused by the intervention of a

transcendent supernatural power, and generally acts outside the realm of natural causes and effects.

The miracles of Christ had at least two purposes. They displayed the power of God and they demonstrated the precepts of God, and in both of these ways they authenticated the claims of the Messiah who performed them. In their demonstrating the power of God they were called *dunameis*, powers (Matt. 11:20; Mark 6:2; Luke 10:13), for they were evident displays of transcendent power in this lower world of ours. That these displays were distinctly connected with the authentication of the Messianic claims is evident from Matthew 14:2 and Luke 19:37. The display of the power of God in the miracles of Jesus of Nazareth should have proved to all that this was Messiah.

Miracles also taught certain divine precepts which could not be taught in any other way. In contrast to the parables, for instance, "there was nothing miraculous in the parables; all was natural and inevitable: the seed growing, the leaven working, the light shining; but not by parables could He show how the blind might see, the dumb speak, and the deaf hear; miracles had to be performed to teach these lessons."[10] That this was one purpose of the miracles is corroborated in Johannine theology where they are called *semeia*, signs (John 4:48), which means "deeds that symbolize spiritual truths." Nevertheless, the deed itself as well as the truth was important, for the miracles of healing, for instance, were cited by the Lord Himself as sufficient and valid proof that He was the Messiah (Matt. 11:4-6).

C. *The King Authenticated by His Person*

The Messianic teaching of Judaism was concerned with a person and an era.[11] The nature of the person of the Messiah was well-defined in the Old Testament under the two con-

[10]W. G. Scroggie, *A Guide to the Gospels* (London: Pickering and Inglis, 1948), p. 555.

[11]Cf. J. Crichton, "Messiah," *The International Standard Bible Encyclopaedia* (Grand Rapids: Eerdmans, 1943), III, 2039-40.

cepts of the King and the Servant of Jehovah. The concept of the King was formed on the basis of such passages as Genesis 49:8-12; II Samuel 7:11 ff.; Isaiah 7:10-17; 9:6; Jeremiah 23:5; 30:9; Micah 5:2; Zechariah 3:8; 6:12; 9:9. Several important features concerning the Messiah are found in these passages: (1) the permanence and universality of His reign as seen in the Davidic covenant, (2) the humble origin of Messiah in the Davidic line (Micah 5:2), (3) the fact that He would be a priest as well as a king (Zech. 6:11), and (4) the prophecy of Isaiah that Messiah would be divine because He would be Immanuel. Thus the Old Testament concept of Messiah as King clearly included the fact that He was to be the Son of God (cf. Matt. 16:16; 26:63; John 1:34, 49; 11:27).

The Servant of Jehovah concept emphasized the suffering of Messiah (Isa. 41:8; 42:1-7, 19 ff.; 43:10; 44:1 ff., 21; 49:3-6; 50:4-9; 52:13—53:12). While it is true that the title is sometimes used of the whole nation of Israel and sometimes of the pious remnant, it is equally true that the conception of the Servant of Jehovah culminates in an individual human being who would suffer vicariously for His people. In their desire to be free from the Roman yoke in the time of Christ, the Jews had lost sight of the aspect of suffering; but that was nonetheless a part of the concept of Messiah.

This dual idea of the divine King and human Servant in the concept of the Messiah finds its embodiment in the divine-human Jesus Christ. Therefore, all proofs that He was the divine-human One authenticate His claims to be the Messiah.

That He was divine is demonstrated by the names and titles previously discussed, by the fact that divine attributes are ascribed to Him (Matt. 11:27), by the fact that He performed divine acts (John 5:25-29), and by the attestations that He was God by demons (Matt. 8:28-29), angels (Luke 2:9-11), His enemies (Matt. 27:54), His friends (Matt. 16:16), and the Father (Matt. 3:17; 17:5).

That He was human was evident to all. He possessed a true
body (Luke 2:52; cf. Matt. 26:12, 26; Mark 14:8, 22, 24; Luke
7:44-46; 22:19-20; 24:39). He possessed an immaterial nature (Matt. 26:38; Mark 14:34; Luke 23:46). He experienced the normal development and difficulties of life (Luke
2:52; Matt. 8:24). Thus the very presence of Jesus Christ on
this earth as a display of the union of a divine and a human
nature in one person was a constant authentication of His
claim to be the Messiah as promised in the Old Testament
Scriptures.

III. THE REPUDIATION OF THE KING

The repudiation of the King is easily traced throughout
the remainder of Matthew, and only the outline of it need
be noted.

1. The repudiation by the Gadarenes because of the condemnation of their illegal business (8:34).

2. The repudiation by the scribes when Christ forgave
the sins of the paralytic (9:3).

3. The repudiation by the Pharisees who questioned His
eating with sinners (9:11).

4. The validation by Christ of the repudiation of those
who rejected the testimony of John the Baptist (11:2-19).

5. The repudiation by all the people of the cities to which
His credentials had been presented (11:20-30). In the midst
of the condemnation there was issued a word of invitation to
individuals (not the nation as a whole) to come to Him.

6. The repudiation by the Pharisees (12:1-50). This passage shows the marked contrast between the yoke of the Pharisees and the yoke of Messiah. This was clearly displayed on
the occasion of the healing of a man with a withered hand on
the Sabbath in violation of Jewish traditions. It was further
displayed with a finality in their committing the unpardonable sin, which was unpardonable for the simple reason that
these religious leaders should have known the power of the

Holy Spirit from their study of the Old Testament and consequently should have recognized Messiah, who was performing His miracles in that power.

7. The repudiation by the people of Nazareth (13:53-58).

8. The repudiation by Herod in his beheading of John (14:1-14).

9. Further rejection by the Pharisees (15:1-20).

10. The rejection by the rich young ruler (19:16-26).

11. The rejection by the chief priests and elders (21:23—22:14).

12. Repudiation by the Herodians, Sadducees, and Pharisees (22:15-46).

13. Full and complete rejection at the crucifixion (26:1—27:50).

IV. The Ministration of the King

In the introduction to this division it was pointed out that a Synoptic Theology must certainly include a major section on the teachings of Christ. Such a section, however, should not comprise the whole of the division nor obscure the theological pattern in the minds of the writers; therefore, it is included here as a major section but within the theological framework of the Synoptics.

A. *The Manner of Christ's Teaching*

It is very difficult to distinguish between the preaching and teaching of Christ, for all of His preaching was infused with teaching and His teaching was preached. He was called "Rabbi" not because He came from the schools but because of the quality of His utterances. Before considering the actual content of His teaching it will be profitable to look at some characteristics of His teaching.

1. *It was an occasional thing.* By this we mean not that He taught infrequently, but rather that He taught as the occasion arose. He was constantly alive to the opportunities

and seized upon a variety of situations. He gladly used the synagogue service as an occasion for teaching (Mark 1:21; Matt. 4:23); if an indoor setting were unavailable He preached outside (Mark 4:1):

> The servants of Christ should learn a lesson from their Master's conduct. . . . We are not to wait till every little difficulty or obstacle is removed, before we put our hand to the plough, or go forth to sow the seed of the word. Convenient buildings may often be wanting for assembling a company of hearers. Convenient rooms may often not be found for gathering children to school. What, then, are we to do? Shall we sit still and do nothing? God forbid! If we cannot do all we want, let us do what we can.[12]

2. *It was unsystematic.* This characteristic of our Lord's teaching is in a sense a result of the occasional nature of it. It is the task of the interpreter to systematize the scattered references to various doctrines in the teaching of Christ.

3. *It was profusely illustrated.* This is self-evident from the wide use our Lord made of parables and by His frequent use of the natural world to illustrate the spiritual world.

4. *It made use of interrogation.* This method was frequently used in controversy with the various sects of Judaism (Matt. 22).

5. *It was authoritative.* Perhaps this is the outstanding characteristic of Jesus' teaching manner, and it is to be accounted for in several ways. His teaching was authoritative because of the contrast with the teaching of the scribes and Pharisees (Mark 1:22). It was authoritative because it was fresh (Mark 1:27). Furthermore, it spoke of reality instead of outward show, and it was related to absolute and maximum standards rather than relative and minimum standards (Matt. 5:20-48).

6. *It was subjective.* Teaching generally points to what

[12]J. C. Ryle, *Expository Thoughts on the Gospels, Luke* (New York: Baker & Taylor, 1858), I, 131.

others say. Shammai and Hillel constantly taught in terms of what people ought to do; our Lord taught subjectively by putting Himself up as the standard to follow.

7. *It held attraction for people.* Although Christ's teaching brought division among the people, it nevertheless drew the attention of crowds of people. On one occasion the people testified that His words were gracious (Luke 4:22). He constantly ministered to all—not simply to those who could do something for Him in return (Mark 4:9, 22-23). In addition, there is evidence in the record that His messages attracted both men and women, and because both were in His crowds He suited His teaching to them. The kingdom of Heaven, for instance, was likened to both what a man does and what a woman does (Luke 13:19, 21). The parable of the lost sheep is followed by the parable of the lost coin—one involves a man and the other a woman (Luke 15:4, 8). When the Lord used the lilies as an object lesson (Matt. 6:28) He chose something which could be related to the activities of both men and women ("They toil not, neither do they spin"). Too, when speaking of His return He spoke of two men in the field (*eis*, the male one, shall be taken) and two women at the mill (*mia*, the female one, shall be taken; Matt. 24:40-41).

B. *Christ's Teaching Concerning Sin*

The determining of Christ's view of sin is of very great importance, for on this matter hangs the doctrine of redemption. Fortunately, the references to sin are numerous and explicit in the words of our Lord so that we are not left in any doubt as to His ideas on this subject.

1. *The universality of sin.* Christ did not view sin as something superficial or limited to one portion of the human race. He classified the best of men—His disciples—as evil (Luke 11:13), and He taught them to pray for forgiveness of sin (Matt. 6:12). Furthermore He called to repentance all men with-

out discrimination or distinction (Mark 1:15), which would hardly have been necessary if all men were not sinners. In parable the Lord reiterated this fact of the universality of sin (Matt. 13:47-50; 22:1-14; 25:1-13). This is not to say that the Saviour did not recognize distinctions in degrees of sin (cf. John 8:34; 18:37; 1:47; Mark 2:17; Luke 5:32).

2. *The doctrine of depravity.* By depravity we mean that man is unable by nature to do anything which would make him acceptable before God. That does not mean that man cannot do anything which is not relatively good, but all such goodness is of no avail in gaining eternal life. Our Lord plainly taught that by nature man is evil. The parables of Luke 15 show the lost condition of man, and the encounter with the lawyer is the best example of the true nature of man (Luke 10:25-37). That this sinfulness in man is due to the root of sin within was also clearly a part of Christ's teaching (Mark 7:20-23; Matt. 11:16-19; 12:39; 17:17; 23:1-39). Though all of these facts concerning the depraved nature of man be true, one must never forget the inestimable value placed by the Lord on the soul of man (Matt. 16:26).

3. *The forms of sin.* The root of sin expresses itself in many ways according to the Lord's teaching.

a. Sacrilege (Mark 11:15-21).

b. Hypocrisy (Matt. 16:6-12; 23:1-39).

c. Covetousness (Luke 12).

d. Blasphemy (Matt. 12:22-37).

e. Transgression of the law (Matt. 15:3-6; 19:3-12; Mark 2:23—3:5; 7:1-13).

f. Pride (Matt. 20:20-28; Mark 10:35-45).

g. Disloyalty (Matt. 8:19-22).

h. Immorality (Matt. 5:28).

i. Useless speaking (Matt. 12:36-37).

j. Unfaithfulness (Matt. 15:14-30; Luke 19:12-27).

4. *The forgiveness of sin.* This subject encompasses matters which are yet to be discussed; therefore, it is sufficient to

note at this point that the Saviour based forgiveness on the shedding of His own blood (Matt. 26:28). That this giving of His own life was done in a strictly substitutionary sense is seen by His own statement that it was given as a ransom for (*anti*, in the place of) many (Matt. 20:28; Mark 10:45). The preposition *anti* cannot be construed in any other way than substitution.[13] The Lord often related the matter of our forgiving one another to God's forgiveness of our sins (Mark 11:25, 26; Luke 11:4; 17:3, 4).

C. *Christ's Teaching Concerning Salvation*

1. *The need for salvation.* The need for Christ's salvation is readily seen in His estimate of the nature of man. He declared that by nature man is evil (Matt. 12:34; Luke 11:13) and capable of great wickedness (Mark 7:20-23). Since this corruption is internal (Matt. 15:11, 17-20) man stands in need of repentance (Matt. 18:3).

2. *The death of Christ.*

a. The manner of His death. The manner of the death of Christ is clearly predicted in His teachings. It was to be a violent death (Matt. 16:21; Mark 8:31; Luke 9:22), a fact which is also taught in parable (Matt. 21:39). It was to be death by crucifixion (Matt. 20:19; 26:2). His death was to be preceded by betrayal (Matt. 26:21; Mark 14:18). The involvement of the elders, chief priests, scribes, and Gentiles was also predicted (Matt. 16:21; 20:19).

b. The meaning of His death. From our Lord's own teaching there is no doubt as to the meaning of His death for us. It was a voluntary and vicarious giving of His life as a ransom (Matt. 20:28). It was an expiation for sin (Matt.

---

[13]Even *huper*, which is also used of Christ's death for us, sometimes clearly has the meaning of substitution (Luke 22:19-20; John 10:11; 11:50-51; cf. Philem. 13, where the preposition clearly means "in the place of" and where it is used in a passage which has no connection with the atonement). The new liberalism completely ignores this linguistic evidence and still insists that the death of Christ was merely "representative" rather than "substitutionary" (cf. A. N. Wilder, *New Testament Faith for Today* [New York: Harper, 1955], p. 134).

26:28; Mark 14:24; Luke 22:20), and the uniform scriptural use of blood forbids any interpretation of the Lord's words other than as teaching expiation of sin by death.[14] For Himself, His death would bring exaltation and glory (Luke 24:26).

3. *The universality of His salvation.* The necessity of faith in relation to salvation is seen in the Synoptics mainly in incidents of physical healing (Luke 6:9; 7:50; 8:48, 50; 17:19; 18:42). The most profound exposition of the way of salvation is John's revelation. However, the revelation of the universality of salvation is primarily Lukan and therefore an important part of the Synoptic teaching. It was announced by the angels (2:10—"to all people"), confirmed by Simeon (2:32—"to lighten the Gentiles") and John the Baptist (3:6—"all flesh"), and affirmed in Luke's genealogy which traces Jesus back to Adam; but the universality of salvation is best seen in the parable of the good Samaritan and the incident that provoked it (Luke 10:25-37). The lawyer's motivation was merely discussion and not conviction of heart. Christ's purpose was to lead him to see the bankruptcy of his own heart and thus the need of a Saviour. It was the lawyer's attempt at self-justification in asking who his neighbor was that led to the parable of the good Samaritan and the pushing out of the bounds of love beyond the exclusivism of Judaism.

D. *Christ's Teaching Concerning Angels*

1. *Satan.*

a. His existence. Every reference by Christ to the Evil One is a proof of Satan's existence. Even though modern theology explains these as accommodation by the Lord of His language to the ordinary Jewish belief, it must be realized that such accommodation in reality invalidates His whole message.

It is impossible to conceive of the Saviour being either mistaken in His view or misleading men in His teaching

[14]Cf. A. M. Stibbs, *The Meaning of the Word "Blood" in Scripture* (London: Tyndale Press, 1947), pp. 1-35.

on such a subject, and yet maintain His infallibility on the one hand, or His moral perfection on the other.[15]

b. His personality. Satan's personality is demonstrated by references to his intellect (Matt. 4:6), sensibility (Luke 22: 31), and will (Matt. 13:39; Luke 13:16). It is further demonstrated by the fact that he is treated as a morally responsible being (Matt. 25:41), and by the fact that personal pronouns are used in speaking of him (Matt. 4:10; 10:25; 16: 23).

c. His position. The Lord affirmed the fact that Satan is head of this world system (Matt. 4:8-10; 12:26; John 12:31). The full revelation of the meaning of this is a major part of Johannine theology.

d. His purpose. Satan's purpose in this age is best seen in the parables of Matthew 13 where his character as deceiver and hinderer of God's program is clearly taught.

e. His judgment. The Lord also spoke of the certainty of the judgment of Satan (Luke 10:18; John 12:31; 16:11).

2. *Angels.* In Burntisland, Scotland, stands the first church built after the Reformation, and in this church is the following inscription:

"Though Gods' Power Be sufthint to Governe Us
Yet for Man's Infirmitie He appointeth His Angels
To Watch over Us."

The ministry of angels is generally slighted by Protestants probably because of a fear of going to the extremes that other groups exhibit. Nevertheless angelic agency is important in the providential outworkings of the plan of God, a fact which is seen most clearly in the life and teachings of Christ.

a. The characteristics of angels. According to the Lord's teaching angels do not propagate after their kind; therefore, their number is fixed (Matt. 22:30; Mark 12:25; Luke 20:

[15]J. M. King, *The Theology of Christ's Teaching* (London: Hodder and Stoughton, 1902), p. 298.

36). In the instances when angels appeared they were youthful in appearance (Mark 16:5); they appeared as males (Luke 24:4; but cf. Zech. 5:9); they appeared as supernatural beings and were recognized as such (Matt. 28:3-4); their raiment was often white and dazzling (Matt. 28:3; Luke 24: 4); and they had unusual strength (Matt. 28:2; cf. Mark 16: 3-4).

b. Their ministry to Jesus of Nazareth. (1) In connection with the birth of Christ. An angel announced the birth of the forerunner (Luke 1:11). The same angel, Gabriel, who seems to appear on special occasions, announced the birth of Messiah to Mary (Luke 1:26). Angels also made the announcement of the actual birth to the shepherds (Luke 2: 9). (2) In connection with the life of Christ. Angels ministered to Christ after His temptation (Matt. 4:11), and an angel strengthened Him in Gethsemane (Luke 22:43—the word for "strengthen" used in this verse is used elsewhere only in Acts 9:19, where it indicates bodily strengthening). Evidently, too, angels were always ready to undertake for the Lord any ministry He might have requested (Matt. 26:53). (3) In connection with the resurrection of Christ. An angel rolled away the stone from the tomb (Matt. 28:2) so that the witnesses of the resurrection might look in. It was angels too who first announced the resurrection (Luke 24:4-6, 23). (4) In connection with the return of Christ. Our Lord taught that His return would be in the company of angels (Luke 9:26), and that upon His return at the end of the age the angels would act as reapers separating the wheat from the tares (Matt. 13:39, 41-42, 49-50). They will also be used to gather the elect at His coming (Matt. 24:31).

c. Other ministries of angels. In addition to what has been said the Lord also revealed two other facts about the angels. They rejoice when a sinner repents (Luke 15:10), for their estimate of the value of a soul is far more accurate than that of the Pharisees to whom the parables of this chapter were addressed. In the story of the rich man and Lazarus the Lord incidentally refers to the fact that angels carried Lazarus to Abraham's bosom (Luke 16:22). What this reference may mean in relation to general procedure is almost impossible to say.

3. *Demons.*

a. Their reality. The reality of demons as real, substantial beings whose existence is not dependent on man's being or thinking is everywhere affirmed by Christ. Not all agree to this today, for some have said that the Lord actually did not accomplish the healing of those who were believed to be possessed, but that the Evangelists have erroneously attributed it to Him. Others have said that the Lord merely went through the form of casting out demons even though in reality He knew that there were no demons to be cast out. Still others declare that He went through the form of casting out demons because He believed that there were demons present, but in that belief He was mistaken and merely shared the erroneous belief of His contemporaries. In other words, these explanations mean: either (1) the Evangelists lied, or (2) Jesus acted out a lie, though He knew better, or (3) Jesus was deceived in His own beliefs. If true, number (1) opens the door for denying the historicity of all the Scriptures. Number (2) is in reality deceiving accommodation and is unworthy of any great person—certainly unworthy of the Son of God; and such accommodation concerning demons goes too far—the Lord spoke of the reality of demons on occasions when He was teaching His disciples and not accommodating Himself to large audiences (Matt. 10:8, 17-18). Explanation (3) is an outright denial of the deity of Christ. If the authority of Christ be recognized, the reality of demons is certain.

b. Their nature. Demons are spirit beings (Matt. 8:16; 17:18; cf. Mark 9:25; Luke 10:17, 20). They are unclean (Matt. 10:1; Mark 1:27; 3:11), and some are worse than others (Matt. 12:45). They are organized (Matt. 12:22-30); they recognize the authority of Jesus (Luke 8:28); and they evidently realize that their doom in the abyss is certain (Luke 8:31).

c. Their work. The work of demons is in general, of course, to promote the purposes of Satan and to hinder the purpose of God. Since Satan is not omnipresent, demons are employed to extend his authority and activity. We know from the Gospel records that they can possess men and animals (Mark 5:8-14), that they lead men into moral impurity (Matt. 10:1; 12:43; Mark 1:23-27; 5:12, 13; Luke 4:33-36), and that they can inflict physical and mental disease (Matt. 8:28; 9:32-33; Mark 5:5; 9:17-18).

We have discussed the teachings of Christ concerning sin, salvation, and angelic beings. Other subjects such as the Holy Spirit, regeneration, and sanctification belong to Johannine theology and will be discussed there. The teaching concerning the kingdom and the present Church age finds its rightful place under the eschatology of the Synoptics. The treatment of other topics such as prayer, discipleship, etc., though valuable and appropriate, seems out of bounds for a book of this size and can only be recommended to the individual's investigation.

V. The Condemnation of the King

The story of the King is a story of loneliness. First He was received and acclaimed; He proved Himself in every way; His teaching was recognized; but now the repudiation climaxes in the rejection. This clearly is the outline of the Christology of the theology of the Synoptics. Some aspects of the rejection are merely historical and some are theological, but both are essential to a proper understanding of Synoptic theology as seen from the viewpoint of the human writers.

A. *The Garden of Gethsemane*

In the Garden all forsook Him and He was utterly alone. The theological problem connected with the scene is to explain the seemingly ruffled composure of the Lord in His prayer concerning the passing of the cup from Him.

One explanation is that Jesus was afraid to die. Of course, if this were true it would make Him greatly inferior to many of His followers who in later years died fearlessly. Also, it would lead logically to the conclusion that Jesus was Himself a sinner.

Another explanation for His actions in the Garden is that He was afraid He would die before the proper time of sacrifice on the Cross; i.e., that Satan would thwart the purpose of the Cross by a premature death. But we know that Satan did not have the power over Christ in this regard (John 10: 18).

A third explanation is that going to the Cross would involve a crime against God on the part of man and Jesus did not want to be involved in such a crime; therefore, He prayed that it would not come to pass. But there is no evidence in His thoughts as revealed by His actions in this scene that such an idea existed, for our Lord never associated Himself with His slayers.

The only correct explanation of His behavior is that He was shrinking from the prospect of being the sin bearer of the world. This involved linking Himself with sin, which in itself is a terrible enough thing to account for the actions in the Garden; but that linking with sin also involved being forsaken by the Father, the significance of which is incomprehensible to human minds. It is true that the struggle is that of the human nature, and in a sense it is the will of Christ which was offered in Gethsemane in this brief prayer.

B. *The Arrest*

Immediately the multitude appeared, the betrayer kissed Him, the soldiers fell back evidently because of a flash of His glory (John 18:6), and Peter (probably missing his aim at the man's head) cut off the ear of the servant of the high priest. Our Lord healed the ear, chided the multitude for the display of weapons, and was led away to be tried and condemned.

C. *The Trials*

1. *The trial before the high priest* (Matt. 26:57-68; Mark 14:53-65; Luke 22:54-65; cf. John 18:12-27).

a. The first phase—the informal trial before Annas. Jesus was brought first before Annas, the father-in-law of Caiaphas. Possibly this was done because the house of Annas was near at hand.[16] or, more likely, because Annas was recognized as the legitimate high priest by strict Jews while Caiaphas was the politically expedient high priest set up by the Romans.[17] During this phase of the trial the witnesses were being secured.

b. The second phase—before Caiaphas with two false witnesses. Our Lord was next brought before Caiaphas, but no formal charge was made. When witnesses failed to appear two false ones were produced, but still no formal charge had been made.

c. The third phase—the violence of the high priest and the silence of Christ. The high priest's reaction to the testimony of the false witnesses was violence. He arose and demanded an answer from the prisoner, but Jesus held His peace. This silence on the part of the Lord is not to be construed as His consenting to the proceedings; actually His silence is clear proof of His refusal to countenance the illegal trial. It is a vivid picture of royal serenity.

d. The fourth phase—the placing of Christ under oath. Finally the high priest put Jesus under formal oath to declare whether or not He was deity. Our Lord's answer posi-

[16]A. Edersheim, *The Life and Times of Jesus the Messiah* (Grand Rapids: Wm. B. Eerdmans Publishing Co., 1943), II, 547.

[17]For an extended discussion of this see J. A. Alexander, *The Acts of the Apostles* (New York: Charles Scribner, 1872), I, 134-36.

tively affirmed that He was the Son of God and even went a step further, for He added that they would see the Son of Man coming in the clouds of heaven, thereby identifying Himself with the Old Testament prophecy. Upon this testimony He was accused of blasphemy, because they recognized this as a claim of deity.

2. *The first trial before Pilate* (Matt. 27:2, 11-14; Mark 15:1-5; Luke 23:1-5; cf. John 18:28-38). The trial before Pilate was necessitated by the simple fact that the Jews did not have the authority to put Jesus to death (John 18:31). It was not simply that they were seeking to rid themselves of the matter, for had that been the case they would have been glad when Pilate found Him innocent. It is John who presents the most detail concerning this trial, and his account begins by noting the ridiculously inconsistent scrupulousness of the Jews who refused to enter the house of Pilate (a Gentile) lest they be defiled for Passover. The charge which was pressed before the Roman authority was not that of blasphemy but that of sedition. Therefore, Pilate's inquiry was "Art thou the King of the Jews?" The Lord's reply (John 18:34) was to inquire of Pilate whether he was asking the question from the viewpoint of a Roman or a Jew, for it would make a great deal of difference in the answer whether he were asking Jesus if He were a king according to Roman or Jewish outlook. When Pilate declared that his viewpoint certainly was not Jewish (v. 35), the Lord replied that His kingdom did not concern worldly kingdoms. Then Pilate inquired if He were a king in any sense (v. 37). The Lord said that He was the king of truth, and Pilate's flippant answer was simply "What is truth?" The result of the trial was the pronouncement that Jesus was not dangerous to Rome. The Jews, however, were not satisfied and in their persistence mentioned Galilee, which provided Pilate with an excuse to send Jesus to Herod.

3. *The trial before Herod* (Luke 23:6-12). Herod's ac-

tions on this occasion display vividly the effects of sin in hardening the heart. This is the Herod who married his brother Philip's wife and who beheaded John the Baptist. His interest was in seeing a miracle, and when that was not forthcoming he and his men mocked Jesus and sent Him back to Pilate.

4. *The second trial before Pilate* (Matt. 27:15-26; Mark 15:6-15; Luke 23:13-25; cf. John 18:39—19:16). If Herod is a picture of hardness of heart Pilate is a picture of weakness of character. Although he had found Jesus innocent he thought to scourge Him before releasing Him. Then he grabbed at the straw of the custom of releasing one prisoner at Passover. The Jews' request for the release of Barabbas shows the success of the propaganda campaign of the priests among the people. Pilate turned Jesus over to the soldiers for scourging, perhaps thinking that this would be sufficient and that he could release Jesus then, but the crowd interpreted it as the scourging which preceded crucifixion (cf. John 19:4-5). Pilate again stalled, but when the crowd threatened to go over his head and take the case to Rome he gave in.

D. *The Death*

Mention has already been made of certain theological aspects of Christ's death in His own teaching. At this point, then, consideration needs to be given to the seven words uttered on the Cross as revealing the Saviour's own thoughts during the crucifixion.

1. *"Father, forgive them; for they know not what they do"* (Luke 23:34). This was probably uttered as they nailed Him to the Cross and is a plea for God to be longsuffering. The people did not know what they were doing because they did not know who it was they were crucifying; therefore, these words imply that their ignorance mitigated the criminality of the act, but of course did not exonerate those who com-

mitted it (cf. I Cor. 2:8). In His death, He was forgiving.

2. *"Today shalt thou be with me in Paradise"* (Luke 23: 43). The thief, to whom this word was spoken, probably heard the first prayer for forgiveness and turned in repentance to the Saviour. Even on the Cross the Lord was winning men to Himself, and His word of assurance presupposes that He would live on in resurrection. The word *Paradise* is used by Christ only here, and means the bliss of Heaven itself.[18] It is not some intermediate compartment. In His death He saved men.

3. *"Woman, behold thy son . . . Behold thy mother"* (John 19:26-27). If it were not that spiritual matters are of utmost importance, the Lord might have committed His mother to James or Jude or one of the others of His own family, but because His brethren were as yet unbelievers He committed her to John. In His death He was concerned with things spiritual.

4. *"My God, my God, why hast thou forsaken me?"* (Matt. 27:46; Mark 15:34). The first three sayings were probably all spoken before noon. This one, which is in every way central, was uttered about 3 P.M., after three hours of darkness and silence during which the Son of God bore the sin of the world. In that work He had to be forsaken by God, and yet at the same time there was no splitting up of the Trinity. All that is involved is inscrutable, but He gave Himself, He was made sin, He bore our sins, and His soul was made an offering for sin. His work was to bear sin.

5. *"I thirst"* (John 19:28). Up to this point our Lord had refused the stupefying drink which was usually given to those who were undergoing the tortures of crucifixion (cf. Matt. 27:34, 48). Now that He has accomplished His work while in full possession of all His faculties He requested the drink. His work was consciously done.

6. *"It is finished"* (John 19:30). This is the cry of victory

[18]A. T. Robertson, *Word Pictures in the New Testament* (New York: Harper, 1930), II, 286-87.

in the hour of seeming defeat. The plan of salvation stands completed. This involves especially the work of redemption from sin, reconciliation of man, and propitiation of God. His work was completely done.

7. *"Father, into thy hands I commend my spirit"* (Luke 23:46). This last word reveals clearly the voluntary character of His death, for it was not until He dismissed His spirit from His body that death occurred. No man took His life from Him; His work was voluntarily done.

Thus, the seven sayings of the Cross reveal that in His death He was forgiving, saving, and concerned with things spiritual; and they reveal that His sacrificial work was to bear sin consciously, completely, and consentaneously. No man can fathom all that is involved.

> The value of the sacrifice is not to be discovered in the intensity of the Saviour's anguish but rather in the dignity and infinite worth of the One who suffers. He did not give more or less; He gave *Himself,* He offered Himself, but this self was none other than the Second Person of the Godhead in whom measureless dignity and glory reside.[19]

VI. THE VINDICATION OF THE KING

All the Gospel writers conclude with the account of the resurrection, thus all considered it a vital and necessary part of their theology. Each one seems to use it for his own peculiar purposes. Matthew emphasizes the resurrection as a proof of all that Christ taught (28:6—"as he said"), and he relates it to the power which would be available to His disciples in their carrying out of the commission (28:18). Mark seems to emphasize the appearances of the risen Lord as proof of His resurrection. After all, no one saw the actual rising, and the witnesses are witnesses to the fact that the tomb was empty and to the fact that they saw the risen Christ.

[19]L. S. Chafer, *Systematic Theology* (Dallas: Dallas Seminary Press, 1947), III, 68.

Luke, whose account includes the extended record of the appearance to the two disciples on the Emmaus road, connects the resurrection with new understanding of truth (24:27), a new pattern of life (24:44—"while I was yet with you" indicates a difference between the Lord's preresurrection and postresurrection mode of life), and the new work (24:48).

Thus the resurrection is proved (this is Mark's emphasis); it in turn proves all of Christ's claims (this is Matthew's emphasis); and it is the basis of newness of life (this is Luke's emphasis).

Chapter 3

THE ESCHATOLOGY OF THE SYNOPTICS

I. The Kingdom Proffered

IT IS RIGHTLY OBSERVED that the theology of the Gospels is an eschatology or it is nothing.[1] As we have seen in the previous section even the Christology is essentially eschatological for it concerns the Messiah; therefore, it is not surprising to discover that the bulk of the Synoptic teaching concerns the kingdom.

A. *The Messengers of the Kingdom*

1. *John the Baptist* (Matt. 3:1-12). The first messenger of the kingdom was John the Baptist, whose ministry was a fulfillment of the prophecy of Elijah's return before the Day of the Lord (Matt. 11:10, 14; 17:12).

2. *Jesus* (Matt. 4:17). Our Lord also came announcing the kingdom. A comparison of Matthew 4:17 with Mark 1:14 will show that *euaggelion,* gospel, is not a technical word but that it simply means good news, the content of which must be defined by the context. In this case it was the good news concerning the nearness of the kingdom.

3. *The Twelve* (Matt. 10:1—11:1). The twelve apostles were also commissioned to preach the good news concerning

[1] J. Moffatt, *The Theology of the Gospels* (New York: Charles Scribner's Sons, 1913), p. 41.

72

the kingdom. The extent of their ministry was expressly limited by the Lord to Israelites, and Israelites must be understood to mean Jews, for the Lord specifically forbade them to go to Gentiles or even to the half-caste Samaritans.

B. *The Message of the Kingdom*

In the case of each of the messengers the message was the same—"Repent, for the kingdom of heaven is at hand." The kingdom that was being announced and proffered at this time was no new thing to the Jewish people. They had a clear idea of what was meant, and that was the kingdom of David's son, Messiah. The announcement was that it had drawn near and stood near (perfect tense of "draw near"; cf. Matt. 21:1; 11:9-12; 26:45-46; Rom. 13:12; Jas. 5:8; I Pet. 4:7). As a matter of fact it was so near that the people should have seen the evidences and signs of it. The concept of the kingdom was clear enough, and that the kingdom was near was central in the message. The new and stumbling idea in the message was that repentance was necessary. Actually it was not new, for the Old Testament prophets had often called the people to repentance in connection with their promised blessings, but it was new in the sense that the people of Jesus' day had expected the kingdom to come in power and without any inward change being required on their part. Many of them did repent as evidenced by the many who received baptism at the hand of John. But most did not. Specifically, the Lord described what that repentance involved in the Sermon on the Mount. The people accepted the good news that the kingdom was near but rejected the requirement of repentance which would have brought its establishment.

C. *The Meaning of the Kingdom*

This is the crux of the matter, for if the message of the kingdom concerned the Church that is one thing; if the

Davidic, earthly kingdom that is another. The amillennialist viewpoint is that the kingdom as announced was not the
Davidic kingdom.[2] It was in fact, as explained in the further
ministry of Christ, the Church, and the kingdom of Heaven
and the Church "are in most respects at least equivalent, and
. . . the two institutions are co-existent and largely co-exten-
sive."[3] In such a viewpoint the Sermon on the Mount becomes the law and standard for the Church, the parables of
Matthew 13 also concern the Church and describe it, and the
Olivet Discourse merely concerns the end of all time, not
the cataclysmic events prior to the setting up of the Davidic
kingdom. Why the author rejects this viewpoint has already
been stated in another work to which the reader is referred.[4]

The premillennial concept of the kingdom does not deny
the fact that in some places the word *kingdom* is used of a
universal, timeless, and eternal kingdom (Matt. 6:33). Nor
does it deny the fact that the mysteries of the kingdom of
Heaven (Matt. 13) concern this present age. But it does
affirm that the Messianic, Davidic, earthly, millennial kingdom was that which John, the Lord, and the Twelve announced, that it was rejected by the Jews and therefore (from
man's viewpoint) postponed, and that the promises which
necessitate its being set up on the earth will be literally fulfilled at the second coming of Christ. Whatever variations
there may be within the premillennial camp must not obscure the fact that the basic difference between premillennialism and amillennialism is that premillennialism regards the
Davidic kingdom promises unfulfilled by the Church and
yet to be fulfilled literally. Amillennialism finds no place for
this aspect of the kingdom except in a supposed fulfillment
by the Church. Thus, in the Synoptics, premillennialism rec-

[2]O. T. Allis, *Prophecy and the Church* (Philadephia: The Presbyterian
and Reformed Publishing Co., 1945), p. 71.
[3]*Ibid.,* p. 83.
[4]C. C. Ryrie, *The Basis of the Premillennial Faith* (New York: Loizeaux
Brothers, 1953).

ognizes and distinguishes the eternal kingdom, the mystery form of the kingdom, and the Messianic kingdom.

Within the circle of premillennial interpretation there is one point of variation which should be mentioned. Some premillennialists distinguish between the meaning of the phrases *kingdom of Heaven* and *kingdom of God*. If such a distinction is made it is usually made along this line: the kingdom of Heaven is said to include professing but unreal elements while the kingdom of God does not. This is not an essential matter in the interpretation of the Synoptics. The basic issue is the distinguishing of the eternal, Messianic, and mystery aspects of the kingdom. Some hold that the difference between kingdom of Heaven and kingdom of God is not real but is traceable to the Aramaic original in which our Lord preached.[5] Others say that the two phrases are synonymous because they appear in similar parables, and what is said of the kingdom of Heaven is also said of the kingdom of God.[6] Still others say that there was probably no essential difference as far as the early preaching was concerned, but that the difference is real by virtue of usage in the record. This is a difference which was made more by the Holy Spirit in the work of revelation and inspiration than by the early preachers.[7] Such a view recognizes that by usage there seems to be a distinction which cannot be dismissed as a peculiarity of the Jewish flavor of Matthew. (If that is all that is involved then why do not Mark and Luke use kingdom of Heaven at least occasionally as a synonymous phrase to kingdom of God?) But it also recognizes that the essential distinction is between the eternal kingdom, the Messianic, millennial kingdom, and the mystery form of the kingdom (whichever phrase is used in any instance).

Matthew seems to emphasize this basic distinction simply

[5]G. E. Ladd, *Crucial Questions About the Kingdom of God* (Grand Rapids: Eerdmans, 1952), pp. 122 ff.
[6]G. N. H. Peters, *The Theocratic Kingdom* (Grand Rapids: Kregel, 1952), I, 283.
[7]Cf. Ryrie, *op. cit.*, pp. 98-99, and Peters, *op. cit.*, I, 195.

by the space he devotes to (1) the Sermon on the Mount (which is related to the Messianic kingdom), (2) the parables of the thirteenth chapter (which is related to the mystery form of the kingdom), and (3) the Olivet Discourse (which is also related to the future establishment of the Messianic kingdom). In Matthew the eternal kingdom is referred to infrequently (cf. 6:33; 12:28; 13:38, 43; 19:24; 21: 31). However, the question is, What kingdom was at hand according to the preaching of John the Baptist and Christ? Obviously it was not the eternal kingdom, for that was already in existence. Equally clear is the fact that it was not the mystery form of the kingdom, for that was not revealed until later in our Lord's ministry. Therefore, the kingdom that was preached as at hand must have been the Messianic kingdom. This was in exact accord with the concept of the kingdom which the Jews had at the time Christ began His ministry. They were looking for the Messianic kingdom, not anything else, and although the Lord later revealed other things about the concept of the kingdom He did not nullify that which He had previously spoken. The kingdom proffered was the millennial kingdom. It was a genuine offer which was just as bona fide as the offer of the Gospel is today to every non-elect person. Man's reaction or ability to respond does not determine the validity of an offer. When the Jews rejected this offer it was according to the program of God, and the Messianic kingdom was postponed. This idea of postponement is a concept which many object to as if it impugned the character of God or the Cross of Christ. Let it be recognized that to say the kingdom was postponed is just as proper as to say that God postpones certain blessings in one's life because of unbelief. To say that a postponed kingdom implies that had it been received there would have been no Cross (and thus the concept involves minimizing the Cross) is to err greatly. The Cross has always been in the plan of God and depended neither on the acceptance nor rejection by Israel of the Messianic kingdom. Had the kingdom offer been accepted at the first advent of Christ the Messiah still would have had to die, for a vicariously suffering Messiah was part and parcel of the kingdom concept of the Old Testament. The fact that the kingdom was rejected and thereby postponed in no way minimizes the Cross.

Thus the kingdom proffered was the Messianic, millennial kingdom promised to David and his seed, affirmed everywhere in the teaching of the Old Testament prophets, anticipated with keen expectation by the Jews at the time of Christ, and proclaimed by John and Jesus during the early part of the latter's ministry.

II. THE KINGDOM PROCLAIMED

Matthew's Gospel is ordered theology. Having presented the King through His genealogy, His birth, and acclaim by the wise men, His baptism, and His temptation; and having emphasized the preaching of the kingdom as at hand (3:2; 4: 17), Matthew then records the Sermon on the Mount. From the very order of the Gospel one would suspect strongly that the Sermon on the Mount had something to do with the Messianic kingdom. The parables of the mysteries of the kingdom do not appear until much later, and the revelation of the Church to be built in the future is even later than that. Therefore, even though the chronological order of these events and discourses may not be the same, the theological order is clearly set forth by Matthew. Objections that we are seeing too much in Matthew's order border on disrespect to the Holy Spirit whose orderly and holy arrangement this is.

However, before discussing exactly how the sermon relates to the kingdom, it would be well to survey other basic views concerning the interpretation of the passage. (1) The first view regards the Sermon as a means of salvation for the world. This is generally the view of the liberal, whether the salvation is individual or cultural. For instance, Harnack says that in the Sermon Jesus goes through

> the several departments of human relationships and human failings so as to bring the disposition and intention to light in each case, to judge man's works by them, and on them to hang heaven and hell.[8]

Another states it this way:

> In all this it is made clear that what matters is character and conduct. Salvation comes to those who turn with a single mind to worship and obey God, walking in the way that has been opened up by Jesus.[9]

Several objections must be raised against this view. First, the sermon was not addressed to the whole world but to the disciples as representative Jews expecting the Messianic kingdom (Matt. 5:1-2). Second, there are no mentions of redemption, justification, and other basic themes related to spiritual salvation. Third, in order to make this speak of salvation one would have to show that the kingdom of Heaven (Matt. 5:20; 7:21) means Heaven or the Church, and not the Messianic kingdom. This would be difficult if not impossible to do. Fourth, to make this a way of salvation would be to preach a gospel of works.

(2) The second basic view is that the sermon is for the Church. "It is the voice of the Chief Shepherd. It is the charge of the great Bishop and Head of the Church."[10] It is a "statement of the practical way in which *agape* is to work itself out in daily conduct here and now. The sermon expresses therefore the only righteousness acceptable to God in this age or in any."[11] Another concludes that "the Sermon

[8] A. Harnack, *What Is Christianity?* (London: Williams & Norgate, 1904), p. 72.

[9] Major, Manson, and Wright, *The Mission and Message of Jesus* (London: Ivor Nicholson and Watson, 1937), p. 470.

[10] J. C. Ryle, *Expository Thoughts on the Gospels, Matthew* (New York: Baker and Taylor, 1858), p. 32.

[11] C. F. H. Henry, *Christian Personal Ethics* (Grand Rapids: Eerdmans, 1957), p. 308.

on the Mount is intended for the guidance of regenerate persons in an unregenerate world."[12] Whatever is recognized by those who hold this view of the eschatological element in the Sermon, that element is definitely secondary to the principal emphasis of the Sermon as a code of personal ethics for the Church today.

Several objections must be raised. First, in order to interpret the Sermon in relation to the Christian and the Church the principle of literal interpretation must be abandoned. Miller, who holds this view, says quite clearly:

> Many of the sayings of the Sermon are metaphorical or proverbial statements, and are not to be understood in a literal or legal sense. . . . But rather the principles behind the concrete instances are to be sought and applied anew to the life of the present as Jesus applied them to the life of His own time.[13]

Any interpretation which must discard literal interpretation ought to be doubted seriously.

Second, such an interpretation is contrary to the theological pattern of Matthew. If the Holy Spirit was fulfilling the Saviour's promise to teach the disciples as well as to remind them of things (John 14:26), and if Matthew's treatment is a theological setting forth of the meaning of Christ's teachings, then one should not ignore the place Matthew gives to the Sermon—a place which definitely relates it to the Messianic kingdom and not to the Church.

Third, there is in the Sermon a striking and embarrassing absence of Church truth as later revealed in the Epistles. It is readily granted that this does not conclusively prove that the Sermon is not for the Church, but it is admittedly very strange that this most complete of all the teachings of Jesus does not mention the Holy Spirit, or the Church *per se,* or

[12]C. F. Hogg and J. B. Watson, *On the Sermon on the Mount* (London: Pickering & Inglis, 1933), p. 19.

[13]R. B. Miller, "Sermon on the Mount," *The International Standard Bible Encyclopaedia,* IV, 2735.

prayer in the name of Christ. These things Christ did mention during His ministry (cf. John 14:16; 16:13, 24; Matt. 16:18). Of all the teaching in the Sermon on prayer, for instance, the Lord later said that it did not reveal the proper basis (John 16:24), which is a rather important omission from that which is "the rule of daily life for the Christian believer."[14] The usual reply to such an objection is that the Sermon has to be supplemented by the teaching of the rest of the New Testament. But that supplementation appears more to involve an essential difference and makes one suspicious of this interpretation. Even Hogg and Watson admit that "taken alone, beautiful as it is, it were law and not gospel."[15] Therefore, it appears that the additional information supplied by the rest of the New Testament is in reality different information and so essentially different as to raise serious question about the validity of this interpretation.

(3) The Sermon on the Mount is kingdom truth. All Scripture is profitable; therefore, whatever be the interpretation of the Sermon it will have application to the Church. Even the most ardent dispensationalists teach its application to the Church: "A secondary application to the church means that lessons and principles may be drawn from it."[16] Thus to say that it is kingdom truth is not to deny its relevance to the Church.

That the Sermon concerns the kingdom is established (1) by the principle of literal interpretation and (2) by the principle of Biblical Theology as displayed in Matthew's theological Gospel (which is based on John 14:26). The King was presented, and He in turn offered Israel her kingdom. It is only logical that He would outline the laws of that kingdom. This is Matthew's divinely inspired order.

Some, however, say that the Sermon is kingdom truth and then proceed to make the kingdom God's universal rule at all times. In other words, "kingdom" is made synonymous with

[14]Henry, *loc. cit.*
[15]*Op. cit.*, p. 105.
[16]L. S. Chafer, *Systematic Theology*, V, 97.

"Church," and even though it is said to be for the kingdom, in reality it is meant that it is for the Church. By "kingdom" we mean the Messianic, millennial, Davidic kingdom, offered by Messiah at His first coming but not to be established until His second coming. The Sermon was preached in relation to this concept of the kingdom, and whatever application it may have, it was in a context of Messianic kingdom expectation that it was preached, and that must be its primary interpretation.

Most who follow this basic view understand that the Sermon relates to the kingdom as it will be established in the future. In this connection, then, it is often called the constitution of the kingdom. Obvious objections, however, will be raised by some to relating the Sermon exclusively to the Messianic kingdom as it will be established in the future millennium. The objections are based on the simple fact that there are some things in the Sermon which picture conditions that are entirely different from what is known of the millennial age from other Scriptures. For instance, if the kingdom is established, why pray "Thy kingdom come"? Or again, if righteousness reigns why are those who are persecuted called blessed? In order to avoid these objections it is sometimes said that the Sermon refers to the time of the *offering* of the kingdom (both during the life of Christ and during the tribulation). This view does not take into account fully that some things in the Sermon do picture millennial conditions (cf. 5:13-16, 39-44; 7:1-6), and it may fail to recognize that even in the millennium unredeemed people will be in need of the message of repentance.

In light of the foregoing discussion it seems best to this writer to consider the Sermon on the Mount in a fourfold light. (1) Basically and primarily it is a detailed explanation of what the Lord meant by repentance. It was a call to those who heard it to that inner change which they had dissociated from the requirements for the establishment of the Messianic kingdom. Therefore, (2) it has relevance to any time that the kingdom is offered, and that includes the days of the tribulation as well as the days when Christ spoke. But (3) it does picture certain aspects of life in the millennial kingdom and thus in a certain restricted sense is a sort of constitution of the kingdom. However (4) as all Scripture, it is profitable for any people, and since it is one of the most detailed ethical codes in the Bible it has a special application to men's lives in any age. One must avoid relegating it all to the future or all to the time of the offering of the kingdom and at the same time one must never miss its importance in application to the Church today. By interpretation (based on Matthew's use of it) the Sermon on the Mount explains repentance in detail in relation to citizenship in the kingdom. The phrase *citizenship in the kingdom* will serve to emphasize the three interpretative aspects as outlined above and will in no way contradict the applicative value of the Sermon. In summarizing the Lord's teaching Matthew's record will be followed.

A. *Characteristics of Kingdom Citizenship* (5:1-16)

1. *Characteristics in relation to God* (5:3-6). Four characteristics are required in relation to God: a poverty of spirit which involves a recognition of one's worthlessness before God, godly mourning in the heart as a result of realizing the poverty-stricken condition, meekness (the word means domesticated), and hungering and thirsting after righteousness. These are spiritual requirements for entrance into the Messianic kingdom.

2. *Characteristics in relation to man* (5:7-12). Again there are four characteristics: mercifulness, purity in heart, peacemaking, and suffering persecution. Citizens of the kingdom should expect to be characterized in these ways, and these four, like the first group, primarily concern entrance into the kingdom.

3. *Characteristics in relation to the world* (5:13-16). There will be a need for witness during the millennium which the subjects of the kingdom must fill. They are to be preserving as salt and prominent as a city on a hill. Even though no unredeemed person may enter the millennial kingdom, many redeemed will enter with unglorified bodies to whom children will be born who will stand in need of this witness.

B. *Code of Kingdom Citizenship* (5:17-48)

In this section of the Lord's sermon there are six laws presented. Each is marked off in the text by the phrase, "Ye have heard that it was said by them of old time . . . but I say unto you" (vv. 21, 27, 31, 33, 38, 43). As laws they doubtless have special relevance to the standard of conduct expected during the reign of Christ, and as authoritative pronouncements (which stood in sharp contrast to the Law and its Pharisaic interpretations) they have relevance to the time of the preaching of the kingdom as setting forth the requirement of inward righteousness in contrast to the external righteousness of the Pharisees (cf. 5:20).

1. *The law of murder* (5:21-26). Although the rabbis were very strict in their teaching against murder, Jesus looked at the causes of murder. Anger starts the process; then follows calling one's brother *raca* (from a word meaning to spit out); finally the brother is accused of being a fool. These are the things which lead to murder. Therefore, in order to avoid the consequences the Lord advised being reconciled to the brother (in religious matters) or settling with an adversary out of court (in secular matters). This law, as all of them, had meaning when Christ announced it to those who were seeking entrance into the kingdom and who needed to examine their hearts, and there is no reason why it will not be in force during the kingdom.

2. *The law of adultery* (5:27-30). Again the Lord pointed His finger at the heart of man. The rabbis defined adultery

as the illicit sexual relationship of a married man and a married woman.[17] The Lord broadened the definition to include anyone who commits the act, regardless of his marital status. But He also went further by pointing out that the seat of sin is in the heart. In rationalizing, the Jews had said that the eye drew them into adultery. Our Lord says that such an idea is nonsense, for the heart does it. But He used their illogical reasoning and carried it to its logical conclusion, for, He said, if it is the eye pluck it out, or if it is the hand that leads into this sin cut it off. If, however, it is the heart, change it. The Lord was not saying that the act is no worse than the look; He was trying to point out the source of the act and what needed to be done to the heart.

3. *The law of divorce* (5:31-32). It would appear from this law that the Lord allowed divorce in the single instance of adultery. If this be so, then this particular teaching did not rise above that of the school of Shammai. It is true that the school of Hillel allowed divorce for many causes, and on the basis of this some have said that in this declaration the Lord simply restricted divorce to the one proved instance in order that women who were divorced for trivial reasons would not be branded as adulteresses. However, such an interpretation does not put the Lord's teaching above that of the scribes and Pharisees as represented in the school of Shammai.

Because this, as all of the Sermon, seems to be of a higher standard than that of the Pharisees, is it possible that the Lord was actually disallowing divorce in all instances? The liberal thinks so, and he views the excepting clause as an interpolation which really altered the sense of the Lord's original utterance.[18] The conservative of course cannot accept such an explanation, and the usual explanation is that in

[17]Major, Manson, and Wright, *op. cit.*, p. 428.
[18]Cf. C. Gore, *The Question of Divorce* (London: John Murray, 1911), p. 23, and W. C. Allen, *A Critical and Exegetical Commentary on the Gospel According to St. Matthew, International Critical Commentary* (Edinburgh: T. & T. Clark, 1907), p. 51, and G. Salmon, *The Human Element in the Gospels* (London: John Murray, 1908), pp. 130-31.

this one circumstance divorce is allowed. It seems to this author that such an explanation actually contradicts Mark 10:2-12; Luke 16:18; and I Corinthians 7:10. Therefore, it is suggested that the Lord was forbidding divorce altogether and that fornication (*porneia*) denotes marital relations within the prohibited relationships of Leviticus 18. In other words, the one who may have married too near a relative should seek annulment, but for all others divorce is disallowed. This follows the meaning of *porneia* in I Corinthians 5:1 and Acts 15:29.[19] If this be the true explanation, then our Lord was replacing the Law with God's ideal of no divorce.

4. *The law of oaths* (5:33-37). In introducing the Old Testament teaching concerning oaths the Lord summarized requirements set forth in Leviticus 19:12 and Numbers 30:2. Rabbinic interpretation had said that only if the name of God were involved in an oath was it swearing; thus one could do a great deal of swearing without breaking their interpretation of the Law. Our Lord showed that even though God's name was not mentioned, God could be involved in oaths by involving His works. A name stands for the person, and the person is revealed by and related to his works; therefore, to defame the works is to take the name in vain. To involve Heaven, Jerusalem, or self is to involve God. Further, the Lord adds, if you need emphasis in your speech, do not resort to oaths, just repeat yourself (v. 37).

5. *The law of nonresistance* (5:38-42). The law said that one could recompense evil with evil (Exod. 21:22-26; Lev. 24:17-20; Deut. 19:18-21); Christ said, "Resist not evil," and He did not qualify the statement in any way. Rather, He explained it and illustrated it in various areas of life (in indignity, v. 39; injustice, v. 40; inconvenience, v. 41; and indigence, v. 42).

6. *The law of love* (5:43-48). In introducing this law the

[19]Cf. W. K. L. Clarke, *New Testament Problems* (London: SPCK, 1929), pp. 59-60, for a detailed explanation of this view.

Lord quotes Leviticus 19:18 and summarizes the sense of such passages as Deuteronomy 23:3-6 and 7:2. The Lord's new law rules out the hating of one's enemies and substitutes in its place godly love which displays itself toward all.

C. *Conduct of Kingdom Citizenship* (6:1—7:12)

In this section the King deals with matters of conduct which should epitomize citizens of the kingdom. These matters apply whether the kingdom is about to be established or already established.

1. *Conduct in almsgiving* (6:1-4) —simplicity and secrecy.

2. *Conduct in prayer* (6:5-15). In this section the Lord says that the place of prayer should be in private where there could be heart-to-heart fellowship and communion with God (vv. 5-6). (This was in sharp contrast to the practice of the Pharisees, who made a point of being caught in the streets at the time of prayer so that everyone could see how religious they were as they stood there praying.) He also says that the point of prayer is not to beseige God with vain repetitions but to ask Him for that of which He already knows we have need (vv. 7-8). Finally, our Lord gave the great pattern prayer (vv. 9-15).

3. *Conduct in fasting* (6:16-18). The Lord says to do your fasting while in secret, conducting yourself normally otherwise.

4. *Conduct concerning money* (6:19-24) —lay up treasure in Heaven.

5. *Conduct concerning anxiety* (6:25-34). The citizen of the kingdom need never be anxious because (1) the one who gave life in the first place will take care of it (v. 25); (2) God who feeds the birds will surely feed His children (v. 26); (3) it is futile to think we can add to the length of our lives (v. 27); (4) God who clothes the lilies will also clothe His children (vv. 28-30); (5) it is a characteristic of the heathen to

worry (vv. 31-32a) ; (6) God knows what we need (v. 32b) ; and (7) priority belongs to spiritual things (vv. 33-34).

6. *Conduct concerning judging* (7:1-6). This is a section which undoubtedly has particular applicability when the kingdom is established, for the tenses of the verbs show that the judgment persisted in (present tenses) brings instantaneous punishment (aorist tenses). In relation to its application today this passage is often abused, for some take it to mean that the Lord condemned all judging. The condemnation is only on hypocritical judging; indeed, the Lord recommends casting the mote out of the brother's eye if one's own spiritual condition is such as to be able to see clearly (v. 5). This is a condemnation of hypocrites, not critics; but in the kingdom the way that professing hypocrites judge will evidently reveal their unregenerate condition and result in their condemnation.

7. *Conduct concerning prayer* (7:7-12). The section closes with an exhortation to ask and a promise of receiving.

D. *Cautions Concerning Kingdom Citizenship* (7:13-29)

Following the teaching concerning the judgment of hypocrites, the Sermon closes with warnings to prove the reality of one's profession. The Lord speaks of two ways (7:13-14), two kinds of trees (7:15-20), two professions (7:21-23), and two builders (7:24-29). These warnings, of course, have special pertinence to any time that the kingdom is proclaimed, for right relationship to God is essential for entrance into the Messianic kingdom (cf. 7:21).

III. THE KINGDOM POSTPONED

Such a title as "The Kingdom Postponed" will immediately raise questions in the minds of some. How can one speak of a postponement of the kingdom when the passage under discussion in this section, Matthew 13, speaks of the kingdom? The answer to that question is, of course, that postponement is used here in relation to the millennial or Davidic kingdom. But, it will be asked, if the Davidic kingdom is postponed that means that had it been received by the Jews it would not have been necessary for the Lord Jesus to have been crucified. The postponement of the kingdom is related primarily to the question of God's program in this age through the Church and not to the necessity of the crucifixion. The crucifixion would have been necessary as foundational to the establishment of the kingdom even if the Church age had never been conceived in the purposes of God. The question is not whether the crucifixion would have been avoided but whether the Davidic kingdom was postponed.

In the divinely inspired theological framework of Matthew there is no better way to express God's purposes concerning the Messianic kingdom than with the word *postponed*. It has already been demonstrated that we must recognize divine guidance of the order of the Gospel as well as the facts of it (John 14:26). In Matthew's arrangement he has presented Christ as King of the Jews proclaiming the Davidic kingdom as at hand (3:2; 4:17; 10:7). He has also shown the distinct line of rejection of the King (cf. especially chapters 11-12). In many respects there is a climax of that rejection in the committing of the unpardonable sin, although, of course, the rejection continues throughout the entire account. However, there is no record of the King's preaching the kingdom at hand after this climax of rejection in chapter 12; rather, the mysteries of the kingdom are then introduced by the King.

The word *mystery* is a technical word used to describe a secret which is unknown to one until initiated. The kingdom of Heaven as referring to the eternal, timeless reign of God was certainly not unknown in Jewish theology. The kingdom of Heaven as referring to the Davidic, Messianic, millennial kingdom was likewise well known to the Jews of Christ's day (cf. Dan. 7:14). Therefore, the mysteries of the kingdom could not refer to the eternal kingdom nor to the

Messianic kingdom, but the meaning of the word *mystery* requires that they refer to some other aspect of the rule of God which was unknown up to that time. If the reference is not to eternity nor to the millennium there is only one other period in the history of the world left, the time between the first and second comings of Christ. Obviously, that period includes the time during which Christ is building His Church, but the mysteries of the kingdom of Heaven have to do with the rule of God over the whole world, not with the government of the Head over the Church. They concern conditions during the course of the time during which Christ is absent from the earth.

The form of this revelation is parabolic. The word *parable* means a casting alongside; thus a parable is the putting side by side of two truths—one truth from the realm of nature and the other from the realm of super-nature. Parables are vehicles for the conveying of doctrine in order that it might be clear and at the same time hidden (Matt. 13:11 ff.). Since they contain truths from the two realms one will expect to find figurative language in parables, but as in all figures of speech the literal meaning of the figure will be evident. Each parable has to be interpreted as a whole, and one parable must not be used to teach the whole story conveyed by all of them together. It goes without saying that the interpretation of those in Matthew 13 must follow the pattern set down by the Lord in His own interpretation of the first two.

To summarize: these parables reveal some of the principal features of the rule of God during the time when Christ is absent from the earth. That there would be such a time was not known previously; therefore, these are the mysteries of the kingdom; and in the meantime the promised Davidic kingdom is merely postponed.

A. *The Sower* (13:1-23)

1. *Identifications*. The sower is Christ; the seed are persons who have received the Word in some way or other and who are sown into the world for a testimony (cf. vv. 19-20, 22-23, "he that was sown"). The Word plays a vital part in the parable, but the seed are persons who have received that Word. The field into which they are sown is the world.

2. *Interpretation*. During the course of this age many people will receive the Word and in turn automatically become testimonies to the world, and there will be many more who receive the Word and make some sort of profession but who do not bear fruit than those who receive and bear fruit. One kind of person hears but does not understand; another hears and has an emotional experience but soon withers; another's profession is unfruitful because of worldliness; while another group is fruitful in varying degrees. All make profession, all are sown for a testimony, but only one group bears fruit for the kingdom.

B. *The Wheat and the Tares* (13:24-30, 36-43)

1. *Identifications*. Again the sower is Christ, and the field is the world. The good seed are children of the kingdom, and the tares are children of the Devil. The reapers who do their work at the end of the age are angels. All these identifications are certain because it is the Lord who makes them.

2. *Interpretation*. During the course of this age Satan will plant such good counterfeits among the true followers of Christ that they will be indistinguishable to men and inseparable until separated by angels at the return of Christ.

C. *The Mustard Seed* (13:31-32)

1. *Identifications*. The sower and the field are doubtless the same as in the preceding parables.

2. *Interpretation*. The principal point of this parable is the unusual or unexpected growth of Christendom during the course of this age.

D. *The Leaven* (13:33)

1. *Identifications.* If leaven means the same here as it does everywhere else in the Scripture (and there is no indication in the parable that it does not) it stands for something evil (Exod. 12:15; Lev. 2:11; 6:17; 10:12; Matt. 16:6; Mark 8:15; I Cor. 5:6; Gal. 5:9).

2. *Interpretation.* Obviously the interpretation of this parable hinges entirely on one's identification of the leaven. If it represents evil doctrine the Lord is saying that this present time will be characterized by evil teaching permeating the truth. If the leaven represents the Gospel it is strange to find it hidden rather than published, and the resultant idea of the Gospel leavening the whole world is an outright contradiction of Scripture (I Tim. 4; II Tim. 3:1-7) and of the facts of contemporary history.

E. *The Hid Treasure* (13:44)

1. *Identifications.* Again there is no reason to change the identity of the man from Christ. The Jewish hearers would have thought of the treasure as their own nation (Exod. 19:5; Ps. 135:4).

2. *Interpretation.* Jews will be a part of the saved multitude of this age, and their salvation, as that of all who are saved, is based on the death of Christ.

F. *The Pearl of Great Price* (13:45-46)

1. *Identifications.* Still the man is Christ. The identification of the pearl is perhaps more obscure, but to the Jew the pearl was not so precious as it was to Gentiles.

2. *Interpretation.* This parable evidently teaches that Christ gave Himself also for Gentiles. By Paul this is called a mystery (Eph. 3:1-6).

G. *The Dragnet* (13:47-50)

1. *Identifications.* The net is the Word of the kingdom.

The fish are those who respond to the Word, and the separation is the judgment at the end of this age.

2. *Interpretation.* The emphasis of this parable seems to be on the separation, not the gathering into the net. Most particularly, then, it describes the separation at the end of the tribulation which is further described in Matthew 25:31-46.

The introduction of these mysteries concerning God's rule affirms the idea that the Messianic, Davidic kingdom has been postponed. The latter promises have not been abrogated nor taken over by the Church; they will yet be fulfilled, but in the meantime God is ruling in other ways, and those ways have been described in these mysteries of the kingdom.

IV. THE KINGDOM PROPHESIED

A. *The Importance of the Olivet Discourse*

Matthew's divinely ordered theology, we have seen, concerns the King and the kingdom. He uses "kingdom" primarily in relation to the Messianic, Davidic, millennial kingdom. In the author's progress of the revelation of the kingdom he has emphasized the offer in the preaching of John, Christ, and the twelve; he introduced early in his Gospel the detailed message of the kingdom in the Sermon on the Mount; he then showed how the Lord revealed certain mysteries of previously unknown truths concerning the kingdom because of the revelation of the introduction of this age. In view of this doctrinal development there is an obvious question: Are the promises of the Davidic covenant for the earthly, national, Messianic, Davidic kingdom abrogated? The answer of the Synoptic Theology is an emphatic *No*, for the Olivet Discourse, which Matthew places as near the end of the Gospel as possible, contains two passages which concern the millennial kingdom and which were spoken after the time at which the Lord introduced the truths concerning the mysteries of the kingdom.

All of the various interpretations of this passage (Matt. 24,

25; Mark 13:1-37; Luke 21:5-36) need not concern the student. Many among both liberal and conservative interpreters consider it as referring to the destruction of Jerusalem in A.D. 70. However, if literal interpretation means anything such an interpretation must be rejected. This is not to say that the discourse does not include prophecy of that event (actually this is Luke's emphasis particularly), but that which happened in A.D. 70 would not begin to fulfill all that is found in the discourse. Therefore, many other interpreters understand that the Lord had reference also to His second coming, and, strange to say, both amillennialists and premillennialists are found in the group.[20] Even without a detailed exposition of all the words and phrases in the discourse which have a time element in them, it is evident that all of them refer to the great tribulation or to other events connected with the second coming of Christ (cf. Matt. 24:3, 6-7, 14-15, 21, 29-30, 37, 42, 44; 25:10, 19, 31). If the discourse as a whole refers to the time of the second advent, the two particular passages concerning the Messianic kingdom must also be interpreted of that time; and, therefore, those two passages, the parable of the ten virgins (25:1-10) and the judgment of the Gentiles (25:31-46), which speak of the millennial kingdom, demonstrate that it was in no way abrogated by any other teaching which Christ introduced.

B. *The Disciples' Questions* (Matt. 24:1-3; Mark 13:1-4; Luke 21:5-7)

Three questions from the disciples provoked the discourse. As the Lord was showing them the temple and predicting its destruction they asked (1) when that destruction would be, (2) what would be the sign of His coming, and (3) what would be the signs of the end of the age. Obviously in their minds the events would be simultaneous, and in His answer the Lord did not attempt to correct that impression, for this

[20]Cf. F. E. Hamilton, *The Basis of Millennial Faith* (Grand Rapids: Eerdmans, 1952), pp. 67 ff.

was one of the many things they could not understand until after the resurrection (John 16:12).

C. *The Signs of the End of the Age* (Matt. 24:4-26)

The answer to the first question concerning the destruction of Jerusalem is not found in Matthew's record, for his concern is with the King and the kingdom, and that which happened in A.D. 70 is related to neither. He immediately launches into the record of what the Lord had to say about the signs of the end of the age, for when they appear the time of the establishment of the kingdom is near. Signs in the physical realm include the disturbances mentioned in verses 6-7. Outstanding signs in the spiritual realm will be the many false Christs who will appear (v. 5), the persecution of the Jews and general disinterest in religion (vv. 10-12), the appearance of the abomination of desolation with resultant consequences (vv. 15-22), and the world-wide preaching of the gospel of the kingdom (v. 14).

D. *The Sign of Christ's Coming* (Matt. 24:27-31)

The second advent of Christ will be visible (v. 27) and accompanied by a great carnage on earth (v. 28). The Lord designates the time of it as "immediately after the tribulation" and states that unusual physical phenomena will attend it (v. 29). At this time also will be seen the sign of the Son of Man whose appearance will bring mourning to the children of Israel (v. 30; cf. Zech. 12:10-12). The final regathering of the Jews from the corners of the earth will be effected at the Lord's return by angelic agency (v. 31).

E. *The Illustrations* (Matt. 24:32—25:46)

Included in the discourse are a number of illustrations of the return of the Lord. The fig tree (24:32-35) is an illustration of the rapidity with which the age will come to an end and the necessity of being alert to signs which appear in the world. The days of Noah (24:36-39) point out the fact that the return of Christ will be unexpected because of the unpreparedness of the normalcy of life which men will attempt to experience in those days. The illustrations of the two (24:40-42) and the faithful servant (24:43-51), teach the need for preparedness in view of the separation which the return of Christ will bring.

The illustrations which follow (the ten virgins, 25:1-13; the talents, 25:14-30; the judgment of the Gentiles,[21] 25:31-46) include warnings of judgment as well as exhortations to preparedness. In each the reward is the kingdom of Heaven and the punishment is Hell. If these words are plainly understood, then they obviously teach that the kingdom of Heaven is yet to be established at the return of Christ. Thus the Davidic kingdom could not have been superseded by the Church.

Beyond any question the Synoptic theology is primarily a theology of the King and His kingdom. This is the divinely guided emphasis of Matthew, the theological Gospel of the Synoptics, and it is the key to the interpretation of the meaning of the life of Christ. Without this basic viewpoint the material becomes a mass of contradictions; with it, it shows the progressive unfolding of the revelation of the purposes of God in the manner of true Biblical Theology.

[21]The word *ethnos*, Matt. 25:32, is translated in the New Testament by "people" two times, "heathen" five times, "nation" sixty-four times, and "Gentile" ninety-three times. The author understands this judgment to be on individual Gentiles, not national groups, at the end of the tribulation for their treatment of Christ's brethren, the Jewish people.

Part II

THE THEOLOGY OF ACTS

Chapter 1

BACKGROUNDS

I. THE AUTHOR

SINCE BIBLICAL THEOLOGY EMPHASIZES the historical conditioning of revelation, a word is necessary concerning the author of the Acts of the Apostles. Dr. Luke was evidently a Greek and not a Jew, for in the record of Colossians 4:12-14 he is separated from those who are said to be of the circumcision.[1] Some hold that he was born in Antioch in Syria[2] while others suggest Philippi as his home town.[3] Evidently he was a free man, and possibly he was born and reared in Antioch but practiced medicine in Philippi. Where he received his medical training is entirely a matter of conjecture though of necessity it would have been either in Alexandria, Athens, or Tarsus. The facts pertaining to his conversion are likewise lacking. The prologue to the Gospel would indicate that Luke was not an eyewitness of the ministry of Christ. It is possible that he was converted in Antioch through the ministry of those who fled Jerusalem because of persecution. It is equally possible that he was converted through the ministry of Paul during the years that Paul was in Tarsus before being called to the work in Antioch.

[1]The Luke in Romans 16:21 is undoubtedly a different person, as also in Acts 13:1.
[2]A. T. Robertson, *Luke the Historian in the Light of Historical Research* (Edinburgh: T. & T. Clark, 1920), p. 23.
[3]R. B. Rackham, *The Acts of the Apostles* (London: Methuen & Co., 1951), p. xxx, prefers Antioch in Pisidia, but this view is not widely held.

In spite of the fact that Luke is usually remembered as a physician, it must be recognized that he was primarily a missionary. Being the author of the third Gospel would qualify him as such; but he also did public, itinerant missionary work. The Macedonian call was answered by Luke as well as Paul (Acts 16:13, 17). Luke evidently was left in charge of the work in Philippi for approximately six years. Later he preached in Rome (Philem. 24). The Lord also used him in a personal ministry to the physical needs of the Apostle Paul (Col. 4:14), and since he was with Paul at the end of his life perhaps he made arrangements for his burial (II Tim. 4:11).

II. The Method of Research

Luke's declaration concerning his method of research is found in the prologue to the Gospel, and although some of the details in the statement relate primarily to the Gospel rather than to the Acts, nevertheless the general method is applicable to both works.

A. *The Purpose*

The method which Luke used was geared to the writing of an historical, not a polemical or apologetic treatise. If this was his avowed purpose, and if his method of research was a valid one, then even apart from the superintending work of the Holy Spirit, there is a strong presupposition in favor of the historical accuracy of the writings.

B. *The Method*

Luke's method of producing these historical books involved investigation of sources and sifting of the evidence.

1. *Sources.*

a. Personal participation. In the book of Acts there are two so-called "we" sections (16:9-40; 20:5—28:31). These indicate that Luke was personally involved in the journey from Troas to Philippi (on the second missionary journey of Paul) and from Philippi (on the third journey) to Rome, including two years in Caesarea and two years in Rome. For these events he had his personal recollections and possibly written diary-type notes.

b. Paul. For five or six years Luke was with Paul before the writing of Acts. This, of course, provided him with information for the record in Acts 7; 9; 11:25-30; 13:1—16:8; 17:1—20:4. In other words, Luke had reliable evidence available from these two sources for the majority of the material in Acts. It is also remarkable to note that his association with Paul did not affect his historical purpose by giving it a doctrinal cast.

c. Other eyewitnesses. Silas, Timothy, Titus, Aristarchus, James, Philip and his daughters are among those to whom Luke had access in gathering material for the Acts (Acts 19: 29; 20:4; 21:8, 18; Col. 4:10; Philem. 24). These provide authentic sources for practically all of Acts.

2. *Sifting.* The other principal characteristic of Luke's method is the careful sifting of the evidence collected. He declared that he "closely traced all things accurately" (Luke 1:3), which means (1) that he sifted the facts before he wrote (the verb is in the perfect tense) and (2) that he made accurate use in his writing of the sifted evidence. The picture is of a physician's skill of diagnosis being applied to the sifting of the material in thorough preparation for writing.

III. The Date

The controversy concerning the date of Acts centers in whether it was written before or after A.D. 70. All agree that Acts was written not long after the Gospel, and those who use a post-70 date often do so on the grounds that since predictive prophecy must be disallowed Luke 21 has to refer to a past event and thus Luke and Acts are both post-70. Beside this denial of prophecy there are other serious difficulties with a

post-70 date. For instance, why are so many important incidents omitted from Acts if it were written after the destruction of Jerusalem? Surely Luke would have mentioned the
burning of Rome, the martyrdom of Paul, and the destruction
of Jerusalem itself.[4] From the ending of Acts as we have it
one would judge that it was written about 63 in Rome during
Paul's first imprisonment.

IV. THE AUTHORSHIP

Throughout this brief discussion the Lukan authorship has
been assumed. In brief the proof of this is usually developed
along these lines: (1) the author of Acts was clearly a companion of Paul (for the "we" sections show this); (2) by
process of elimination, that companion was Luke; (3) the
same man who wrote the "we" sections wrote the rest of the
book; and (4) this conclusion is corroborated by the inci-
dence of medical terms found in the work (cf. 1:3; 3:7 ff.; 9:
18, 33; 13:11; 28:1-10).

[4]Cf. the discussion in H. Alford, *The Greek Testament* (London: Rivingtons: 1859), II, 17-19.

Chapter 2

THE PHILOSOPHY OF THE PLAN
OF ACTS

ANY INQUIRING MIND cannot help wondering what motivated Luke in his sifting and selecting of the material
that comprises Acts. Why does Paul receive so much prominence? Why is it that the westward progress of the gospel is
that which is chiefly traced in the historical record? Why are
certain incidents on the missionary journeys reported in detail while others are passed over briefly? Like the Gospel,
Acts was also planned in an orderly way; what philosophy
motivated the plan of Acts is the subject of this section.

I. THE BASIC PURPOSE OF THE PLAN

It is quite apparent that the basic purpose of Acts will not
be much different from that of the Gospel because both are
addressed to the same individual for a similar purpose; namely, to instruct this person in the ministry of Jesus of Nazareth.
The Gospel is the first part of the instruction and is stated by
Luke to be but a beginning of the story (Acts 1:1); therefore, the book of Acts is obviously a continuation of the account of the ministry of Christ. The word *began* in Acts 1:1
not only describes the content of the Gospel but also that of
Acts, for it implies that Acts will deal with that which Jesus
continued to do after His resurrection.

In addition to the word *began* there is another noteworthy

feature of the introduction to Acts; i.e., the immediate and repeated mention of the Holy Spirit (1:2, 4-5, 8). The acts of the risen Christ are immediately related to the work of the Holy Spirit; thus this second treatise to Theophilus is a chronicle of what the risen Christ did through the Holy Spirit. The recording of these acts is the basic purpose of the book.

II. THE SPECIFIC DEVELOPMENT OF THE PLAN

To say that Luke's basic purpose was to record the acts of the risen Christ through the Holy Spirit is not to answer any specific questions concerning the selection of material. All of the works of the risen Christ are not included, for there is obviously geographical, chronological, ethnological, and personality selectivity. It is not difficult to distinguish four distinct lines along which the basic plan is developed, and since they are discernible, it is safe to assume that Luke planned it so.

A. *The Great Commission Line*

The most obvious line of development in the Book of Acts is that which follows the Great Commission. This is the basis for the customary analytical outline of the book.

1. *The introduction of the Great Commission line.* The theme is introduced at the outset (1:6-8) on the occasion of the disciples' questions concerning the Messianic kingdom. In His answer the Lord did not suggest any abrogation of the kingdom promises or any alteration of their literal character —He merely said that the disciples' concept of the timing of the fulfillment of those promises was wrong. They knew what was coming, but they were not to know when; and in the meantime Christ introduced a new program and sent new Power for the carrying out of it.

2. *The evidence of the Great Commission line.* The selectivity along this line is apparent, for every reader of Acts has noticed that the first seven chapters concern the work in Jeru-

salem; chapter 8, the work in Samaria; and the remainder of the book, the uttermost part of the earth.[1]

3. *The end of the Great Commission line.* Rome is clearly the goal toward which the chronicle tends, for the Gospel's reaching Rome is the climax of the book. Though this fact may also be related to the acceptance line of selectivity, it has some bearing here. This would be especially true if one accepts the suggestion of Bruce that *ap' eschatou tēs gēs,* from the uttermost part of the earth, means Rome.[2] If the basic philosophy of the plan of Acts is built on the continuing acts of the risen Lord through the Holy Spirit, and if the commission was the last command given in person, then it is apparent why Luke gave such prominence to this line of selectivity.

B. *The Acceptance Line*

Also discernible is selection which demonstrated the fact that the acts of the risen Christ through the Holy Spirit were well received by the civil authorities. Indeed, there seems to be a deliberate attempt on the part of Luke to mention as often as possible the good relations which the messengers of the Gospel enjoyed with the civil authorities. Sometimes the amount of religious opposition recorded in the book tends to obscure the civil approbation, but the student should notice the following passages: 13:7; 16:35; 17:9; 18:12; 19: 31, 37; 26:30-32; 28:21.

This evidence, however, must not lead one to the conclusion that Acts was written as a document to be used in Paul's defense during his trial in Rome. It merely demonstrates another manner in which the basic philosophy of the plan was worked out. Concluding the record in Rome completed the author's purpose, for he had then demonstrated the acceptance of Christianity in the capital of the empire.

[1] Of course chapter 12 refers again to the work in Jerusalem, but this is entirely in line with the *kai . . . kai* (both . . . and) of 1:8, which shows that the progress of the Gospel was to be out from Jerusalem but not to the exclusion of Jerusalem.

[2] F. F. Bruce, *The Acts of the Apostles* (Chicago: Inter-Varsity Christian Fellowship, 1952), p. 71.

C. *The Pauline Line*

Another obvious purpose of Luke was to choose certain acts which would show the greatness of the apostle Paul's character and which in turn would vindicate his apostleship.

1. *The reason for this line.* There were certainly other apostles whose lives and works Luke might have reported. Why then does Paul receive the prominence? The reasons are two: (1) It was necessary to establish Paul's character because of the discrediting of him in Galatian and Corinthian quarters. (2) It was necessary to vindicate the authority of his writings by the record of his labors for the Lord. It would not have been enough simply to say that they were inspired, but the historical account of how God used Paul lent support to their authority. We can see the impact of this even today if we can imagine how the Pauline Epistles would be received if the book of Acts did not appear in the New Testament.

2. *The evidence of this line.* It appears to be with designed purpose that Paul is promoted along identical lines with Peter in the record. For instance, the account includes the healing of a lame man by both (3:2; cf. 14:8), exorcism by both (5:16; cf. 16:18), an encounter with a sorcerer (8:18; cf. 13:8-11), and spectacular personal power (5:15; cf. 19:12). Too, frequently in the book there is emphasis on Paul's direct authority from Christ as if to counter any argument that Paul was not an apostle because he never companied with the Lord in the days of His humiliation (cf. 9:1 ff.; 22:17-21; 26). Thus the promotion of Paul is one of the clear lines of selectivity in the planning of Luke's history.

D. *The Jewish Rejection Line*

The last clear line is that which traces the rejection of Messiah by the Jewish nation. This might be considered as a part of the larger consideration given to the entire matter of Jewish-Gentile relations in the Church. However, that larger area is more related to doctrine than planning. To point up the rejection seems to be part of the planned purpose of the book in order to serve as a backdrop for the record of the acts of the risen Christ in relation to Gentiles. The rejection of the kingdom is the obvious point of the detailed record in 3:12-26). The rejection of the King is apparent throughout the early chapters (cf. 7:51; 9:1), but the principal rejection is the rejection of Christianity itself, and Luke mentions this repeatedly (9:23; 13:46; 14:19; 15:1; 17:5, 13; 18:14; 21:27; 23:12).

These four selective lines of development appear to be Luke's chosen procedure in exhibiting the acts of the risen Christ through the Holy Spirit in his historical record. While we may discern the lines of development and surmise reasons for them, we must never lose sight of the fact that the superintending work of the Holy Spirit in inspiration was guiding and guarding in every detail. Along these lines, distinguishable yet interwoven, the book developed by the hand of the diligent and precise historian who was its author.

Chapter 3

THE THEOLOGY OF ACTS

I. THE DOCTRINE OF GOD

A. *God*

1. *His existence.* Everywhere throughout the Book of Acts the existence of God is assumed because of the apostolic preachers' background in the Old Testament. Even among the heathen at Lystra this was so (cf. 14:15), though at Athens the knowledge of the existence of the true God was not assumed by Paul (17:22 ff.). Generally speaking, however, it is taken for granted as in the Old Testament.

2. *His characteristics.* A number of characteristics of God are rather incidentally mentioned in the book.

a. He is Creator (14:15; 17:24). This truth about God was particularly affirmed among Gentile audiences though it was well-known and acknowledged by the Jews (cf. 4:24).

b. He is sovereign. The apostles recognized God's sovereign relationship over themselves when they addressed God as the Master [*despota,* from which the word despot is derived (4:24)] and perceived that He was in absolute control of events and circumstances (4:28). He was also recognized as the God of sovereign election (13:48; cf. Dan. 6:12, where the same word is used in the Septuagint), and as the ruler over all nations (17:26).

c. He is beneficent. His beneficence is seen particularly in the realm of natural blessings (14:17) and in the temporary staying of judgment (17:30).

3. *His revelation.*

a. He is near to all men (17:27; cf. Deut. 4:29; Ps. 145:18).

b. He appeared and spoke in times past (7:2, 6, 31).

c. He revealed Himself through providential workings, often employing angels (5:19; 7:53; 8:26; 10:3; 12:7).

d. He reveals Himself directly. This is probably one of the outstanding features of the apostolic age. The "naturalness of the supernatural" is everywhere apparent. He was seen of Stephen (7:56), Paul (9:5), and Ananias (9:10).

e. He reveals Himself through the written Word (4:25).

4. *His works.* Ultimately all things are of God, but certain particular works are ascribed to Him in Luke's account. They are:

a. The resurrection of Jesus (4:10; 5:30; 13:37),

b. The salvation of Gentiles (2:21; 13:47; 26:18; 28:28),

c. The rebuilding of the tabernacle of David (15:16),

d. The future judgment (17:31),

e. The sending of the Spirit (2:17),

f. The anointing of Jesus (10:38), and

g. The exalting of Christ (2:33-35; 4:11).

B. *Jesus Christ*

1. *Designations and descriptions related to His person.*

a. He is human. The humanity of Christ is mainly demonstrated in the book by references to the historic human Jesus of Nazareth and by identifying Jesus with the Christ. That Jesus was a real human being is assumed and accepted in Peter's Pentecostal message; that Jesus is the Christ is the point of his message (2:36). References to specific incidents in the earthly life of Christ are few, but those which are mentioned constitute proofs of His humanity (2:23; 8:32; 10:38).

b. He is divine. The principal theological proof of the

deity of Christ is in 13:33 where eternal sonship is affirmed. "*To-day* refers to the date of the decree itself . . . but this, as a divine act, was eternal, and so must be the sonship it affirms."[1] Deity is also another point of Peter's message at Pentecost, for he shows by the resurrection, exaltation, and subsequent sending of the Spirit that Jesus of Nazareth is Lord, thus proving Him to be divine.

c. He is the rejected and suffering Saviour. The rejection is the point of Peter's quoting Psalm 118:22 in 4:11. It is doubtful that the emphasis was on Christ's being made head of the corner, but rather it seems to have been upon the setting at nought. Therefore, this is not so much a revelation of Christ's headship over the Church as it is an emphasis on rejection.[2] The suffering Saviour is a recurring theme throughout the book (3:18; 8:32-35; 17:2-3; 26:22-23).

d. He is the resurrected one. This was the keynote theme of apostolic preaching as exemplified in the sermons at Pentecost and Antioch in Pisidia (2:25-28; 13:32-35). The resurrection is of course closely connected with the ascension (1:9-11) and exaltation (2:33-35).

e. He is the coming one. At the time of the ascension the promise of Messiah's return was affirmed to the upward gazing disciples (1:9-11). It was also reiterated in Peter's second recorded sermon (3:21).

All of these relatively incidental references to the person of Christ, while not forming any major theological area of the book, display the lofty, complete, and orthodox concept of Jesus which the apostolic preachers and the chronicler had.

2. *His ministry.*

a. In salvation. All the Old Testament quotations concerning salvation in the book speak of the universality of the salvation which Messiah would provide. Such inclusiveness

[1]J. A. Alexander, *The Acts of the Apostles* (New York: Charles Scribner, 1872), II, 29.
[2]*Contra* L. S. Chafer, *Systematic Theology* (Dallas: Dallas Seminary Press, 1947), IV, 62-63.

is based on the universal promise of the Abrahamic covenant (Gen. 12:3) which assured that in the Seed would all the families of the earth be blessed (cf. Acts 2:21; 3:25-26; 10:43; 13:16 47; 26:23; 28:28). However, there is an exclusive aspect to His salvation in that it is provided only through the name of Jesus of Nazareth (2:36; 4:12; 13:39).

b. In teaching. If we consider all that can be found concerning that which our Lord taught His disciples during the forty days between the resurrection and ascension (1:3-9; 13:31), we have at best only a sample of the many things He must have said.

(1) Concerning self. On the Emmaus road He attempted to show the two that their concept of Messiah was greatly warped, and this was a concept that was generally shared by all until the coming of the Spirit (Luke 24:26-27).

(2) Concerning time of the kingdom. Of the times and seasons of the long-promised Messianic kingdom He taught them that they could have no knowledge (1:6-7). There was no rebuke on the Saviour's part to the question nor any implication that the kingdom was not to come in literal fulfillment of the promises. The time they could not know about; the kingdom they did know about and no rethinking about it was necessary.[3]

(3) Concerning the Spirit. Although the ministry of the Spirit was well-known and perhaps widely experienced in the Old Testament, the Lord announced that the baptism of the Spirit was yet future (Acts 1:5). (Whatever happened as recorded in John 20:22 could not have been the baptism; otherwise the future tense in Acts 1:5 loses all significance.)

(4) Concerning service. The service of the disciples, He told them, was to have new power in the person of the Holy Spirit and a new program in that it would extend to the uttermost part of the earth (1:8). The motivation of it was to be love for Himself (John 21).

[3]*Contra* G. B. Stevens, *The Theology of the New Testament* (Edinburgh: T. & T. Clark, 1899), pp. 261-62.

c. In other ways. The entire book is the record of Messiah's work; therefore, any list will be incomplete. Nevertheless, among the more notable things which He did are: the sending of the Spirit (2:33), the adding to the Christian group (2:47; 4:12), the performance of miracles (4:10; 9:34; 13:11; 16:18; 19:11), and the manifestation of His personal presence (7:56; 9:5, 10-11; 18:9).

C. *The Holy Spirit*

1. *His deity.* A direct statement of deity is found in the well-known passage in chapter 5 where Peter uses God and the Holy Spirit interchangeably (5:3-4). His coming was an act of sending by the risen Son (2:33).

2. *His work in relation to Christ.* He is said to have anointed the Lord during His ministry on earth (10:38). This probably is equivalent to indwelling and occurred at the baptism of Christ. That is not to say that the baptism means anointing but just that both things happened at the same time.

3. *His work in the future.* If one interprets the quotation from Joel 2 in Acts 2 as having a future fulfillment, then the Spirit will someday be poured out on all flesh with certain unusual accompaniments.[4]

4. *His work in relation to the Church.* This is the principal area of the Spirit's work as far as the record in Acts is concerned.

a. He baptizes (1:5; 11:15-16). This ministry was with the purpose of forming the Body of Christ.

b. He governed the early Church (13:2-4).

c. He filled the workers for witness (1:8; 2:4; 4:31; 5:32; 9:11-20). That this should be the case was the normal expectation of the Church (6:3, 5; 11:24).

d. He led the early Church leaders. Outstanding illustrations of this are Philip (8:26-30), Peter (10:19; 11:19), Paul

[4]Cf. the author's article "The Significance of Pentecost," *Bibliotheca Sacra,* October, 1955, pp. 333-35.

(16:7; 20:23; 21:4, 11), and the prophets, of which Agabus is an example (11:28; 21:4).

Although the reader of Acts is distinctly conscious of the Spirit's work, it is always, as it should be, the work of promoting the glory of Christ and not Himself. These are the acts of the risen Christ through the Holy Spirit as He moved upon men.

Note concerning tongues.

a. The recorded occurrences of tongues. Tongues were heard at Pentecost (2:6), in Caesarea (10:46), and at Ephesus (19:6). There is no specific mention of tongues in Samaria (8:17) though the verb *saw* in verse 18 may indicate tongues.

b. The meaning of tongues according to Pentecostalism.[5] According to the Pentecostal position tongues do not mean (1) linguistic ability, (2) Christian eloquence, (3) a temporary gift which was the exclusive possession of the apostolic age, (4) the babblings of fanaticism, or (5) a display of the power of Satan. They are, according to Pentecostalism, (1) the initial physical evidence of the baptism with the Holy Spirit, (2) a devotional gift, and (3) a sign of confirmation and judgment.

c. The meaning of tongues in Acts. (1) The use of tongues (foreign languages, as is clearly stated in 2:6) was God's way of spreading the Gospel quickly to all nations. (2) Tongues were also a sign of confirmation to the Jewish people of the truth of the Christian message (cf. Isa. 28:11 where it was predicted that other tongues would be a sign of confirmation to the Jews). Sometimes the confirmation was to those who stood by and observed (as in Acts 10) and sometimes it was to those who received the gift (as in Acts 19). (3) From the Book of Acts alone one must admit that it might be difficult to prove that tongues were not the initial evidence of the baptism with the Holy Spirit. But from the

[5]Carl Brumback, *"What Meaneth This?"* (Springfield, Mo.: Gospel Publishing House, 1947).

viewpoint of Systematic Theology it is not difficult, for I Corinthians 12:13 and 30 say all are baptized by the Spirit but all do not speak in tongues. Therefore, tongues are not the required evidence of the baptism. In order to answer this argument, some Pentecostals attempt to distinguish between the baptism *by* the Spirit (in Corinthians) and the baptism *with* the Spirit (in Acts), but such a distinction is highly artificial (for the same Greek preposition, *en* is used in Acts 1:5 and I Cor. 12:13).

Regulations concerning the use of tongues belong to Paulinism and not to the theology under discussion.

II. The Doctrine of the Scriptures

A. *The Use of the Old Testament*

In the speeches in Acts there are about 110 references from the Old Testament taken from eighteen to twenty books. The predominance of quotations are Messianic passages from Deuteronomy, the Psalms, and Isaiah. As would be expected, there are more quotations from the Old Testament in the earlier speeches in Acts because of their address to Jewish audiences, and the passages quoted are Messianic in order to identify Jesus of Nazareth as the Christ. A. Rendel Harris and F. F. Bruce[6] believe that many of these quotations were taken immediately from Books of Testimonies which were collections of proof texts from the Old Testament on various subjects. These scholars cite the interdependent exegesis of the quotations (as in 2:25 ff. and 13:33 ff.) and the fact that missing is the usual formula "that it might be fulfilled." Such could easily have been the immediate source though the ultimate origin is the Old Testament.

B. *The Inspiration of the Old Testament*

That the Old Testament was from God was affirmed by the early Church (1:16; 4:25; 28:25). The authority of the

[6]Cf. F. F. Bruce, *op. cit.*, p. 19.

Scriptures was also recognized (3:18, 21; 13:46-47; 15:15-18; 26:22-23) .

C. *The Form of Quotation of the Old Testament*

Two problems arise in the matter in which the form of quotation is made from the Old Testament. One is the use of the Septuagint instead of the Hebrew text (as in 15:13-18) , and the other is the problem of paraphrase or interpretative changes (as in 26:18 where "from the power of Satan to God" is added to the original quotation from Isa. 42:7, 16) .

Any detailed discussion of possible solutions to the problem is beyond the scope of the consideration of this book, but simply and briefly there are three suggestions pertinent to the solution. (1) In the New Testament often the Septuagint is used in order to make something clearer than the Hebrew text does. In some instances the Septuagint may even be more accurate. (2) Actually, paraphrases are no real problem.[7] The minds of the writers of the New Testament were filled with Scripture, and they often merely quoted the sense of it even though prefixing the paraphrase with the phrase "the Scripture says." The word *says* is thus used in a general sense, and since quotation marks were unavailable in the Greek language, such a general sense is not only possible but quite probable in many cases. It would be like saying today, "The Scripture says Christians shouldn't lie to each other." In such an example the verb *to say* is used in a general sense and in no way indicates or introduces a direct quotation, and yet the sense of the Scripture has been quoted accurately. (3) Any solution must ultimately take into account the superintending work of the Holy Spirit in both Testaments. In reality all quotations in the New Testament of the Old Testament are quotations by the Author of the Author Himself.

[7]Roger Nicole, "Old Testament Quotations in the New Testament," *The Gordon Review*, 1:7-12, February, 1955.

III. The Doctrine of Salvation

A. *The Condition of Salvation*

There is only one condition for salvation everywhere stated in the preaching of the early Church, viz. faith.

1. *There is a faith which is not unto salvation.* There are two notable examples of the exercise of such faith in the book—Simon (8:13) and Agrippa (26:27). In order to be saving faith it must be rightly placed, and the faith of these two was not directed toward Jesus of Nazareth.

2. *Saving faith must be in Jesus Christ.* This idea is the most often repeated statement in Acts concerning salvation (10:43; 11:17, 21; 14:23; 16:31; 18:8). On occasion the record says that saving faith is directed toward God, but in such instances a knowledge of Jesus is presupposed, so that the faith is toward God as revealed in His Son (e.g., 16:34).

3. *The message of faith is made known through God's messengers.* It is through men that God delivers His message both by word of mouth (15:7) and by deed and life (13:12).

4. *The act of believing is through grace and therefore is rooted in the eternal counsels of God.* Belief, though a human act, is nonetheless accomplished through the grace of God (18:27), and those who believed had already been enrolled or set in the rank of ones having eternal life (13:48; cf. II Tim. 3:11 for the same word). This emphasis on the divine sovereign aspect of salvation is somewhat surprising to find in an historical book, but it shows that the doctrine was a fixed part of the theological substructure of Luke's thinking.

5. *A synonym for faith is repentance.* Often the idea of believing is expressed by the word *repent* (2:38; 3:19; 5:31; 8:22; 11:18; 17:30; 20:21 26:20). Like faith, it is the human requirement for salvation and yet it is the gift of God (5:31; 11:18). Both Peter and Paul preached repentance, which means that it cannot be assigned to Petrine theology. The

word means to change one's mind, and by its usage in the Book of Acts it means to change one's mind about Jesus of Nazareth being the Messiah. This involved no longer thinking of Him as merely the carpenter's son of Nazareth, an imposter, but now receiving Him as both Lord and Messiah. Thus, repentance as preached by the apostles was not a prerequisite to nor a consequence of salvation but was actually the act of faith in Jesus Christ which brought salvation to the one who repented.

6. *Faith alone is sufficient.* A deviation from the sufficiency of faith appeared early in the Church. Some of the brethren of the circumcision tried to make circumcision an additional condition for salvation (15:5). The reason that this arose was that some considered Christianity merely a group within Judaism. Therefore, when Gentiles came into the Church they thought they should come as Jewish proselytes and be circumcised. The question came to a head when a Church council was called in Jerusalem to settle it. Because of the other decrees of the council suggesting the limiting of certain liberties, we sometimes overlook the decision which was made concerning the all-important question of whether circumcision was necessary in addition to faith for salvation. The decision is clearly stated: "Wherefore my sentence is, that we trouble not them which from among the Gentiles are turned to God" (15:19).

B. *The Consequences of Salvation*

1. *Eternal life* (13:48).

2. *Justification* (13:39). Justification, the declaration that the sinner is righteous, was something that the Mosaic law could not do.

3. *Remission of sins* (2:38; 10:43; 22:16).

C. *The Constraints of Salvation*

1. *Constrained to be baptized.* In every recorded instance,

immediately upon receiving Jesus as Saviour the believers
were baptized.

a. The kind of baptism. Baptism in the Book of Acts was
in the name of Jesus, and this was different from the baptism
of John the Baptist (cf. 13:24; 19:4).

b. The meaning of baptism. Baptism always means identification. Jewish proselyte baptism (which was practiced in
Christ's time) [8] meant the identification of the Gentile proselyte with Judaism. Baptism into the mystery religions had
the same significance. John's baptism identified the people
with his message. Likewise, Christian baptism was an act
of identification with the Christian message and with the
Christian group.

c. The method of baptism. Even non-immersionists admit
that immersion was the common practice of apostolic times
and that there were sufficient pools in Jerusalem to permit
even the immersion of 3,000 converts on the day of Pentecost.[9] The mode of Jewish proselyte baptism which was a
similar and contemporary rite, was clearly and invariably
immersion,[10] and it is difficult to imagine a different mode
being practiced by the Christian Church.

d. The basis of baptism. In every instance the reason for
being baptized was that salvation had already been experienced. Baptism was not unto salvation but on the basis of
salvation.[11]

[8] A. Edersheim, *The Life and Times of Jesus the Messiah* (Grand Rapids:
Eerdmans, 1943), II, 745-47.
[9] T. M. Lindsay, "Baptism," *The International Standard Bible Encyclopaedia* (Grand Rapids: Eerdmans, 1943), I, 390; J. Calvin, *The Institutes
of the Christian Religion* (Grand Rapids: Eerdmans, 1953), IV, xv, 19.
[10] Cf. Edersheim, *loc. cit.*, and E. Schürer, *A History of the Jewish People
in the Time of Jesus Christ* (Edinburgh: T. & T. Clark, 1890), II, ii, 319 ff.
[11] Acts 2:38 is no exception. A. T. Robertson explains the meaning of the
words "unto the remission of your sins." In themselves the words can express
aim or purpose for that use of *eis* does exist as in I Cor. 2:7 . . . But then
another usage exists which is just as good Greek as the use of *eis* for aim
or purpose. It is seen in Matt. 10:41 . . . where it cannot be purpose or aim,
but rather the basis or ground. . . It is seen again in Matt. 12:41 about
the preaching of Jonah . . . They repented because of (or at) the preaching of Jonah . . . I understand Peter to be urging baptism on each of
them who had already turned (repented) and for it to be done in the

2. *Constrained to testify of Christ.* This seemed to be a natural and normal consequence of salvation, so that as a result others were saved daily (2:47; 8:4; 9:20; 18:5, 26; 26:19-20).

3. *Constrained to help one another.* The new community brought strange people together, but that new relationship was one of love and mutual help (2:44; 11:27-30; 15:36; 18:23; 21:20-26).

4. *Constrained to restrict their liberty.* When Gentile believers were made aware of the offensiveness of certain practices to fellow Jewish believers, they gladly restricted their liberty in Christ for the sake of their brethren (15:19-29). It was not a question of being restricted because of the whims of a few but because of the large numbers of Jews who needed to be won to the new faith.

IV. THE DOCTRINE OF THE CHURCH

However limited the treatment of the theology of Acts may be in standard Biblical Theologies, ecclesiology always receives some attention, for "the picture which the Acts furnishes of the life of the primitive Christian community is an interesting and graphic one . . ."[12]

A. *The Beginning of the Church*

The Church is Christ's (Matt. 16:18). He chose and trained its first leaders during His earthly lifetime. Some of His teaching was in anticipation of the formation of the Church. His death, resurrection, ascension, and exaltation were the necessary foundation on which the Church was to be built. But, although the Lord is the founder of the Church and the one who laid the groundwork during His earthly life, the Church did not come into functional existence until

name of Jesus Christ on the basis of the forgiveness of sins which they had already received" (*Word Pictures in the New Testament* (New York: Harper, 1930), III, 35-36).
[12]G. B. Stevens, *op. cit.*, p. 262; cf. R. F. Weidner, *Biblical Theology of the New Testament* (New York: Revell, 1891), I, 161-64.

the Day of Pentecost. There are a number of considerations that prove this.

(1) The chief argument relates to the baptism of the Holy Spirit. The Lord had spoken of this work of the Spirit just before His ascension (1:5) as being yet future and unlike anything they had previously experienced. Although it is not expressly recorded in Acts 2 that the baptism of the Spirit occurred on the Day of Pentecost, it is said in Acts 11:15-16 that it did happen then in fulfillment of the promise of the Lord. However, it is Paul who explains that this baptism places people in the Body of Christ (I Cor. 12:13). In other words, on the Day of Pentecost men were first put into the Body of Christ. Since the Church is the Body of Christ (Col. 1:18), the Church could not have begun until Pentecost and had to begin on that day.

(2) A second argument concerns the exaltation of Christ and the sending of the Holy Spirit (2:33). It is obvious that Peter's emphasis would be incongruent with the idea that the Church began some years after Pentecost as well as with the idea that it began before Pentecost, for it is dependent on the resurrected and ascended Lord (cf. Eph. 4:8-11).

(3) From Pentecost on there is a new distinctiveness. The day itself was certainly unlike other Pentecosts before, and the group that was formed was immediately distinctive. The converts' submission to water baptism marked that large group off from other Jews immediately. Even though the word *Church* does not appear in Acts until 5:11, and even though there was a certain intermixture with Judaism, there was a distinguishably new group after Pentecost (2:38).

(4) Peter called Pentecost the beginning (11:15). This beginning could not be put sometime after Pentecost, for Peter associates the beginning with the Lord's promise concerning the baptism of the Spirit which the Lord had said would be fulfilled "not many *days* hence" (1:5).

Note on ultradispensationalism. The Bullinger or more

extreme type of ultradispensationalism usually places the Church entirely after the Book of Acts, while the more moderate type represented by O'Hair places it within the Book of Acts either at 18:6 or 13:46 or sometimes, more rarely, with the conversion of Paul in chapter 9. In either type two things are clear: the Church did not begin on Pentecost, but when it did begin is indeterminable.[13]

The principal arguments for their placing the beginning of the Church after Pentecost are two. (1) Since Pentecost was a Jewish feast and since the Church is unrelated to Judaism and the Old Testament, the Church could not have begun on Pentecost. (2) Since Peter applied Joel's prophecy to Pentecost, the implications of Pentecost must be Jewish and not Christian. The first argument overlooks the validity of types and would run into difficulty with Passover and Firstfruits being used as types of the work of Christ. The second shows misunderstanding of how Peter did use Joel's prophecy on Pentecost, for Peter did not say that the prophecy was then being fulfilled.[14]

B. *The Organization of the Church*

1. *The apostles.* In the earliest days of the Church when all its members were in Jerusalem the apostles assumed the places of leadership. The apostles guided the doctrine of the new group, which was a factor in binding the Church together (2:42).

2. *Elders.* When Luke first mentions the elders he introduces them without preface as though they were to be regarded as a matter of course (11:30). We are to understand from this that the elders were adopted by the Christian Church from the Jewish synagogue organization (cf. 4:5; 6:

[13]Cf. E. W. Bullinger, *The Mystery* (London: Eyre and Spottiswoode, n.d.), p. 40; J. C. O'Hair, *A Dispensational Study of the Bible*, p. 32.
[14]Cf. the author's article, "The Significance of Pentecost," *Bibliotheca Sacra*, October, 1955, pp. 333-35.

12; 25:15). Evidently elders as an organized group antedate the deacons, and elders bore the same relation to groups elsewhere as the apostles first bore to the Church in Jerusalem. Paul's appointing of elders to take the leadership of churches he founded would bear this out. It also seems that there were several elders over each congregation (14:23; 15:2, 4; 21:18) and that their responsibilities extended to both spiritual and temporal matters (11:30; 14:23).

3. *Deacons.* As far as the record in Acts is concerned the word *deacon* seems to be used entirely in an unofficial sense. That is not to say that the office of deacon was not recognized during the Acts period (cf. Phil. 1:1); but the word is used in Acts in the general sense of those who serve (1:17, 25; 6:1, 2, 4; 11:29; 12:25; 19:22; 20:24; 21:19). Those who were chosen in Acts 6 as a result of the dispute among the widows should probably be termed helpers rather than deacons, for theirs was a distinctly subordinate function and not an office in the Church.[15] The development of the office probably took place in the following way:

> There were subordinate duties to be fulfilled toward the Christian society as a society, not easily included under *episkopē*—"superintendence,"—and those who performed these habitually come to be charged with them. In the course of a generation the performance of the duty hardens into a distinct office.[16]

C. *The Life of the Church*

The life of the early community involved many things.

1. *Doctrine* (2:42). The apostles had a huge job on their hands instructing the multitudes who came to Christ. The content of their teaching was the facts and meaning of the life of Jesus of Nazareth. Teaching was combined with preaching (4:2; 5:21, 25, 28, 42; 28:31), but doctrine had a

---

[15]As was pointed out many years ago by Vitringa, *De Synagoga Vetere* (Franequerae: Johannis Gyzelaar, 1696), p. 914.

[16]Gregory Dix in *The Apostolic Ministry*, ed. Kenneth E. Kirk (London: Hodder & Stoughton, 1946), p. 244.

prominent place in the life of the early groups (11:26; 15:35; 18:11, 25; 20:20).

2. *Fellowship*. The presence of the definite article in 2:42 probably points to the spiritual fellowship which bound the Christians together. The group also fellowshiped in material things (4:32). It is ridiculous to call this action Christian Communism, for any sale was voluntary (4:34; 5:4), and the right of private possession was never abolished. The group controlled only that which was given it, and the distribution was according to need and not equally. This was Christian fellowship in action, for the principal means of expressing fellowship is through the giving of material things.

3. *The Lord's Supper*. In Jerusalem the Lord's Supper was observed daily (2:42), though doubtless we are not to understand daily in each house but daily as far as some place in Jerusalem is concerned. Weekly observance seemed to become the customary procedure as time went on (20:7, 11). and when Paul visited Troas he was included with the local believers in the memorial supper.

4. *Prayers*. Prayer permeated the life of the Church, and as it is the most important aspect of any work for the Lord it is the secret of the success of the early Church. There were prayers on regular occasions and prayers for special needs (1:24; 3:1; 4:23-31; 6:4, 6; 9:40; 10:4, 31; 12:5, 12; 13:3; 14:23; 16:13, 16; 20:36; 28:8).

5. *Persecution*. The life of the early Church was filled with persecution (4; 5; 7; 8; 12; 15; 21). Persecution was either by heretics (like the Judaistic legalizers) or by the political rulers. (Herod's persecution in chapter 12 is essentially religious and not political, for he was acting to please the Jews and not the Romans.)

6. *Discipline*. The notable example of discipline in the life of the Church is the case of Ananias and Sapphira (5:1-11). In some instances subtraction is not retrogression.

In summary, these are the outstanding features of the ecclesiology of Acts. (1) The Christian Church was a new group with a distinctly recognizable beginning. (2) It was not a purely democratic group, but from the beginning had regularly constituted leadership charged with the oversight of its affairs. (3) The basis of the life of the Church was the love-bond which welded individual believers into a community. In other words, the fellowship was the basis of Church life. It accounted for the interest in doctrine, the sharing of material goods, the frequent remembrance of the Lord in the Supper, the emphasis on prayers, persecution from the religious leaders, and the necessity for discipline within its own circle.

V. Missions

A. *The Principles of Missions in the Book of Acts*

In a history of the missionary work of the Church one would expect that the Holy Spirit would reveal certain principles concerning missionary work which serve as guides for today.

1. *The groundwork principle.* The basis of all missions is the individual disciple. Our Lord had set the pattern for the groundwork on individuals in the Great Commission when He commanded His disciples to make disciples. This work, according to Matthew 28:18-20, involves going, baptizing, and teaching (the three participles in the verses stand in contrast to the single imperative, "make disciples"). In other words, laying the groundwork involves more than evangelism; it also includes teaching the new converts. This is what the early Church did, and the historical record bears that out, for the chief designation Luke uses for the early Christians is the word *disciple* (6:1, 2, 7; 9:1, 19, 25-26, 38; 11:26; 13:52; 14:22, 28; 18:23, 27; 19:9; 20:1, 30; 21:4, 16).

2. *The geographic principle.* In relation to geography the disciples were commanded to go everywhere, and this they did, though not always voluntarily. On the Day of Pentecost

there were providentially assembled men from many nations who carried the message back home. On another occasion God used persecution to scatter the seed (8:1, 4). Missionary work to unreached areas soon became a normal desire and purpose of the Church (13:1-3; 15:40). The aim was to reach those who were unreached (cf. Rom. 15:24).

In applying the geographic principle today three cautions should be observed: (1) this must not be done to the neglect of the work at home (note Paul's continuous interest in the collection for the Church in Jerusalem); (2) this must not be done spasmodically (cf. 18:11; 19:10); and (3) there should not be a loss of interest in works with which one was associated in the past (cf. II Cor. 11:28).

3. *The group principle*. The ultimate goal of laying the groundwork of individual disciples in every place was the establishing of local churches. This came about spontaneously because individuals who were converted and taught saw the need for group activity. The disciples did not go to a community and announce that they were going to establish a church—that developed spontaneously; neither did they go into a city and make converts without establishing a church (14:23). The main goal of missionary work is the establishment of the local, organized church. The New Testament Epistles addressed to churches attest the validity and success of this principle.

B. *The Procedures of Missions in the Book of Acts*

Basically the procedure was to preach and teach the Word continually. However, there were particular ways in which this was done.

1. *Itineration*. The missionaries were always on the move, not spasmodically but systematically (11:22-26; 15:36). Even the settled pastor is told to itinerate (II Tim. 4:5).[17]

2. *Attacking strategic centers*. Beginning in Jerusalem and spreading to Antioch, Ephesus, Philippi, Athens, Corinth,

[17]The word *evangelist* includes the idea of itinerant ministry.

and ending in Rome, the message was brought to the centers of population first. From there it radiated to the surrounding areas (19:10; cf. I Thess. 1:8).

3. *Oral preaching.* This is undoubtedly the principal method of missions. Whatever other aids to witness may be given, there can be no substitute for oral preaching (2:40; 5:42; 8: 4-5, 35, 40; 13:5; 28:31). Preaching was done in the synagogues (9:20; 13:14; 14:1; 17:1, 10; 18:4; 19:8); in houses (10:34); in the church (13:1); by a river bank (16:13); in jail (16:25); in street meetings (17:22); and at work (18: 2-3).

4. *Literature.* The existence of Acts itself, to say nothing of the Epistles, is evidence of the importance placed on the written ministry in instructing believers.

5. *Training national workers.* This is an outcome of making disciples. Sometimes such training was related to groups, like the elders (14:23; 19:30; cf. I Thess. 5:12), and in other cases it was of individuals (16:1; 18:26). This procedure made for multiplication of the missionary effort rather than mere addition.

VI. Eschatology

A. *The Kingdom of God Was the Subject of Apostolic Preaching*

Throughout the record it is reported that the early evangels preached the kingdom (8:12; 14:22; 19:8; 20:25; 28:23). In these references the phrase has various shades of meaning. In two instances it is linked with the phrase *name of Jesus* (8:12; 28:23). In one place it is used as a synonym for the Gospel of the grace of God (20:25). It is preached to both Jewish and Gentile audiences (cf. 19:8; 28:23), and has an element of future realization in the concept (14:22). Chiefly, however, the idea seems to be the basic idea of kingdom; i.e., the sovereign ruling power of God. Thus the phrase as used in the apostolic preaching means the things concerning the power and plan of God working to bring salvation through Jesus the Messiah, which salvation will consummate in future glory. It is closely akin to the Jewish idea of the universal kingdom.[18]

B. *The Promise of the Messianic Kingdom is Reaffirmed*

Mention has already been made of Jesus' reaffirmation of the Messianic kingdom promises (1:6-7), but Peter also confirmed these promises (3:12-26). The occasion was the healing of a lame man, but the theme of Peter's message to the crowd that gathered was similar to that which he had preached on Pentecost—Jesus whom you killed is Messiah. Then after the appeal for repentance he promised forgiveness of sins and the times of refreshing associated with the coming of Messiah (3:19). Although the phrase *times of refreshing* is found only here in the New Testament, it evidently is synonymous with "restitution of all things" in verse 21 and thus refers to the millennial kingdom (cf. 1:6; Luke 2:25). Thus Israel's hope is in no way abrogated but rather is reaffirmed even after the beginning of the Church. Just as in the Synoptics so also in Acts the meaning of the word *kingdom* must be determined by its usage.

C. *The Program of the Ages Is Outlined* (15:13-18)

As a preface to summing up the decision of the Jerusalem council, James, after reviewing the fact that through Peter's ministry God first visited the Gentiles, quotes a prophecy from Amos 9:11-12. If it be admitted that "after these things," which is not a part of the Amos passage, is a deliberate change made by James under the guidance of the Holy Spirit, then there is set up an order of events which clearly outlines God's program of the ages. The order is: (1) God visits Gentiles; (2) after this Christ will return; (3) the millennial kingdom will be established and in it Gentiles will return to the Lord.

[18]Cf. S. Schechter, *Some Aspects of Rabbinic Theology* (New York: Macmillan, 1923), pp. 80-96.

Those who object to seeing an order of events in this passage generally hold either that the Church now is fulfilling
entirely the prophecy of Amos[19] or that there is a partial fulfillment now in the Church and another fulfillment during
the millennium.[20] The latter, of course, allows for a premillennial scheme while the former is a tenet of amillennialism.
However, it appears that the change in the Amos quotation
is intentional and that an order is deliberately set up. This
is entirely consistent with the confirmations of the millennial
promises found elsewhere in the book and discussed above.

This, then, is a survey of the theology of Acts. In relation
to the scheme and purpose of Biblical Theology it is of the
greatest importance, for it traces the history and expansion
of the infant Church against the background of Judaism. As
Stevens so aptly says: "The wonder is not that the Church's
progress was slow and gradual, but that it was so sure and
continuous."[21]

In Luke's careful planning and developing of the record
certain features stand out in the progressive revelation of doctrine. (1) Primarily it is the new entity, the Church, which
is the outstanding aspect of the progress of New Testament
revelation as revealed in the theology of Acts. Not only does
this include the fact of the existence of the Church but the
new bond and resultant life is a vital part of it. The missionary enterprise, too, must be included in this new concept.
(2) Also paramount in the theology of Acts is the doctrine
of salvation through faith in Jesus of Nazareth, the Messiah,
for all men regardless of national background. The annulling
of all ritual requirements, such as circumcision, is an important step in progressive revelation. (3) This new program, however, does not abrogate or replace God's purpose
in the Davidic, Messianic kingdom. This is reaffirmed in
Luke's account.

[19]O. T. Allis, *Prophecy and the Church* (Philadelphia: Presbyterian and
Reformed Publishing Co., 1945), pp. 135-36.
[20]F. F. Bruce, *The Acts of the Apostles*, pp. 297-98.
[21]*Op. cit.*, p. 274

Part III

THE THEOLOGY OF JAMES

Chapter 1

HISTORICAL BACKGROUND

I. THE AUTHOR

THE AUTHOR OF THIS EPISTLE styles himself as the servant of God and of the Lord Jesus Christ. Four men named James are mentioned in the New Testament: James the father of Judas not Iscariot (Luke 6:16), James the son of Zebedee (Matt. 4:21), James the son of Alphaeus (Matt. 10:3), and James the half-brother of the Lord (Matt. 13:55; Gal. 1:19). The first two mentioned are not possible candidates for author of the Epistle. Some identify the last two as the same person by making Clopas (John 19:25) the same as Alphaeus, thereby making Mary the wife of Clopas the same person as Mary the mother of Joses and James the less (Mark 15:47; 16:1; Luke 24:10; Mark 15:40). This would mean that those who are called the brethren of the Lord were actually cousins (Mark 6:3). The chief difficulty with this view is simply that it ends in a contradiction: James the son of Alphaeus was one of the twelve disciples (Acts 1:13) —a believer; yet those who are called the brethren of the Lord (which according to the view would include this James) were unbelievers.[1]

Eusebius and many others after him identify the author with the brother of the Lord. It has been shown that this could not mean cousin as if Mary had no other children be-

[1]Cf. A. Carr, *St. James, Cambridge Greek Testament* (Cambridge: Cambridge University Press, 1896), pp. xii-xiii.

side Jesus. It could mean step-brother in the sense of a son of Joseph by a previous marriage, which would also preserve Mary's position as the mother of Jesus only, or it could mean half-brother in the sense of a natural son of Joseph and Mary after the birth of Jesus. The former view was held in the second to fourth centuries while the latter gained prominence after that time and is supported by the "until" of Matthew 1:25.

Accepting the view that the author was the half-brother of Jesus we can know certain facts about his life. His childhood was spent in the Nazareth home of Joseph and Mary with Jesus, and undoubtedly many things to which he was exposed in those early days came back to him with new meaning after his conversion. The pious Jewish home also contributed to his knowledge of and reverence for the Old Testament which is displayed often in the Epistle. During the ministry of Jesus there was evidently not much contact with the home or family, for He separated Himself from them at the very beginning (John 2:12) and was rejected by his townspeople shortly thereafter (Luke 4:31 ff.). All of this time His brethren remained unbelievers (note the imperfect tense in John 7:5).

In the upper room after the ascension James suddenly appears on the scene as a converted man (Acts 1:14). Paul fills in the gap by telling us that the risen Lord appeared to him (I Cor. 15:7). Very quickly James was not only received by the Christian brethren but was recognized as the head of the Church in Jerusalem (Acts 12:17; 15:13-21; 21:18; Gal. 2:9), a position which he held until his death. Eusebius says he was a Nazarite and an ascetic who used no wine, no meat, no razor. But he did use his knees, for according to tradition, he was found so often in the temple praying for the sins of his Jewish brethren that they became as hard as camels' knees. It is said that his death occurred at the hands of the scribes and Pharisees who took him to the pinnacle of the temple and flung him down. The fall did not kill him, and as they were stoning him to death James, like his Lord, prayed for their forgiveness.

From a life like this what kind of theology could be expected? One would expect it to be centered in the Word, for the godly Jewish background would certainly affect it in this respect. One would also expect a very practical theology—one that lives out that Word. Too, one would expect to find evidences of James's making up lost time, so to speak, in saturating himself with the words of Christ. These, too, would then become part of his concept of the Word, being put on an equal plane with the words of the Old Testament. And this is what we find, for James's theology is pre-eminently a theology of the Word. It reveals a reverence for the Old Testament, a knowledge of the teachings of the Lord, and a relevance of both to the problems of everyday life.

II. THE DATE AND READERS

The Epistle is addressed to the twelve tribes scattered abroad (1:1), but this must be understood to be limited to believing Jews (2:1, 7; 5:7). No other limitation is necessary though some have limited it to the churches in Judea or the eastern dispersion. The address can be taken as widely as James makes it. It is to all his brethren in the flesh who had become Christians.

The background gleaned from the Epistle itself shows a very early kind of persecution of believers of such type as was found in Palestine only before the year 70.[2] The use of the word *synagogue* (2:2) also attests to a very early date for the letter. There is no reference to the controversy which was settled at the Jerusalem council in 49, but 2:15-16 may be a reference to the famine mentioned in Acts 11:27-30. This would put the writing of the Epistle between 44 and 50.

[2]*Ibid.*, p. xxviii.

III. The Circumstances of the Churches

In writing to the scattered groups of Jewish believers James draws on scenes from his own experience in Judea to use as warnings and examples. From this we can paint a fairly complete picture of the conditions and circumstances of these early groups of believers.

Most of James's readers were evidently from the lower and poorer classes of society (2:5). Being in the employ of their richer fellow countrymen they were subjected to all sorts of oppression and injustice (2:6; 5:4). In such a situation it is not surprising to find that the Christians were courting the favor of the rich and treated them with special partiality when they came into the assembly of believers. This James denounces in no uncertain terms.

Within the Church itself there were abuses. Apparently there was little organization of assemblies at this time, and some of the believers taking advantage of the situation displayed an excessive eagerness to become teachers. This led to an over-emphasis on speaking and hearing rather than practicing (1:22; 3:1). Sometimes it ministered to pride and contention (4:1). Evidently many of the Christians had never yet fully dedicated themselves to the Lord but were still running their affairs according to their own plans (4: 7-15). It is a picture of conditions in the Church throughout all its history, including today, but it is a picture which we do not usually associate with the first half of the first century. James quickly dispels in this letter the auroral glow of spiritual perfectness which we generally associate with the first century Church.

Chapter 2

THE THEOLOGY OF THE EPISTLE

I. THE DOCTRINE OF GOD

THE THEOLOGY OF JAMES is closely akin to Old Testament Theology. This is clearly seen in the doctrine of God. James's designations of God include "the Lord" (4:15; 5:11-12), which is definitely after the manner of Old Testament expression; "Father" (1:17, 27; 3:9) ; and "Lord of Sabaoth" (5:4).

His characterizations of God also reflect the Old Testament ideas of jealousy and judgment. His Spirit who dwells within us is envious, desiring to have full control (4:5) ; therefore, whoever is a friend of the world constitutes himself an enemy of God (4:4). Wrathful judgment is also assured on those who oppress unjustly (5:1-6). At the same time God is also pictured as the giver of wisdom (1:5) and of good gifts (1:17) and as merciful toward the humble (5:11). This undoubtedly reflects the Lord's teaching (cf. Matt. 5:43-48; Mark 10:18), for in James's total presentation of God "we see the God of the Old Covenant clothed in the qualities which distinguish Jesus' conception of the Father in heaven."[1]

The other persons of the Godhead receive scant mention in the Epistle. By name Christ is mentioned in only two places (1:1; 2:1; cf. 1:7; 5:8-9) , and yet that is no measure

[1] G. B. Stevens, *The Theology of the New Testament* (Edinburgh: T. & T. Clark, 1899), p. 280.

of the importance James placed on the person of the Lord. He is indispensable to faith (2:1) and therefore is in the substructure of several important passages in the Epistle concerning salvation (1:18; 2:14-26). The Holy Spirit is mentioned only once (4:5) as the One who indwells believers and demands undivided allegiance.

II. THE DOCTRINE OF THE WORD

Although the Epistle of James is intensely practical, the central theological doctrine is undoubtedly that of the Word. If the Synoptic theology is eschatological and Johannine theology theological, then James's is bibliological. This centrality of the Word certainly stems from James's Jewish background and rearing in a godly Hebrew home. The godliness of his mother is fully displayed in such a passage as Luke 1: 46-55, and the naturalness of her use of the Old Testament Scriptures shows how deeply embedded the Word was in her heart and mind.

> From childhood the Jews knew many of the Old Testament lyrics by heart; and, just as our own poor, who know no literature but the Bible, easily fall into biblical language in times of special joy or sorrow, so Mary would naturally fall back on the familiar expressions of Jewish Scripture in this moment of intense exultation.[2]

There are fifteen discernible quotations from the Old Testament in the Magnificat. This is the well from which James drank deeply in his childhood and youth.

A. *The Employment of the Word*

The Epistle of James contains 108 verses in its five chapters. In that brief space the author refers or alludes to Genesis, Exodus, Leviticus, Numbers, Deuteronomy, Joshua, I Kings, Job, Psalms, Proverbs, Ecclesiastes, Isaiah, Jeremiah, Ezekiel,

[2]A. Plummer, *A. Critical and Exegetical Commentary on the Gospel According to St. Luke, International Critical Commentary* (Edinburgh: T. & T. Clark, 1910), p. 30.

Daniel, Hosea, Joel, Amos, Jonah, Micah, Zechariah, and Malachi.[3] This is nothing short of remarkable. By doing this James obviates the need for any formal statement of inspiration; he merely assumes it as most of the writers of Scripture do. He does speak specifically of the authority of the Scriptures in 4:5-6 and has no hesitation about citing Scripture to prove his point.

In addition to this extensive use of the Old Testament, the Book of James reflects the teachings of Jesus more than any other book in the New Testament apart from the record of them in the Gospels.[4] Referring to the Sermon on the Mount alone as a conveniently compact presentation of the Lord's teachings, one will find in James at least fifteen allusions to those teachings. Again this is a remarkable fact. As far as James is concerned it shows how he must have sought out and pored over the words of Christ after his own conversion and how enthralled he was with them. As far as the words of Christ are concerned, James's intermixture of them with the Old Testament places them in the same category as the inspired, authoritative Word of God. The Epistle is saturated with the Word and bespeaks for its author his high view of that Word and the deep foundational place it held in his own theological thinking.

B. *The Epithets of the Word*

James's view of the Word is also clearly seen by the epithets he employs to describe it.

1. *The Word of truth* (1:18). The Word of truth is the Word of God used in the spiritual creation of spiritually dead men. It is the Word which conveys truth—thus it is a phrase practically equivalent to "the gospel."

2. *The Scripture* (2:8, 23; 4:5-6). In the time of Christ

---

[3]Cf. J. B. Mayor, *The Epistle of St. James* (London: Macmillan, 1897), pp. cx-cxvi.

[4]Cf. W. G. Scroggie, *Know Your Bible* (London: Pickering & Inglis, 1940), II, 297-98.

"the Scriptures" was a designation used of the Old Testament and withheld from other Jewish literature.[5]. Therefore, when James uses this title he would be using it in that sense and assigning to the Old Testament all the inspiration and authority current in the belief of the times. To quote the Scripture was to end all argument (4:5-6).

3. *The perfect law of liberty* (1:25; 2:8). This is one of the most difficult phrases in the book, and yet it seems to be James's regular way of designating the Word of God. Obviously we cannot say that the law of liberty is the entire Bible, for it was not written when James used the phrase. Just as obvious is the fact that it includes the Old Testament (2:8) and yet is not coextensive with the Old Testament (1:25-27). From what has already been said about James's use of the Old Testament and the teachings of Christ, it would seem best to define the law of liberty as the Word of God revealed in the Old Testament and brought to fruition in the teachings of Christ.

C. *The effects of the Word*

As would be expected in this Epistle James assigns some practical benefits to the Word.

1. *The Word is a means of regeneration* (1:18) *and is implanted to save the soul* (1:21).

2. *It is a mirror reflecting the defects of a man* (1:23-25). Consequently, it is to be carefully gazed at (1:25) and carried out with diligence (1:22). It is significant that James makes this particularly applicable to men (cf. 1:23 where *aner*, male, not *anthropos*, person, is used) as if to point out the fact that men, more than women, need to be careful to be sensitive to respond to what they see in the Word.

3. *It is a guide for Christian living* (2:8).

4. *In the day of judgment it will serve as a standard for judgment* (2:12).

[5]James Orr, "The Bible," *International Standard Bible Encyclopaedia* (Grand Rapids: Eerdmans, 1943), I, 461.

That upon which the Word has effect relates to soteriology, anthropology, hamartiology, Christian living, and eschatology. This shows how basic the doctrine was in the thinking of James.

III. THE DOCTRINE OF FAITH

A. *The Background of the Doctrine*

James's teaching about faith finds its background in Pharisaism, not Paulinism. Alford explains this clearly:

> the Jewish Pharisaic notions were being carried into the adopted belief in Christianity, and the danger was not, as afterwards, of a Jewish law-righteousness being set up, but of a Jewish reliance on exclusive purity of faith superseding the necessity of a holy life, which is inseparably bound up with any worthy holding of the Christian faith.[6]

As the Pharisees trusted outward observances so the Jewish believers stood in danger of trusting an outward creed without the inward heart reaction which would produce good works.

James's teaching is not in conflict with Paulinism. The idea is an anachronism and theologically unsupportable. It is obvious that James wrote before Paul and that he speaks of the works of faith, not the works of the law against which Paul wrote later.

B. *James's Use of* Pistis, *Faith*

It is farthest from the truth to say that the conception of faith is lacking in the Epistle, for its pre-eminence is implied from the very first (cf. 1:3 ff.). James conceives of it as an active principle (1:6; 5:15) based on real trust in Christ who is its object (2:1). Certainly James's purpose is not to eliminate faith as a leading principle of the Christian life but

---

[6]H. Alford, *The Greek Testament* (London: Rivingtons, 1859), IV, Prolegomena, 102.

rather to guard against the danger of thinking faith to be only an intellectual assent to a creed which is never activated to produce good works. The difference between James and Paul is not that of faith versus works, but a difference of relationship. James emphasizes the work of the believer in relation to faith and Paul the work of Christ in relation to faith.

C. *The Central Passage* (2:14-26)

Even in the central passage the contrast is not between faith and works but between a dead faith (vv. 14-20) and a living faith (vv. 21-26). Dead faith, James emphatically says, cannot save (v. 14). It is extremely important to the argument to remember that the question of whether faith can save is confined by the hypothesis that it is to be understood in relationship to a man who *says* he has faith but produces no works. The question is not whether faith can save but whether such faith, that is dead faith, can save. That this is dead faith which James cites is clearly shown by the lack of response to almsgiving, a matter of great importance to Jews. Thus it can only be concluded that such non-working faith, even though it be related to an orthodox creed (v. 19) is dead (v. 17) and void of quality (v. 20).

Living faith, on the other hand, is illustrated by Abraham and Rahab, who out of their works showed their faith. Paul later uses Abraham as an illustration of the saving efficacy of faith apart from circumcision while James uses him for an entirely different purpose—proving by his works the living character of his faith. A working faith is a living faith as vividly illustrated in the final picture of the relationship of body and spirit (v. 26), for as they are inseparable so are faith and works.

IV. THE DOCTRINES OF MAN, SIN, AND SATAN

For a short epistle the author has a good deal to say about

these subjects. He believed in the creation of man by God (3:9) as a being composed of material and immaterial parts (2:26; 3:9). Some of the likeness of the original creation is retained in spite of the ravages of sin (3:9), and this is the basis for guarding what is said about one's fellow man. The author sets forth no real theory as to the origin of sin but he states details which show his belief in the universality of sin among all men (3:2) and the inherent nature of sin in man (1:14-15; 2:1 ff.; 3:1 ff.; 4:1 ff.).

Although sin is described specifically as trespass (2:9, 11), offense (2:10), an active principle (2:9; 5:15), and lacking the good (4:17), James's principal emphasis is to relate sin to the nature of God. Thus sin is defined as that which is against a righteous God (5:9; 4:5) as well as that which is against the revelation of God in law (2:9-11). Thus the ramifications of James's lofty conception of God and His Word are clearly seen in his definition of sin.

Some of the areas in which man may sin are thought (4:8), word (3:1 ff.), deeds of omission (4:17), deeds of commission (5:1-6), and attitude (4:12-17). Some of the results of sin mentioned are sickness (5:15), unanswered prayer (4:2), lack of blessing (1:25), increased judgment (2:13), and spiritual death (2:14-26; 5:20). Specific sins which were prevalent in the groups to which the Epistle was written were the sin of partiality (2:1-3), sins of the tongue (3:1-12; 5:12), contention (4:1-3, 11-12), and worldliness (4:4-5).

Everywhere the existence of a personal Devil is assumed in the Epistle. His relation to the sin of man is most clearly seen in 4:1-7 where the Christian is exhorted to resist the Devil in order to have victory over worldliness. The same passage also relates Satan to the cosmos.

V. THE SPIRITUAL LIFE

As far as quantity of material is concerned the doctrines related to the spiritual life receive the most attention in the

Epistle. To speak of the theology of James as bibliological is not a contradiction for the Word is foundational in the theological substructure of the writer. Nevertheless there is a connection between the two ideas, for the author's dealing with the specifics of the spiritual life are related to and based on the Word as epitomized in the law of liberty.

A. *The Doctrine of Dedication*

Dedication is an urgent matter. This is seen from the condition of the churches to which James was writing and it is also implied in the aorists used in 4:7-10. The tense further signifies that dedication should be a settled matter in the life of the believer.[7] The idea is to have these things done which are involved in dedication. Dedication as James conceives of it in this passage is not a piecemeal thing but a complete and settled action which includes several factors.

1. *Submission* (v. 7). To his proud readers James says first that it is necessary to put oneself under God.

2. *Selection* (v. 7). Dedication involves deciding whether one is on God's side or the Devil's. James does not say that the believer is to keep on drawing near to God but that he is to decide whose side he is on and take his firm and fixed stand there.

3. *Separation* (v. 8). Hand and heart (external and internal) must be cleansed in order to live a dedicated life.

4. *Seriousness* (v. 9). One who turns to God will also turn from the sin of the past. Very strong language is used here to describe the reaction a believer should have to the kind of life he has lived when an undedicated and worldly Christian. A proper sense of shame concerning the past will reflect itself in a sober and serious outlook toward the future. Dedication is a serious matter.

5. *Subjection* (v. 10). If God's will be taken then self is denied. And yet the paradox is that it is the one who abases

[7]A. T. Robertson, *A Grammar of the Greek New Testament in the Light of Historical Research* (New York: Hodder & Stoughton, 1919), pp. 855-56.

himself who is ultimately exalted by God. This kind of dedication is the basis of spiritual living and was the urgent need of the groups addressed in this Epistle.

B. *The Doctrine of Dependence*

The continuing effects of a once-for-all dedication depend on the maintaining of a proper attitude of dependence on God in all the matters of everyday living. The two ideas of dedication and dependence are closely associated in James's mind (4:7-10, 13-17). Evidently in his thinking the brother who makes his own plans for the morrow (v. 13) is a sample of an undedicated Christian. Two ideas run through this passage (4:13-17). (1) There should never be presumption on the part of the believer though there should be planning. (2) There always should be a realization of the transitory nature of life and a complete resignation to the perfect will of God.

[handwritten marginal note: I Prayer Fault — ① Do not ask ② Wrong motives]

C. *The Doctrine of Prayer*

[handwritten marginal note: II Prayer Favors ① Grace of God]

One would expect to find the man who was known as "camel-knees" writing a lot about prayer. There are three major sections dealing with prayer in the Epistle and scattered references elsewhere (1:5-8; 4:2-3; 5:13-20).

[handwritten marginal note: III Prayer Fervor — agony of prayer]

1. *The requirements of prayer.* Prayer involves (1) the realization that one is asking from a superior (4:3 where *aitēo*, which has that meaning, is used); (2) the realization of a personal need (4:2; 5:16 where *deēsis* is used); (3) the presence of working faith in the life of the one who prays (5:16); (4) complete unselfishness on the part of the petitioner (4:3); (5) asking on the basis of promises in faith and without doubting or disputing with oneself (1:6). Lack of any of these requirements would constitute a hindrance to prayer.

2. *The objects of prayer.* Though many things are mentioned in the Epistle as specific and proper objects for prayer,

all can be catalogued in three groups—prayer for physical needs, mental needs, and spiritual needs.

Regulations for prayer for physical afflictions are found in 5:13-20. Though this is a difficult passage to interpret it is clear that prayer is a necessary part of the procedure in the case of the healing of the sickness of one involved in sin. Confession, sacramental anointing, presence of the elders, and prayer must all be involved in such a case if the affliction is to be relieved.

Mental problems can also be solved by prayer (1:5-8). God will always answer the prayer for wisdom with liberality (or better, simplicity) and without upbraiding; thus God is never involved in His answering our prayers in secondary motives or in complaint on account of favors unreturned. On our part, however, the prayer must be in faith without wavering.

Personal and corporate spiritual needs also find their supply in answer to prayer (4:1-3). The background of this passage has already been discussed; the principal point to notice in connection with prayer is the necessity for completely unselfish praying if spiritual problems are to be solved.

D. *The Doctrine of Speech*

1. *Misuse of the tongue means a dwarfed life* (3:1-5). James puts the utmost importance on proper speech for a truly spiritual life, for, he says, although we all oftentimes offend, the most frequent offense comes from the tongue. Therefore, one who is victorious over these sins may be said to be a mature man, and contrariwise, he who sins in speech is dwarfed in his spiritual development (cf. Matt. 5:34-37, 48). Control of speech will include control of the entire body just as bits control horses, rudders ships, or a small spark a forest fire.

2. *Misuse of the tongue means a defiled life* (3:6-8). The misused tongue will reveal inner defilement and foulness.

3. *Misuse of the tongue means a deceitful life* (3:9-12). When the tongue which should be used to bless God curses man the words *deceit* and *hypocrisy* are certainly not too strong to use to describe James's thought about the matter.

E. *The Doctrine of Wisdom*

In 3:15-18 James gives the antidote to all the sins of the Christian life. It is simply the use of right wisdom. Worldly wisdom is not from above but is earth-bound, sensual, devilish, and can only produce jealousy, faction, confusion, and vile deeds. Heavenly wisdom comes from God (1:5; 3:17); is displayed in good works, meekness, and peace; and is epitomized as pure, peaceable, forbearing, easily entreated, full of mercy and good fruits, without variance, and without hypocrisy. If used it would give victory over the very sins which plagued these groups to which James wrote.

VI. ECCLESIOLOGY

As was said in the introduction, the state of the Church in James's day was not developed. Religion was more personal than corporate, for the distinctive Christian groups were not yet so recognized among those to whom this Epistle was addressed. Thus he describes true religion as that which is concerned with widows and orphans and a separated life. Both duties are individual and more private than public. In ministering to widows and orphans one does not expect recognition from the crowd or return from those ministered to. This is the most unselfish kind of love and coupled with the unspotted life of separation from the world constitutes true religion.

Church organization has not evidently developed to include any officers other than elders (5:14) who were undoubtedly a carry-over from the synagogue organization (2:1\

rather than a distinctively Christian innovation. Some Christian groups were still meeting in synagogues and had not yet been forced to separate themselves.

The principal ecclesiastical problem (apart from the individual worldliness which of course had corporate ramifications) was the partiality displayed in the assemblies (2:1-11). The very wealthy people who were oppressing the believers (5:1-6) were being courted and favored by being given the chief places in the church meetings while those who were poor were despised by the believers. It is the perpetual problem of respecting the outward appearance of man and paying court to those whom we think can help us in return. James's condemnation of this prevalent sin is severe. He says (1) it touches the heart of the Christian faith, for if God had dealt with us in respect of persons where would any of us be? (2:1, 4a); (2) it causes one to place himself as a judge (v. 4b); (3) it degrades those whom Christ honors; i.e., the poor of this world (v. 5); (4) it honors those who have shown themselves unworthy of honor by their actions (v. 6); (5) it is plainly sin even though it seems to be a trivial matter and one practiced everywhere (v. 9); (6) it breaks the Law (v. 10; cf. Lev. 19:15; Deut. 1:17; 16:19); and (7) it will severely judge those who have practiced it (v. 13).

In trying to summarize the theology of James one is tempted to say that it is intensely practical, but this would leave a misimpression. His system is intensely theological, being rooted in the teachings of the Old Testament and molded by the teachings of Jesus. The chief point of the book is that "Christianity is principally an energetic moral life, which has its principle in the word of truth, by which the Christian is newly begotten by God."[8] The principal substructure is bibliological, for it is the Word of truth which begets us unto the new life, and it by the royal law of liberty

[8]C. F. Schmid, *Biblical Theology of the New Testament* (Edinburgh: T. & T. Clark, 1877), p. 360.

that that life is to be governed. The main emphasis of the Epistle is devoted to the exposition of the aspect of salvation as practical, energetic, Christian life. This is the heart of the theology of James.

Part IV

THE THEOLOGY OF PAUL

Chapter 1

PREPARATORY QUESTIONS

I. What Is the Particular Importance of the Apostle Paul?

THE LIFE OF PAUL IS WELL KNOWN. Born in Tarsus of Roman citizenship, he was educated in the ways of Judaism in the family circle first and then in the school of Gamaliel in Jerusalem (Acts 22:3). Whether or not Paul ever attended the rhetorical schools of Tarsus is an open question.[1] After his conversion the apostle spent three years in Arabia (Gal. 1:17) where his theological system was shaped. He returned to Damascus but soon had to escape over the city wall in a basket (Acts 9:23-25). After visiting in Jerusalem he returned to his home town of Tarsus where, as far as the record states, he was unoccupied with any public ministry for five or six years. He responded to the call of Barnabas to help with the work at Antioch from which city he departed on the first missionary journey. The important events in the remainder of his ministry are listed below in a brief chronology of Paul's life.[2]

[1]Cf. W. M. Ramsay, *The Teaching of Paul in Terms of the Present Day* (London: Hodder & Stoughton, n.d.), pp. 40-48.
[2]Profitable comparison with the chronology of F. F. Bruce may be made by the student (*The Acts of the Apostles,* Chicago: Inter-Varsity Christian Fellowship, 1952, pp. 55-56).

Date	Event	Chapter Reference in Acts
30	Death and resurrection of Christ...............	1
30	Pentecost	2
35	Conversion of Paul	9
35-37	Paul in Damascus, Arabia, Damascus............	9
37-43	Paul in Tarsus	9
46-48	First Missionary Journey	13-14
49	Church council at Jerusalem	15
50-54	Second Missionary Journey	16-18
52-53	Writing of I and II Thessalonians from Corinth	
54-58	Third Missionary Journey	18-21
56	Writing of Galatians from Ephesus	
56	Writing of I Corinthians from Ephesus	
57	Writing of II Corinthians from Ephesus	
58	Writing of Romans from Corinth	
58	Journey to and arrest in Jerusalem	21-23
58-60	Paul in prison in Caesarea	24-26
60-63	Paul sent to Rome and imprisoned there for two years	27-28
62	Writing of Ephesians, Colossians, Philemon, and Philippians	
64-65	Writing of I Timothy and Titus from Macedonia	
66	Second imprisonment of Paul in Rome	
66	Writing of II Timothy	
66	Death of Paul	

The life of this man is of particular importance for at least three reasons. (1) His personal conversion is one of the strongest apologetics for the truth of the Christian message. The power of a risen Saviour to transform an imperfect and rebellious human life is probably nowhere more clearly seen than in the life of Paul. (2) His academic activity is of the utmost importance to the doctrinal foundations of Christianity. The years he spent in rabbinic training, the Arabian years of solitude, the revelations he received, and the letters he wrote were all used by the Lord in the shaping of the doctrine of the Christian Church for all time. (3) His missionary activity extended throughout practically the entire civilized world. Paul was always reaching out to unreached places (Rom. 15:24), and being particularly the missionary to the Gentiles he touched the untouchables for the Saviour (Eph. 2:14). He defined his convictions sharply, cherished them intensely, and carried them out consistently in action.

The secret of these things which make Paul distinctive is found on the Damascus road where he said, "What shall I do, Lord?" (Acts 22:10). The obedience of faith effected his conversion, and the obedience of yieldedness affected the remainder of his life. Paul's unreserved "what" (notice that he did not proposition the Lord with "which") made him willing to spend time in solitary study as well as to be busy writing in the midst of an already crowded schedule of missionary activity. The continuing character of Paul's dedication accounts for his ceaseless missionary activity. This activity included the time of testing when Paul had to return home and live as a Christian among those of his family and friends who had seen him leave Tarsus to become a rabbi. It meant the hardships and privations described by the apostle in II Corinthians 11:23-28. Later in his life there were doubtless temptations to settle down in one of the many churches he had founded instead of reaching out to unreached places (cf. Acts 16:6-13). It finally ended in a martyr's death. And yet the distinctively important ministry of Paul did not end with his death, for every believer since has benefited from the life and ministry of this man who said, *"What* shall I do, Lord?" and who lived to the fullest that complete dedication.[3]

---

[3]A note concerning the meaning of the name *Saulus Paulus* is in order. *Deissmann* (*Bible Studies* [Edinburgh: T. & T. Clark, 1901], pp. 313 ff.) has shown that the phrase in Acts 13:9, *Saulos ho kai Paulos*, can only be taken to mean "Saul who was also called Paul." "The *ho kai* admits of no other supposition than that he was called *Saulos Paulos* before he came to Cyprus; he had, like many natives of Asia Minor, many Jews and Egyptians of his age, a double name." The choice of the Graeco-Roman second name, Deissmann says, was made without particular purpose though sometimes a name was chosen which sounded similar to the first name. This might have been

II. What Was the Influence of Judaism on Paul?

If Paul was an educated Jew, what effect did this have on his life? To think about a question like this is not to intimate any minimizing of the supernatural changes which the Lord wrought in Paul's life. Nevertheless, Paul was a trained Jew by race and rearing even after his conversion, and certain things in that background were carried over into his Christian life and activity, though other things were changed or rejected.

A. *Paul Was a Hebrew Patriot*

Glimpses of Paul's patriotism to his people appear frequently in his writings (Acts 22:3; 26:4; Rom. 3:1; 9:1-3; II Cor. 11:22; Gal. 1:14; Phil. 3:4-6). Paul owed his ability to make tents to the patriotism of his father who carried out the injunction of the Talmud to teach his son a trade. Too, Paul's early instruction in the Law can be traced to the work of his father. At least these two things, his trade and his training in the Law, were carried over into Paul's Christian life.

B. *Paul Was a Pharisee*

As a Pharisee of the Pharisees (Phil. 3:5) Paul undoubtedly exhibited the characteristics of Pharisees that are found in the New Testament. He would have considered himself righteous (Matt. 5:20); he knew the Scriptures (Matt. 23:2); he obeyed the Pharisaic interpretation of the Law (Mark 2:24; Acts 26:5); he tithed (Luke 18:12); he fasted (Matt. 9:14); and he was diligent in prayers (Mark 12:40; Luke 18:11). In his unconverted days he was, as the name *Pharisee* connotes, a separatist. Certain of these traits, such as praying, undoubtedly merely carried over into Paul's Christian

the case with Saul who was also called Paul. Luke's record of this in Acts 13 simply and clearly shows that when Paul began to turn to the Gentiles he was presented to them under his Greek name which he had had as a second name all along. Certainly the two names in no way represent the old and new natures in the apostle.

life; but Paul's basic attitude toward Pharisaism was radically changed when he became a believer. One needs only to look at Paul at the council in Jerusalem or read his letter to the Galatians to see how basically his Pharisaic attitudes had changed. Pharisaism gave Paul habits of discipline for his life as a Christian, and Christianity gave him freedom from the legality of his life as a Pharisee.

C. *Paul Was a Student of the Old Testament*

To his training under Gamaliel Paul owed much of his knowledge of the Old Testament. This is of course displayed everywhere in his writings in the extensive use of Old Testament quotations. Paul also studied Jewish interpretations of the Old Testament, but at best these were insufficient until he came to recognize Jesus of Nazareth as the promised Messiah. As a Pharisee, Paul's hope for the Messiah burned brightly; as a student, he investigated it; as a Christian, he realized it.

D. *Paul Was a Missionary*

The school of Hillel to which Paul belonged as a pupil of Gamaliel welcomed proselytes (Matt. 23:15). Its goal was at least one proselyte per year per Jew, and Paul was beyond question active in this regard in the practice of his Jewish religion. His mind was schooled to think missions, and his activity was geared to that end even before he came to the Saviour.

Paul's ancestral faith was unquestionably part of God's preparation for the man who became the great leader of Christianity, but it was only preparation. By no means, however, are we to understand that Paul the Christian was merely a revamped Jewish Paul. Although there were carry-overs from one to the other, there were also radical changes. Actually it can be said that all Paul was as a Hebrew was transformed by Christ. His intense Hebrew patriotism gave place to an interest and concern for all men; indeed, this patriot was the apostle to the Gentiles. His Pharisaic separatism was replaced by a separation unto Christ. All of Paul's studies in the Old Testament were suddenly enlightened by the revelation which he discovered in Christ. Unguessed meanings leaped out of the pages of the Old Testament (cf. II Cor. 3:1-14). The missionary of the school of Hillel became the zealous propagator of the Gospel of God's grace in Christ. To be sure, there was a natural preparation in Paul's Hebrew background which can be seen in his later life, but this in no way implies that his theology was a natural outgrowth of Judaism. The total man—his life, his thinking, his theology— was supernaturally transformed that day when he recognized Jesus the Saviour on the Damascus road.

III. WHAT WAS THE INFLUENCE OF HELLENISM ON PAUL?

A. *The City of Tarsus*

Geography affects all men. As a country boy is different from a city boy, so, for instance, John the Baptist was different from Paul. Tarsus, the capital of Cilicia, was a key city in the east-west trade routes of the day. It was situated on the Cydnus River which flowed into a lake south of Tarsus. This protected harbor made Tarsus a convenient transshipping point for overland trade to and from Asia Minor. The mountains to the north of the city, broken only by the Cilician Gates, gave Tarsus the protection of a natural fortress. The city, boasting a population of nearly half a million, was a center of learning. Even though it is debatable whether Paul ever attended the university of Tarsus it is clear that cosmopolitan Tarsus left its mark on the boy. The fact that he learned a trade was due to Judaism, but the particular trade he learned is traceable to the city in which he was reared, for Tarsus was a tent-making center, since the raw material grew nearby. Paul's Roman citizenship was a result of the environment in which he was born, and as a Roman citizen Paul was a citizen of the world. Too, he was every whit a gentleman, as witnessed by his bearing before governors and kings. Undoubtedly Paul's cosmopolitan interests were cultivated early in Tarsus. His knowledge of the Greek language came from the same source. In the right sense he was a man of the world, and much of this he owed to the influence of the city of Tarsus.

B. *The Mystery Religions*

In a very real sense the mystery religions were rivals to Christianity, for, appealing to the masses, they offered the average person salvation from fate. It is inconceivable that Paul was not acquainted with these movements which were going on all around him. It is an easily proved fact that "in all the main centres of his missionary operations the Apostle Paul must have been brought into constant touch with the influences of the Mystery-Religions."[4]

It is apparent that some of the same terms which were used in the mystery religions are found in the basic doctrines of Pauline theology. The word *mystery* itself, which is almost exclusively a Pauline word in the New Testament, is a good example. *Gnōsis,* knowledge, *sophia,* wisdom, *teleios,* mature, and *pneuma,* spirit, are other examples; but, as Kennedy shows, these conceptions *for Paul* had their roots not in the mystery religions but in the Old Testament. Paul's readers, however, were able

> to catch the meaning of a more or less technical terminology, due not merely to a course of instruction in the Old Testament, but to their acquaintance with a religious vocabulary already current among the Mystery-associations.[5]

Though Paul may show acquaintance with mystery terminology and even though Paul may have used some of those terms

[4]H. A. A. Kennedy, *St. Paul and the Mystery-Religions* (New York: Hodder and Stoughton, n.d.), p. 115.
[5]*Ibid.,* p. 198.

in a deliberate attempt to interest Greek readers in the Gospel of God's salvation, this by no means proves that Paul's theology was in any way derived from or dependent upon the theology of those cults.

This essential difference between the teachings of the mystery religions and those of Paul is very evident in some of the central conceptions of the mystery religions. For instance, the salvation which these groups offered was a salvation from the tyranny of an omnipotent Fate, and although Paul's conception of salvation may be said to be many-sided, it is primarily a salvation from sin. Or again, though some have attempted to show a dependence of the ordinances of Christianity on those of these cults, Kennedy has proved that it is "vain to endeavour to find points of contact between Paul and the Mystery-cults on the side of ritual."[6] The conclusion is evident—Paul's acquaintance with the mystery religions does not admit of recognizing any dependence upon them.

C. *Stoicism*

There is no doubt that certain resemblances can be found between some of the teachings of Stoicism and Paulinism. Comparisons can be made with the Stoic doctrines of (1) the world soul, (2) natural law, (3) conscience, and (4) world citizenship. Traces of similarities in Paul's writings might be seen in such passages as (1) Acts 17:28; Romans 11:36; I Corinthians 8:6; Colossians 1:16; (2) Romans 2:14; (3) Romans 2:15; I Corinthians 10:25; II Corinthians 1:12; 4:2; 5:11; (4) Acts 17:26. However, real as some might make these similarities, the study and comparison of Stoicism and Paulinism makes it apparent that there was a vast difference between these and all doctrines of the two systems. (1) The Stoic concept of a governing Force has no relation to the Christian doctrine of a God who can be known and fellowshiped with through Jesus Christ. (2) The Stoic concept of natural law is that of an internal thing something like

⁶*Ibid.*, p. 282.

an inner light. Paul did speak of natural law but a natural law which came from God and is external to man. No man, according to Paulinism, can act acceptably before God, because of his fallen nature. (3) If there is any relationship between Stoicism and Paulinism it could only possibly be in the teaching on conscience. But again there are vast differences in the concepts, because, for the Stoic, conscience merely led a person to a belief in fatalism, while Paul clearly taught that conscience obeyed would lead to penitence. The Stoic did not believe that he needed outside help, since human virtue was all-sufficient. The Christian concept of the doctrine of conscience would bring one to the realization of his need before a personal God. (4) The brotherhood of Christianity is based not on world citizenship but on the death of Christ.

As far as Stoicism is concerned Paul's theology in no way shows dependence on its teachings. Theologically and philosophically the two systems are diametrically opposed. Paul did not build on the Stoic system; rather he tried to win men out of it (Acts 17:18).

> Tens of thousands of souls were seeking release and self-conquest and victory over the world, but Paul could see with piercing clearness that the lines which the Stoic quest for these things was following could never by any possibility lead to the peace and freedom which he himself had actually found in Christ. It was on a wrong track altogether: and was Paul, realizing this, likely to borrow much? What could the religion of frustration give to the religion of fulfilment? Across the pages of Seneca, Epictetus, and Marcus Aurelius the shadow lies. Beneath their bravest words the feeling of futility lurks. What is God, after all, but just Fate—*heimarmene?* And what can man do, caught in the toils of a harsh determinism, but bow his head and submit? Nor can he look forward with any life of the heart to what may come hereafter, for immortality too has slipped away; and Epic-

tetus could only bid a father kissing his child remember that it was a mortal thing he loved, and whisper while he kissed "To-morrow thou wilt die." This was the direction in which Stoicism had its face; and the road led —as Paul saw—straight out towards unyielding despair.[7]

IV. WHAT WAS INVOLVED IN PAUL'S CONVERSION?

The conversion of the apostle Paul has been the subject of almost endless discussion. In his own writings Paul makes reference to it only a few times. He epitomized it as seeing the Lord (I Cor. 9:1); he related it to the supernatural elective purposes of God (Gal. 1:15); he spoke of the suddenness of it (I Cor. 15:8; Phil. 3:12); he testified to the fact that it was an act of new creation by God and not merely a change of habits of life (II Cor. 4:6); and he acknowledged the merciful character of it (I Tim. 1:13). In addition, Luke records Paul's conversion and testimony of it in three places in the Acts. This record of Luke furnishes the principal facts on which to base conclusions concerning the nature of Paul's conversion.

A. *Conviction*

Conviction preceded the conversion of Paul. The Lord Himself reminded Paul that it had been difficult for him to kick against the goads. Many suggestions have been offered as to what specific things had been goading Paul and bringing conviction to his heart. (1) Probably the principal goad was the martyrdom of Stephen. Again and again Paul's mind would have recalled Stephen's last words testifying to the fact that Christ was risen. Stephen saw the Son of Man and spoke to Him with his dying breath. He also evinced the same spirit as Jesus when he said, "Lay not this sin to their charge." (2) The lives and testimonies of the Christians was another thing Paul had to reckon with.

[7]James S. Stewart, *A Man in Christ* (London: Hodder and Stoughton, 1935), pp. 63-64.

Paul certainly had no intention of being infected with the new heresy; but that, in Tertullian's words, he was "struck with an inward misgiving," unconfessed probably even to himself, in witnessing the lives which its protagonists led, seems beyond doubt.[8]

He did not persecute them because he was impressed; but he couldn't help being impressed when he persecuted them. (3) A third goad was Paul's knowledge of the historical Jesus of Nazareth. Whether or not Paul ever saw Jesus in person in the days of his earthly life is unimportant to this point; he did know of the claims of Jesus, for he had talked to those who had seen and heard Him (cf. Acts 20:35; Gal. 1:18). Informed by associates in Pharisaism, Paul's keen mind had analyzed this new faith which posed a serious threat to Judaism. But all his intellectual conviction of the wrongness of Jesus' claims coupled with intense persecution of those who believed them could not remove the goad which the knowledge of the historic Jesus was in Paul's life.

B. Conversion

The conversion of Paul has had many explanations. Enemies of Paulinism in the early Church propagated the idea that Paul purposely acted out a fraud by pretending to be a Christian in order to take revenge on the Jews because he had been jilted in love.[9] The modern counterpart of this ancient view proposes that Paul feigned revelations in order to give vent to irregularities of action and lawlessness. It is difficult to imagine how Paul convinced his missionary companions to play along with him, and this explanation cannot be reconciled with Paul's positive Gospel message.

Rationalistic attempts have also been made to explain Paul's conversion by attributing it to a combination of physical weakness, a violent storm, and delirium caused by the

[8]*Ibid.,* p. 121.
[9]Philip Schaff, "The Conversion of Paul, False Explanations," *History of the Christian Church* (Grand Rapids: Eerdmans, 1950), I, 307.

burning Syrian heat.[10] A fanciful explanation at best, it in no way coincides with the historical record of the Acts and Paul's Epistles.

Perhaps the most popular non-conservative view of Paul's conversion is that which may be called the subjective vision hypothesis. This supposes that Paul's conversion was a natural psychological process which started with a gradually developing intellectual conviction that the Christian way might be the right way and which climaxed on the Damascus road in a subjective visionary experience in the soul and mind of Paul. In one form or another the view has had many able exponents. Strauss, Baur,[11] the Tübingen school, Schmiedel,[12] B. W. Bacon, and McGiffert have all advocated it. The explanation is contrary to the facts of Scripture and must assume the unreliability of those records. It, like Renan's view, pictures Paul as a physically weak person, a question which will be discussed more fully below. Too, it ignores the fact that all of Paul's struggles in Judaism were driving him to greater zeal in his own religion and not developing within him a maturing appreciation of Christianity. Although it is true that there were things goading Paul before his conversion, he may have been entirely unaware of them until the risen Lord revealed them on the Damascus road. This subjective vision theory supposes that Paul was completely aware of these and other things and was consciously wrestling with them before his conversion. Gradual maturing, not sudden conversion, is the explanation offered.

Both the rationalistic and subjective explanations assume to some extent the fact that Paul was a constitutionally weak person. The illness frequently suggested is epileptic insanity. If such be the explanation for Paul's revelations including that which accompanied his conversion, then, as Ramsay

[10]Ernest Renan, *The Apostles* (New York: Carleton, 1869), pp. 171-74.
[11]F. C. Baur, *Paul, His Life and Works* (London: Williams & Norgate, 1876), I, 61-89.
[12]P. W. Schmiedel, "Resurrection and Ascension Narratives," *Encyclopedia Biblica* (New York: Macmillan, 1914), pp. 4081-86.

correctly observed, "it affects the very foundations on which rests our right to accept as in any degree valuable Paul's belief in the truth and power of his own personal experiences."[13] Ramsay has ably shown that epilepsy could not have been Paul's thorn in the flesh; and he concludes that such a theory could only have been advanced "by persons who knew nothing about neurology."[14] In Paul's day when there was no known way of controlling epileptic fits one would have to assume that the disease would have taken its normal course which inevitably results in deterioration and damage to brain and body. But there is no evidence of such in his Epistles.[15]

No matter what explanations one might wish to accept, the Biblical theologian must let Paul speak for himself. To him the experience was one of actually seeing the Lord, who identified Himself as Jesus of Nazareth and who spoke in clear words revealing His plan for the apostle. It was no experience of self-delusion, for throughout his entire life Paul based his ministry on it and persuaded others of the reality of it. Paul's conversion was not the result of evolution but of revolution. It was not even in the manner in which people are ordinarily converted; i.e., by man's preaching of the Gospel. Nor was it merely a supernatural interposition of God intended to produce belief in the fact of resurrection.[16] It was a personal encounter with the risen Christ; and only this can suffice to explain fully the transformation of Saul of Tarsus.

[13]*The Teaching of Paul in Terms of the Present Day* (London: Hodder and Stoughton, 1894), p. 306.
[14]*Ibid.*, p. 319.
[15]What Paul's physical affliction was is not easy to determine. Migraine headaches, ophthalmia, and malaria are suggested. Galatians 4:15 and 6:11 would seem to indicate ophthalmia; however, the mention of the eyes in 4:15 may merely be symbolic of a precious organ, and the large letters of 6:11 are more likely to indicate the importance of the writing rather than the illness of the writer. Malaria apparently accounts for the symptoms which are exhibited in the Epistles. Though there is no deteriorative damage as in epilepsy, it causes severe periodic attacks and also is a chronic affliction.
[16]Cf. J. G. Machen, *The Origin of Paul's Religion* (New York: Macmillan, 1921), pp. 67-68.

V. WHAT ARE THE SOURCES OF PAULINE THEOLOGY?

The sources of Pauline theology are Acts, the missionary Epistles (I and II Thess.), the doctrinal Epistles (Rom., I and II Cor., Gal.), the Prison Epistles, and the Pastoral Epistles. It is only concerning the inclusion of the Pastoral Epistles that there is important debate today. Although the Epistles may be classified as above, this does not imply that there was development in the sense of change in Paul's theology. The earliest Epistles may be simple but they are not rudimentary. We may notice change of emphases in his Epistles, but not change of doctrine. Before Paul wrote I Thessalonians he had known the Lord for about fifteen years. Three of those fifteen were years of revelation and meditation in Arabia; therefore, his theology was fully developed from the time of the first stroke of his pen.

Whether the Pastorals should be included in the sources of Pauline theology has been the subject of recent debate. Those who do not hold to the full Pauline authorship of these books either hold that the letters are pseudonymous and to be dated in the first half of the second century or that they are amplifications by a Paulinist of genuine Pauline fragments of the same era. The arguments of P. N. Harrison against the Pauline authorship have carried the most weight in recent years.[17] His principal arguments are linguistic and historical.[18]

The linguistic argument is dazzling. The statistics and charts are almost overwhelming, but even Harrison is forced to admit that alone it is inconclusive, for Paul, he recognizes,

---

[17]*The Problem of the Pastoral Epistles* (London: Oxford, 1921), pp. 1-184.

[18]It is also recognized that Harrison presents other arguments, but it is not within the scope of this work to deal with each one in detail. His "ecclesiastical atmosphere argument" is that the Church organization of the Pastorals is foreign to and later than that which appears in the "genuine" Epistles. But such passages as Acts 14:23; Phil. 1:1; and I Thess. 5:12 show as much organizational development as we see in the Pastorals among elders and deacons. The order of widows of I Timothy 5 could easily have developed to the extent pictured by the time of the close of Paul's life. After all, ministrations to widows were pretty well organized shortly after Pentecost (Acts 6:1)!

might have written in different style and with unusual vocabulary in treating the subjects of the Pastorals.[19] One wonders why a forger or a devout Paulinist would not make every
attempt to imitate Paul rather than being so dissimilar. Since
the Pastorals cover only 17 of 128 pages of Paul's writings
(in Westcott and Hort's Greek Testament), one is suspicious
that Harrison's linguistic argument is in the nature of comparing the merchandise of a specialty shop with that of a
large department store and assuring the public on the basis
of the comparison, which shows the stock to be different, that
the two stores could not possibly be owned by the same man
or corporation.

The historical argument is that since the Pastorals cannot
be fitted into the life of Paul as recorded in Acts they could
not have been written by Paul. This assumes that Acts brings
us to the end of Paul's life and that he did not experience
two imprisonments in Rome. An array of debatable evidence
from the Fathers is cited by Harrison as proof of this. That
Paul died in Rome is a fact (II Tim. 4:6); the question is,
Does Acts 28 record that time? If so, then it would be difficult to fit the Pastorals into the chronology of Acts. If not,
then they could easily have been written by Paul. The citations from the Fathers at best give only uncertain and debatable support to the theory of one imprisonment, but other
light which Ramsay has thrown on the matter, in this author's mind, completely answers Harrison's argument.[20]

Ramsay pictures the situation at the close of Acts as follows: Paul, of course, had to be detained in Rome until
his prosecutors should appear, for the trial could not begin
until the accusers appeared to state the complaint against
him. Evidently the Jewish accusers did not appear, for they
probably realized that their case was too weak to gain a con-

---

[19]Cf. pp. 46-47.
[20]*The Teaching of Paul in Terms of the Present Day*, pp. 346-71. Philip
Carrington, *The Early Christian Church* (Cambridge: University Press,
1957), I, 170, makes similar observations.

viction. Had not Agrippa said so (Acts 26:31-32)? Recognizing this, they then seemed to employ delaying tactics. If they could not convict Paul, they would keep him out of circulation (but not silent) for as long as the law allowed. And the law considered any man innocent against whom a charge had not been brought after eighteen months. This legal term elapsed, Paul was processed for release, and the two years of Acts 28:30 were fulfilled. It was acquittal by default. Such a picture, which Ramsay has supported conclusively, answers completely Harrison's historical argument and supports the Pauline authorship of the Pastorals. Thus they must be considered as a valid source of Pauline theology.

Chapter 2

THE DOCTRINE OF GOD

BASIC TO PAULINE THEOLOGY is the concept of God. Though in some respects this doctrine is incidentally developed, it nonetheless permeates Paul's thought. That God exists, that He has revealed Himself, and that He is the sovereign ruler of the universe is the foundation on which Paul builds. The existence of God is everywhere assumed—a carry-over from Judaism—and Paul always starts from this principle.

I. THE NATURE OF GOD

Of the attributes of God Paul mentions a number. He is the only wise God (I Tim. 1:17), whose omniscience will be displayed in the day of judgment (Rom. 2:16; I Cor. 4:5). His quality of love was uniquely proved in the sending of Christ (Rom. 5:8; Eph. 2:4). He is the One who is able to do above all things as well as above those things which we ask or think (Eph. 3:20), and this sovereign power of God was primary in Paul's thought (Rom. 9). In addition, God is omnipresent (Rom. 10:6-7; I Cor. 3:16; 6:19), true (Rom. 3:4), just (Rom. 3:26), and merciful (Eph. 2:4).

However, it is the living nature of God which assumed particular importance in Pauline thought. That idea is found in his preaching to the heathen, for it is the living God who saves men (Acts 14:15; 17:24-29; I Tim. 4:10).

His converts were distinguished as those who had turned to the living God (I Thess. 1:9). It is the living God who is the cause of sanctification (II Cor. 3:3), the comfort of the believer in times of distress (I Tim. 4:10), and the object of Christian service (I Thess. 1:9).

II. THE REVELATION OF GOD

A. *The Means of Revelation*

Paul speaks of a number of ways in which the living God has revealed Himself.

1. *God has revealed Himself through Jesus Christ* (I Tim. 3:16; *cf.* Rom. 5:8; II Cor. 4:4; Eph. 1:19-20; II Tim. 1:10).

2. *God reveals Himself to all men through nature* (Rom. 1:20).

3. *The Scriptures reveal the salvation of God* (Rom. 3:21; 16:26; I Cor. 15:3-4; II Tim. 3:15-16).

4. *The providential guiding of history should lead one to seek God* (Acts 17:26-27).

5. *The constitutional nature of man reveals the living character of his Creator* (Acts 17:28-29).

6. *Children of God reveal their Father as they live among men* (Rom. 10:14; II Cor. 3:2).

7. *The Mosaic Law was a means of revelation to the Jewish people* (Rom. 2:12; 9:4).

B. *The Content of Revelation*

In Christ all the attributes of God can be seen by man. From nature man can learn of God's eternal power and Godhood. All can reason to things invisible from things visible, and although the revelation of God in nature is not sufficient for salvation, it is sufficient and just grounds for condemnation if rejected. Through God's dealings with man in the course of history His goodness and longsuffering are revealed (Rom. 2:4). The law of Moses brought specific and detailed revelation of the mind of God for the Jewish people, and with that privilege went special responsibility (Rom. 2:17-29).

C. *The Intent of Revelation*

Not only for the Jew but for all men revelation brings responsibility. A man's reaction to that which God has revealed, whatever be the means or content, will determine His acceptance or rejection by God (Rom. 1:21-32; 2:7-8). To the Christian the availability of knowing the truth of God as it is revealed by the Holy Spirit brings responsibility to mature and not to live carnally (I Cor. 2:10—3:2). Being confronted with God automatically brings responsibility, and all men have been confronted to some extent.

III. THE SOVEREIGNTY OF GOD[1]

The Old Testament, which says much concerning this doctrine, was the legacy which Paul received as a Jew. Further, in acquiring a knowledge of the teachings of Christ Paul would also have come in contact with this teaching (cf. John 6:37, 44; 10:27-29; 17:11). However, it fell to him to develop it fully and systematically.

A. *The Terminology*

In his Epistles Paul uses at least eight different words to convey the concept of sovereignty. (1) *Proorizō*, which is never found in the Septuagint or classical Greek and only in Acts 4:28 outside of Paul's writings, means a marking off beforehand (Rom. 8:29-30; I Cor. 2:7; Eph. 1:5, 11). Paul always speaks of what this means in terms of the ultimate destiny of those so marked off. (2) *Proginōskō*, to foreknow (Acts 2:23; 26:5; Rom. 8:29; 11:2; I Pet. 1:2, 20; II Pet. 3:17), emphasizes not mere foresight but an active relationship between the one who foreknows and those who are foreknown. (3) *Eklegō*, to choose, as used by Paul emphasizes

[1]Cf. Francis Davidson, *Pauline Predestination* (London: Tyndale Press, 1945), pp. 1-36.

the idea of free choice. Indeed, when Paul uses the verb in describing God's action it is used in the middle voice, indicating that God's choosing was done freely and for Himself (I Cor. 1:27-28; Eph. 1:4). Other words in the Pauline vocabulary are (4) *klētos,* called (Rom. 1:1, 7; 8:28; I Cor. 1:1, 2, 24); (5) *protithēmi,* to purpose (Rom. 1:13; 3:25; Eph. 1:9); (6) *boulē,* will (Acts 13:36; 20:27; Eph. 1:11); (7) *thelēma,* will (Eph. 1:11); and (8) *eudokia,* good pleasure (Eph. 1:5, 9; Phil. 2:13; II Thess. 1:11). Thus, the concepts involved in this doctrine are obviously not built on a single word or a few scattered passages.

B. *The Principal Passages*

There are three chief passages where Paul expounds his fundamental teaching concerning predestination. (1) Romans 8:28-30 is a passage of encouragement. All things work together for good because God has purposed that His own should be conformed to the image of His Son. This assured result is traceable to God's entering into a relationship with the elect in foreknowledge, effecting its outworking through calling and justifying, and guaranteeing its consummation in the predestined conformity to Christ. This ultimate glorification rests on God's foreknowledge, which must be understood in the positive and active sense of entering into a relationship with the elect. To hang the sense of the passage on the mere contemplative foresight of God (which is the usual connotation given to foreknowledge) would be, in Warfield's words, "little short of absurd."[2]

(2) The more famous Romans passage on predestination is found in chapters 9 through 11. This is not a parenthetical section, for it grows directly out of Paul's fundamental doctrine of justification by faith. If all are sinners, and if there is not a difference between Jew and Gentile, then what is to become of the special privileges of Israel? Paul's answer

[2]B. B. Warfield, "Predestination," *A Dictionary of the Bible,* James Hastings, editor (Edinburgh: T. & T. Clark, 1902), IV, 58.

begins by demonstrating that the source of all of Israel's blessings is the sovereignty of God. These blessings were undeserved in the first place, and subsequently they were forfeited by unbelief; nevertheless, in God's merciful sovereignty He will fulfill all that He promised (11:26-36). God's choices, Paul declares, are not necessarily based on natural generation (9:6-9) or human merit (9:10-13), but upon the exercise of sovereign mercy (9:14-24). If God could not have retreated into His own sovereignty and chosen a people He would have been obliged to condemn every member of the human race because of sin. It is sovereign grace that blesses anybody.

(3) If possible an even higher note is struck in Ephesians 1:1-11. The time of choosing is expressly stated to have been before the foundation of the world (1:4). The basis of the choice is God's own good pleasure (1:5, 11). Paul uses the three terms *purpose (boulē)*, *good pleasure (eudokia)*, and *will (thelēma)* in stating the origin of predestination. The purpose of predestination is the glorification of God (1:12), and herein lies the only possible solution to questions which arise from the doctrine. If God in decreeing acted in perfect harmony with all of His attributes, then there is nothing to fear in the outworking of that decree, and there is every assurance that in the end it will glorify Him more than any other plan could.

C. *The Doctrine*

The roots of Paul's doctrine of sovereignty are to be found in his theism. It is because Paul was a firm believer in a living God who is the author of all that is that he was a predestinarian. The effects of his doctrine are best seen in his own life, for it was the deep consciousness of God's choosing and guiding him that motivated his missionary activity (Gal. 1:15-16). The viewpoint of Paul's doctrine is always one of amazement that God deals with any man in grace. His doctrine is not founded on the question, Why are some lost? While all the questions one might like to have answered are not necessarily dealt with, the main outlines of Paul's concept are apparent.

1. *The ultimate source of predestination is the absolute sovereignty of God.* It is God who is sovereign in all the affairs of men, and predestination finds its source in that immutable characteristic of God. However, sovereignty is not to be understood as naked, unrestrained volition, but the action of the most self-obligated Being in the universe, who when He acts has to act righteously, lovingly, justly, and in complete accord with His full personality.

> No man ever had an intenser or more vital sense of God, —the eternal (Rom. 16:26) and incorruptible (1:23) One, the only wise One (16:27), who does all things according to His good pleasure (I Cor. 15:38; 12:18; Col. 1:19, 15), and whose ways are past tracing out (Rom. 11:33); before whom men should therefore bow in the humility of absolute dependence, recognizing in Him the one moulding power as well in history as in the life of the individual (Rom. 9). Of Him and through Him and unto Him, he fervently exclaims, are all things (Rom. 11:36; cf. I Cor. 8:6); He is over all and through all and in all (Eph. 4:6; cf. Col. 1:16); He worketh all things according to the counsel of His will (Eph. 1:11): all that is, in a word, owes its existence and persistence and its action and issue to Him.[3]

The starting point of the doctrine, then, is God who is sovereign, and there was no question in Paul's mind that election rests solely upon Him.

2. *The purpose of predestination is salvation, and the issue of it is service.* It is to be expected that the soteriological ramifications of this doctrine would claim the attention of the great missionary. The whole history of salvation is recorded in the great passage on election in Ephesians 1:1-12.

[3]*Ibid.*

Romans 8:28-30 has been called the most daring passage in the Bible, for those who were foreknown are already glorified, so certain is the outcome of God's elective program. But Paul, the servant of the Lord, also emphasized that this salvation issues in service (Eph. 2:10). He used his own life to illustrate the point (Gal. 1:15-16), and his converts emulated him (I Thess. 1:4, 8-10). The doctrine is thus lifted completely out of the realm of the speculative and contemplative and placed at the heart of the missionary enterprise of the Church.

3. *Predestination does not override human responsibility.* Paul's Epistles are replete with lengthy sections devoted to moral exhortation. The single preposition in II Thessalonians 2:13, "through sanctification of the Spirit and belief of the truth," shows how closely associated in his mind were God's and man's part in salvation. Grace received always brings added responsibility. While it is true that Paul never allows the so-called rights of man to challenge the sovereign, though mysterious, ways of God, he firmly holds to the responsibility of man (cf. I Cor. 9:27; II Cor. 5:10; 6:1).

4. *In relation to the destiny of the wicked, the doctrine of predestination includes the idea of reprobation.* The very idea of election incorporates the idea of the greater number out of which some have been chosen to eternal life. Although Paul is definite in saying that election is pre-temporal and predetermined before birth, he never suggests that there is a similar decree to elect unto damnation. Paul seems content to let this remain a mystery. When he does employ terms which indicate reprobation, Paul indicates that reprobation is in the nature of God's abandoning man to his evil deeds and just deserts. The most direct statements of reprobation are found in Romans 9:18, 21. One might say that in the Pauline writings there is a doctrine of reprobation but not a decree of damnation. There is preterition, non-election, God's passing some by, but never is there inference anywhere

that God delights in the destiny of the wicked, that they are driven against their wills, that election nullifies a "whosoever" gospel, or that any individual can consider himself non-elect and thereby excuse himself in his rejection of Christ. However, the doctrine of reprobation is definitely a part of Pauline theology.

5. *Predestination glorifies God.* "To the praise of his glory" rings throughout the passage in Ephesians 1:1-12. The ultimate purpose of all of God's doings is the glorification of Himself. In such a belief is the only possible resolution of the problems of the doctrine, and with such a belief one can only bow in worship and awe before the one who has devised that infinitely wise plan. Hear Paul as he concludes his discussion of this doctrine in Romans 11:33-36:

> O the depth of the riches both of the wisdom and knowledge of God! how unsearchable are his judgments, and his ways past finding out! For who hath known the mind of the Lord? or who hath been his counsellor? Or who hath first given to him, and it shall be recompensed unto him again? For of him, and through him, and to him, are all things: to whom be glory for ever. Amen.

IV. The Son

Paul's Christology originated on the Damascus road. His exposition of this doctrine is generally unsystematic and is found "in solution" with other arguments and teachings. Nevertheless, the treatment is thorough so that there is no doubt as to Paul's thought on these matters.

A. *The Humanity of Christ*

1. The birth of Christ. Paul mentions both the background and actual birth of the Lord. He was a descendant of Abraham and David (Rom. 9:3-5; Gal. 3:16; II Tim. 2:8). Although there is reasonable doubt that Galatians 4:4 refers specifically to the virgin birth, it says nothing incon-

sistent with the doctrine. That He was of the seed of David (Rom. 1:3) establishes His right to the Davidic throne.

2. *The life of Christ.* Even though Paul may never have seen Jesus in the days of His humiliation, he speaks of a number of events in His life. Paul appeals to the gentleness, meekness, and generally lowly character of Jesus' life (II Cor. 10:1; Phil. 2:1-8). The Lord's sinlessness is affirmed (II Cor. 5:21). But it is the record of events relating to the death of Christ which appears more frequently in Paul's writings (Rom. 6:1-10; I Cor. 2:8; 5:7; 11:23-25; 15:1-3; Gal. 2:20; 3:13). Paul's use of these facts is not in the manner of a mere rehearsal of them, but is usually in connection with doctrinal teaching.

3. *The human nature of Christ.* Paul's statements in this connection are very cautious in order to keep the sinlessness of Christ before the minds of his readers. Thus Paul speaks of the Christ being made in the likeness of sinful men (Rom. 8:3; Phil. 2:7). The humanity was real (I Tim. 3:16) but without sin. Unlike John, Paul does not use the humanity of the Lord as a pattern for Christian conduct. In Johannine thought it is the earthly life of Christ which motivates holy living (I John 2:6); in Paul the emphasis is on the risen Lord to whom believers are joined (Rom. 6:1-10).

4. *The second or last Adam.* This Pauline conception of Christ as the second or last Adam (Rom. 5:15, 19; I Cor. 15:21, 45, 47, 49) has an unemphasized suggestion of the earthly life of Christ in it. However, as the last Adam, Christ not only undoes what Adam did (Rom. 5) but founds an entirely new humanity based on resurrection (I Cor. 15).

B. *The Deity of Christ*

1. *The pre-existence of Christ.* The preincarnate existence of the Lord is mentioned by Paul often (Phil. 2:5-8; cf. Rom. 8:3; I Cor. 15:47; II Cor. 8:9; Gal. 4:4). Preincarnate activity is also ascribed to Him (Col. 1:16).

2. *The deity of Christ.* Paul goes a step beyond pre-existence in asserting the full and undiminished deity of Christ. He was not only made the Son of God but declared so by raising people (*nekrōn*) from the dead (Rom. 1:3-4). He was always God for the divine nature dwells in Christ (Col. 2:9). However, the strongest single passage supporting the deity of Christ is Philippians 2:6: "Who being in the form of God thought it not robbery to be equal with God." Though it is sometimes claimed that this does not refer to the divine nature, parallelism, exegesis, and logic defeat such a claim. Parallelism would suggest that if the form of the servant were real then the form of God must be equally genuine. Exegesis shows that *morphē*, form, "implies not external accidents but the essential attributes."[4] Reason teaches that the verse is asserting the deity of Christ, for "surely it is logically accurate to say that Christ did not grasp to Himself, and covet to retain, a state that was then His own."[5] The verse is a strong statement of the deity of Christ.[6]

C. *The Lordship of Christ*

The designation *Jesus* is rarely used by Paul (cf. Rom. 8: 11; 10:9; I Cor. 12:3; II Cor. 4:5, 11, 14; 11:4; Gal. 6:17). Altogether it is found in only eight undisputed references. The title *Lord* occurs at least 144 times plus 95 more times in connection with the proper name *Jesus Christ*. Lordship obviously loomed large in Paul's thought.

1. *The ground of Lordship.* Christ is Lord not by acquisition but by inherent right (Col. 2:9). Even in the days of His flesh He was Lord (I Cor. 2:8). However, Lordship will be exercised primarily after the resurrection (Phil. 2:9;

[4] J. B. Lightfoot, *Saint Paul's Epistle to the Philippians* (London: Macmillan, 1885), p. 110.

[5] C. J. Ellicott, *A Critical and Grammatical Commentary on St. Paul's Epistles to the Philippians, Colossians, and to Philemon* (London: Longmans, Green, and Co., 1888), pp. 44-45.

[6] Cf. S. N. Rostron, *The Christology of St. Paul* (London: Robert Scott, 1912), pp. 176-86.

Rom. 14:9), but it was a quality eternally inherent in His nature.

2. *The meaning of Lordship.* Sometimes Paul uses the term as an equivalent for Master (Eph. 6:9; Col. 4:1). In other instances the designation *Lord* is especially related to Christ's work as mediator between God and man (I Cor. 11:3; 15:27-28; cf. I Tim. 2:5). In this use there is an idea of subordination to the Father. But "Lord" is also a trinitarian designation (I Cor. 8:6; cf. I Cor. 12:4-6; II Cor. 13:14). In these verses both equality and distinction of the persons of the Godhead are clearly seen.

In summary, it may be said that Pauline Christology, received on the Damascus road, (1) did not slight the humanity of Jesus, (2) included strong emphasis on the full deity, and (3) stressed the ·inherent majesty of the Lord Jesus Christ.

V. The Spirit

Like the teaching concerning Christ the doctrine of the Holy Spirit is not systematically presented by Paul. However, he says a great deal about the Spirit which shows that His person and work occupied a large place in Paul's thought. The revelation of almost all of the specific ministries of the Spirit in the New Testament is Pauline.

Concerning the person of the Spirit, Paul affirms in incidental references His personality and deity. The Spirit exhibits the attributes of personality with intellect (I Cor. 2:10-11), sensibility (Eph. 4:30), and will (I Cor. 12:11; I Tim. 4:1). His many and varied ministries, yet to be discussed, also show personality. Deity is proved by assigning to the Spirit attributes and actions which could only be true of God (I Cor. 2:10-11; Rom. 8:2; II Thess. 2:13; Rom. 8:26-27, cf. v. 34). Further, the Spirit is distinguished from God and from Christ (I Cor. 12:4-6; II Cor. 13:14; Eph. 4:4-6). It is the Spirit who specifically works in believers as

He wills (I Cor. 12:11). His distinct ministries to the Christian can only be properly construed if based on the view that the Spirit is a person distinct from God and from Christ.

Paul's principal contribution to Pneumatology is in the area of the work of the Spirit. Although he mentions the Spirit's work in relation to salvation (Gal. 3:2; II Thess. 2: 13), it is His ministry to the Christian that is Paul's special contribution. He baptizes into the Body of Christ (I Cor. 12:13) and gives gifts to the members of that Body (I Cor. 12:4 ff.). The one aim of these gifts is to minister to the unity of the Body, for unity is wrought through diversity. His teaching about these spiritual gifts is intensely practical, for each is to use his gifts for the benefit of all. Each person has his own place and work. Each has his special endowment to be used for the general good. That is why, for instance, the gift of tongues must be so carefully regulated and why the gift of prophecy is to be preferred. Utility is the test.

Another Pauline emphasis in Pneumatology is within the sphere of ethics. The Spirit is Himself holy, and His work is holiness or sanctification (I Cor. 6:11; Gal. 5:25). The Body itself is the temple of the Spirit (I Cor. 6:19). The inner conflict of life is between the flesh and the Spirit (Gal. 5:16-26), and only by reliance on the power of that indwelling Spirit can victory be gained (Rom. 8:13). In the everyday exercise of the spiritual life the Holy Spirit must be given pre-eminence, for He is the one who teaches the Christian the truth of God (I Cor. 2:13), who enables in prayer (Rom. 8:26), and who leads and guides (Rom. 8:14; Gal. 5:18). It is no wonder that the apostolic command is "Be filled with the Spirit" (Eph. 5:18), for every phase of the Christian life is related to His ministry. Even the virtues which men need for everyday life are the product of His work, for the fruit of the Spirit is "love, joy, peace, long-suffering, kindness, goodness, faithfulness, meekness, self-control" (Gal. 5:22-23).

Not devout fervors alone, not dreams of far-off ideals alone, but the every-day qualities which one needs most in his commonplace life, are the Spirit's work. . . . When the religious ideas of the apostolic age are considered, this correlation of the Spirit with man's ethical and practical life seems to be Paul's greatest contribution to the doctrine under consideration.[7]

The references to the Spirit may be scattered but they are profuse in all the Pauline Epistles and clearly demonstrate the substructural importance of the doctrine in the apostle's thinking.

[7] G. B. Stevens, *New Testament Theology* (Edinburgh: T. & T. Clark, p. 439.

Chapter 3

SIN AND SALVATION

I. THE DOCTRINE OF SIN

A. *The Meaning of Sin*

Paul's concept of sin is Hebraistic, not Hellenistic. The Greek idea was that sin was undeveloped good and a necessary stage in the upward progress of man toward God. A mistake was in the final analysis intellectual, not moral. To the Greek, then, sin was an unfortunate but temporary episode in man's advance in true wisdom and knowledge. To Paul sin was anything but that. It was a matter of the will, a deliberate declension on the part of man alienating him from God. Further, it was a matter of moral depravity, for Paul considered sin a state as well as an act.

The meanings of the many Greek words which Paul uses for sin elaborate his concept. Sin is missing the mark (Rom. 5:12—6:1, 15), which is a positive act involving not only missing the right but hitting the wrong. Missing the mark is not a negative concept of omission but a positive act of commission. Sin is trespass, which is willful disobedience (Rom. 2:23; Gal. 3:19; I Tim. 2:14). Sin is a falling away or deviation from the truth (Rom. 5:15, 17-18). Sin is a disregard of the truth, an unwillingness to hear (Rom. 5:19; II Cor. 10:6). It is unrighteousness (Rom. 1:18; Col. 3:25), ungodliness (Rom. 1:18; Titus 2:12), lawlessness (II Thess.

2:3; Titus 2:14), ignorance (Eph. 4:18), defeat or loss (Rom. 11:12; I Cor. 6:7), and grievous wickedness (Rom. 1:29-31; I Cor. 5:8). From Paul's usage it is evident that (1) the concept of sin was so well defined that in every instance it is clear what kind of sin is in view; and (2) the concept is many-sided; and (3) most of the words appear in Romans.

B. *The Universality of Sin*

Paul's systematic presentation of the universality of sin is found in the first division of the Roman Epistle. The heathen are first condemned for their sin, which is primarily against the revelation of God in nature (1:18-32). The cause of their condemnation is their own willful ignorance of the light of nature (1:18-23). As a consequence God completely abandoned them (1:24-32). The moralist comes under Paul's attention in 2:1-16 (even though the section has primary reference to the Jew, its application is to any who excluded himself from the condemnation of chapter 1). He is condemned by the truth (2:1-5), by his deeds (2:6-11), and by the Gospel (2:12-16). Paul then turns directly to the Jew and shows that he is justly condemned because he did not keep the law of God (2:17-29) and because he did not believe the promises of God (3:1-8). As a climax to the entire section Paul writes in sweeping terms of the condemnation of all men (3:9-20). In this concluding paragraph Paul's method is to state the proposition and then substantiate it by linking together various passages of Scripture in order to prove that all men are sinners and that men are wholly sinners. Man's character (3:9-12) and man's conduct (3:12-18) show both his sinful nature and sinful acts.

C. *The Origin of Sin*

With respect to the origin of sin in the human race Paul teaches that it began with Adam's transgression (Rom. 5:12-

21). Eve was deceived by Satan (II Cor. 11:3; I Tim. 2:14),
Adam was the gateway through which sin entered the race
(Rom. 5:12a), and "all sinned" (Rom. 5:12b). It is the
meaning of the phrase *all sinned* which is of primary importance to an understanding of the origin of sin. No one
questions that through Adam sin came into the experience
of the race, but whether or not this was by the race's being
in Adam is questioned. Finney, for instance, says that Adam
as the head of the race merely influenced his posterity by
exposing them to aggravated temptation. Constitutional sinfulness he stoutly denies.[1] It is sometimes argued that being
"in Adam" means affectation by Adam's sin but not participation in it. "If they sinned, their sin was due in part to
tendencies inherited from Adam. . . . The Fall gave the pre-
disposition to sin. . . ."[2] Barthianism, while stressing the
solidarity of sin in the human race, denies that sin originated
in Adam, for the account of Genesis 3 belongs to a realm of
history which is not historiographical. Brunner declares that
original sin is read into the account.[3]

The only proper explanation of Paul's thought on the
matter is that when Adam sinned the entire race sinned in
him because "all individuals were seminally in Adam, and
actually participated in his sin."[4] It is not that Pauline theology assigns this idea of imputed sin as the only basis for
condemnation, for in other places Paul recognizes that inherited sin and personal transgression also bring condemnation. But this idea of imputation based on actual participation in the sin of Adam is a clear part of Pauline teaching.

D. *The Effects of Sin*

1. *Sin brings death.* Paul traces both physical and spiritual

[1]C. G. Finney, *Lectures on Systematic Theology* (South Gate, Calif.:
Colporter Kemp, 1944), p. 255.
[2]W. Sanday and A. C. Headlam. *A Critical and Exegetical Commentary
on the Epistle to the Romans, International Critical Commentary* (New
York: Scribner's, 1895), p. 134.
[3]E. Brunner, *Man in Revolt* (Philadelphia: Westminster, 1947), p. 142.
[4]G. B. Stevens, *The Pauline Theology* (London: Richard B. Dickinson,
1892), p. 134.

death to sin. In Romans 5:14 the reign of physical death during the time from Adam to Moses, even over those who had not sinned in the same manner as Adam did, proves that all sinned in Adam (cf. I Cor. 15:21). In the same passage he wrote of the sentence of spiritual death passing upon all men through Adam (Rom. 5:12). The proof of the fact that all are separated from God by spiritual death is the universal slavery of man to sin (Rom. 6:16, 23).

2. *Sin causes corruption of character.* Because man is a sinner he sins. Basic character is affected to the extent that there is none that really seeks God or does that which can make him acceptable to God (Rom. 3:9-12). Such character breeds corrupted conduct which exhibits itself in corrupting, deceitful, uncharitable, blasphemous works, and murderous, oppressive, quarrelsome, impious deeds (Rom. 3:15-18).

3. *Sin affected creation* (Rom. 8:18-25). In speaking of the expectation of the Christian, Paul somewhat incidentally remarks that creation too awaits release from bondage to which it was subjected unwillingly. God was obliged to subject the earth to ineffectiveness because of the sin of Adam. Since man lost in the Fall the dominion he had originally been given over the earth, the earth had to be cursed, so fallen man would not have been left living on an unfallen earth. Thus unwillingly, because of man's sin, the earth was put in subjection.

4. *Sin is the reason why Christ had to die.* In all of Paul's Epistles there is repeated emphasis on the truth that Christ died because of sin (Rom. 8:2-3; I Cor. 15:3; II Cor. 5:21; Gal. 1:4; Eph. 1:7; Phil. 3:9; Col. 1:14; I Thess. 5:9-10; II Thess. 2:13-14; I Tim. 2:5-6; II Tim. 1:10; Titus 2:14).

E. *The Relationships of Sin*

Paul deals with sin in relation to two other important concepts—the flesh and the law. Although Paul uses the word *flesh* to designate the material of the body (I Cor. 15:50; Eph. 5:30; 6:12) and as a synonym for the whole of man (Rom. 3:20; I Cor. 1:29), his principal use is an ethical one. Flesh stands for that which is sinful (Rom. 7:18, 25; 8:1-9, 12-16). It is the human nature of man which is governed by sin. The flesh in that sense motivates the entire life of the unredeemed man, and it can only lead to spiritual death, for it stands in enmity with God (Rom. 8:5-8). The Christian's basis of victory depends on a once-for-all crucifixion of the flesh (Gal. 5:24) and a constant controlling of it by the Spirit (Gal. 5:17-23).

The relationship between sin and the law is fully developed by Paul in Romans 7:7-25. Paul makes it clear that the Law is not to be equated with sin, but that the Law reveals certain things about sin. It reveals the fact of sin (and it is the Mosaic law which is in view here, for Paul specifically mentions the tenth commandment, v. 7); it provides sin with a base of operations (v. 8); it reveals the power of sin (v. 9); it reveals the deceitfulness of sin (vv. 10-11), for instead of directing Paul to life, the law showed him the way of death by revealing the deceitfulness of sin; and it reveals the sinfulness of sin (vv. 12-13). The law, which in itself is holy, just, and good, becomes the instrument to reveal sin, the agent of evil. How evil, then, by comparison must sin be because it works the greatest evil through the law which was in reality a preparation for righteousness.

Although the law shows these things about sin, it cannot empower the believer to give him victory over sin (Rom. 7:14-25). The law does not provide the proper motivation, for it says "have to" while grace says "want to." The law can never empower unto sanctification. Legalism is sanctification's chief enemy; to connect the Law with the Christian's sanctification is to defeat him before he starts.

II. The Doctrine of Redemption

Not from Judaism did Paul receive his teaching on redemption, for the idea of a suffering Messiah was a repugnant one. It was on the Damascus road that he became convinced that Jesus was Messiah and that the Messianic concept involved the death of Messiah. That death was included as the culmination of Messiah's work was a conclusion urged also in the early preaching of the apostles as well as by Paul.

A. *The Nature of Redemption*

Paul conceived of redemption in its broadest terms. It was a purchase (I Cor. 6:20; 7:23). It included an irrevocable deliverance (Gal. 3:13; 4:4-5), and it guaranteed release on payment of ransom (Titus 2:14; Rom. 3:24; 8:23; I Cor. 1:30; Eph. 1:7, 14; 4:30; Col. 1:14). The idea of ransom does not make the concept of redemption entirely a commercial one, for redemption is also vicarious. Substitution is seen in Romans 3:24, and Paul's use of *huper*, in place of, also requires the vicarious idea (II Cor. 5:21; Gal. 3:13; cf. Philem. 13).

B. *The Means of Redemption*

Redemption has its ultimate source in God (Rom. 3:24; I Cor. 1:30). It involves the payment of a ransom price (I Cor. 6:20; 7:23), and this was done by the God-man (Gal. 4:4-5). However, it is not the life of Christ which redeems but his death (Eph. 1:7; Col. 1:14—blood stands for death, cf. Rom. 5:9-10). Thus redemption was accomplished through the one righteous act of the Son of God giving His life as a ransom (Rom. 3:24; 5:18).

C. *The Scope of Redemption*

Redemption is for all (Rom. 3:23-25). It delivers from iniquity (Titus 2:14) and from the Law (Gal. 3:13) with the result that those redeemed are adopted as adult sons (Gal.

4:5). Eventually it will include the resurrection of the body (Rom. 8:23).

D. *The Results of Redemption*

In relation to sins, redemption includes forgiveness (Eph. 1:7) and thus becomes the basis for justification (Rom. 3:24). In relation to Law, redemption provides freedom and release. Because the Redeemer came under the Law those who believe can be redeemed from its curse and received as sons. In relation to ethics, redemption by its very nature means that the one redeemed owes something to the one who redeemed him (I Cor. 6:20; Titus 2:14). Though God's emphasis to the believer is always one of appeal to be His slave, it is nevertheless a reasonable requirement by the very nature of redemption.

III. THE DOCTRINE OF JUSTIFICATION

A. *The Meaning of Justification*

Justification is a legal term which means to announce a favorable verdict, to acquit, to vindicate, to declare righteous (cf. Deut. 25:1). Paul himself distinguishes it from forgiveness, though forgiveness is necessarily included in it (Acts 13:39). He also makes the lack of justification synonymous with condemnation, and since the latter is a sentence of disapproval the former must be a sentence of approval (Rom. 5:16; 8:33-34). Thus it is a forensic act of the pronouncing of a judgment rather than the moral process of making one just through the infusion of righteousness.

B. *The Means of Justification*

Faith, righteousness, grace, redemption in Christ are all related to justification (Rom. 3:21-26). It is an act of grace on God's part; it is made possible on the basis of the sacrifice of Christ; the human requirement is faith, which brings imputed righteousness to the believer; and the fact that the

believer is righteous in Christ is the basis of the announcement which is justification or declaration of righteousness.
This righteousness is obtained by being placed in Christ.

> God does not merely acquit, or impute righteousness to,
> a man though he is guilty; that is not even human jus-
> tice, much less divine. The Christian, as we have seen,
> is "translated" from the old condition in which right-
> eousness was impossible into the new condition of one-
> ness with Christ. Christ is perfectly righteous, and *in
> Him* the Christian is . . . righteous.[5]

However, people are not translated into the kingdom of
Christ either against their own will or indiscriminately or
automatically. Faith is the necessary condition (Eph. 2:8-9),
and such faith that means an abandonment to God that He
might do that which we cannot do for ourselves. In Romans
4, Paul illustrates from the life of Abraham that all a man
must do is believe in order to gain God's righteousness. He
makes three points about the sufficiency of faith: justification
did not come to Abraham by faith plus circumcision (4:9-
12); justification did not come to Abraham by faith plus Law
(4:13-17); and justification comes to anyone by faith alone
(4:18-25).

C. *The Results of Justification*

Justification brings peace (Rom. 5:1) and practical holiness (Rom. 6-8). The Pauline logic is simple: because we
are righteous in Christ (which is the basis of justification)
we should live righteously in this world (cf. Col. 3:1). Paul's
soteriology is everywhere ethical in its ramifications.

[5]A. H. McNeile, *St. Paul, His Life, Letters, and Christian Doctrine* (Cambridge: University Press, 1920), p. 293.

Chapter 4

THE DOCTRINE OF THE CHURCH

THE CONCEPT OF THE CHURCH looms large in Paul's thought. This is attributable to at least two reasons: his relation to the revelation of the mystery of the Body accounts for his concept of the Church universal, and his desire to organize his converts into self-governing and self-propagating groups accounts for the emphasis on the local church. Paul uses the word *church* more than sixty times in his Epistles both to indicate a local organization (I Cor. 1:2) as well as the whole body of believers (I Cor. 12:28; Col. 1:18), but his thought as a whole contains certain basic avowals which taken together set forth his doctrine of the Church.

I. THE CHURCH IS A MYSTERY

The first of these avowals concerns the mystery character of the Church, the Body of Christ. The word *mystery* of course does not mean something difficult to understand but something imparted to the initiated only.[1] It occurs in the Septuagint only in Daniel 2 in reference to the secrets of Nebuchadnezzar's dream. In the New Testament the word appears 27 times, 21 of which are in the writings of Paul.

Paul uses the word in reference to the basic features of the Church. The fact that he uses it in other connections (Eph. 6:19) does not mean that the Church is not a mystery;

[1] Cf. D. M. Edwards, "Mystery," *The International Standard Bible Encyclopaedia* (Grand Rapids: Eerdmans, 1943), III, 2104.

it simply means that these other facts were also unknown in Old Testament times. That there would be both Jews and Gentiles in one body in the Church was unknown and is a mystery (Eph. 3:1-12). This one body is called by Paul a new man, not a made-over Israel (Eph. 2:15). The living, organic nature of the people of God, the Church, is also called a mystery (Col. 1:24-27; 2:10-19; 3:4, 11). The relationship of the Church as the Bride of Christ is characterized by the same word (Eph. 5:22-32), and the fact that some who belong to this Body will not have to die but will be translated is also a mystery (I Cor. 15:51-57). Thus this truth concerning the Body of Christ, the Church, the new people of God, Paul considered a mystery unknown before New Testament times. His own definition in Romans 16:25 is borne out by this usage.

Does this mean that Paul actually believed that the Church was completely hidden in the Old Testament? What he wrote in Colossians 1:25-26 would so indicate, and it is not mitigated by the *as* in Ephesians 3:5. All Paul is saying in the latter passage is that even though it was known in the Old Testament that Jews and Gentiles would both share in blessings it was not known how that would be brought to pass within the one Body of Christ.[2] His very use of the word *mystery* plus the direct statements such as Colossians 1:25-26 do indicate that in his mind the mystery of the Church was completely unknown in Old Testament times.

Does Paul claim to be the sole recipient of the revelation of the mystery? On theological grounds it could not be so, for the Church was known and recognized before Paul's time (Acts 8:1-3; Phil. 3:6; Gal. 1:13; I Cor. 15:9). James's speech before the Jerusalem council (Acts 15) also shows

---

[2]The use of *hōs*, as, in Ephesians 3:5 may be declarative, in which case it has the force of a participle (cf. A. T. Robertson, *A Grammar of the Greek New Testament in the Light of Historical Research* [New York: Hodder & Stoughton, 1919], pp. 953-69). Thus the verse may be paraphrased, "The mystery which was not made known in other generations, *having* now been revealed to his holy apostles and prophets."

prior understanding of the fact that in this age Jews and Gentiles would be on the same basis. Further, on the basis of his own testimony in the principal passage on the matter Paul disavows any claim to being the sole recipient or agent of the revelation of the mystery (Eph. 3:1-12). All he says in this passage is that, generally speaking, the mystery was unknown before he revealed it, but it is quite clear that he recognized that God had revealed it to the other apostles and prophets as well as to himself (v. 5). This was done by the Holy Spirit, not by Paul, thus making it clear that Paul was not the first nor the only agency of this revelation. Even when he speaks of himself as the agent he is not at all emphatic about his position (note the unemphatic *emoi,* to me, not standing at the first of the sentence in verse 3). Thus he makes no claim that the revelation of the mystery was only to him. By contrast, when Paul is speaking of the proclamation of the mystery (v. 8) he does claim that that was his principal responsibility. To say, as Paul does in this passage, that he received something from God is not to say that God had not also given it to others, as indeed He had to the apostles and prophets. It is nevertheless true that although it cannot be said that Paul was the sole recipient of the revelation of the mystery, he was the principal agent of the revelation of it to others, for it is to his theology largely that we owe our knowledge of the Church as a mystery.

A corollary to the mystery character of the Church is the distinction of the Church to this age. This other way of affirming the same truth is seen in what Paul has to say about the beginning and the end of the Church. Concerning the former, Paul's thought is emphatic in placing stress on the necessary relation of the Church to the resurrection and ascension of Christ. It is built upon His resurrection (Eph. 1:19-20; Col. 3:1), and its functioning is dependent upon the giving of gifts to individual members, which gifts in turn are dependent upon the ascension of Christ (Eph. 4:7-12).

If by some stretch of imagination the Body of Christ could be said to have been in existence before the ascension of Christ, then it will have to be concluded that it was an inoperative body. In Paul's mind the Church is built on the resurrection and ascension, and this makes it distinctive to this age.

In writing of the conclusion of the Church when the saints will be translated and resurrected Paul uses the phrase *dead in Christ* (I Thess. 4:16). This seems to distinguish those who have died in this age from believers who died before Christ's first advent, thus marking the Church off as distinct to this age and a mystery hidden in Old Testament times but now revealed.

II. The Church Is an Organism

The Church as an organism is the complex structure of the Body of Christ which carries on living activities by means of the individual believers, who are distinct in function but mutually dependent on and governed by their relation to Christ, the Head. Thus it is natural to find the Pauline revelation of the Church as an organism chiefly pictured under the figure of the Church as the body. Related in a secondary way are two other figures—the Church as a building (I Cor. 3:11; Eph. 2:20), and the Church as a bride (Eph. 5:22-32), but the principal revelation is found under the figure of the body.

A. *The Entrance into the Organism*

The fact that there is a definite act and time of entering the Body is affirmed throughout the Pauline writings (I Cor. 6:15; Eph. 5:30; Col. 2:19). The means of entrance is stated clearly as the work of the Holy Spirit in baptizing believers into the Body (I Cor. 12:13). He baptizes or introduces all who believe into the new element of the sphere of resurrection life in the Body. The context makes it clear that the Spirit's work is not restricted to a certain group of believers, for there were all kinds in the church at Corinth and Paul declares that all have been baptized into the Body. Faith is of course the human requirement, but it is faith in Christ as Saviour. The baptizing of the Spirit automatically and simultaneously follows, placing all believers in that Body.

The principal ramification of our entrance into the organism is summarized in the Pauline doctrine of union. This union involves union with Christ as the Head of the Body and union with all other believers as fellow-members of the Body (I Cor. 12:12-31; Rom. 12:4-5).

B. *The Direction of the Organism*

As in other organisms so in the Body of Christ the direction comes from the Head. Paul teaches the headship of Christ over principalities and powers (Col. 2:10), over all men (I Cor. 11:3), and in particular over the Church (Eph. 1:22; 4:15; Col. 1:18; 2:19). The basis of Christ's headship over the Church, though related to and presupposed by His universal headship over all men, is particularly His work of redemption (Eph. 5:22-32). In other words, the rights of redemption result in the prerogatives of headship.

Specific ideas which are involved in the direction of the Body by the Head are discernible in Paul's thought. First, headship involves subordination (I Cor. 11:2-16). In this passage Paul clearly taught a ranking order of relationships. The head of Christ is God; the head of man is Christ; and the head of woman is man. Thus the order is God, Christ, man, and woman. This does not imply inferiority, for that would be incompatible with Paul's doctrine of the full deity of Christ taught elsewhere (Col. 2:9), but it does teach subordination. Thus the headship of Christ over the Church is intended to convey the idea of the subordination of the Church to the directions of Christ (Eph. 5:24).

Second, headship involves interdependence (Col. 2:19; Eph. 5:30; 4:15). The Head is dependent upon the members to carry out His directions, and in turn the members are dependent on that Head for leadership and upon each other for co-operation in carrying out the functions of the Body. The Body is a living organism.

Third, headship includes inseparable union. If this were not so then we must be able to conceive of a maimed Body of Christ, which idea is nowhere suggested in the Scripture. Indeed, in the illustration Paul uses of marriage as a picture of the relationship between Christ and the Church there is no hint that divorce is possible in this relationship (Eph. 5:22-32). This was of course not true in the relationship between God and Israel.

Fourth, headship means loving direction. As Head, Christ is no autocratic or blind ruler. His direction is saturated with love for His Bride, for whom He gave His life.

C. *The Nurture of the Organism*

It almost goes without saying that the Body is nurtured by the Head (Col. 2:19; Phil. 4:13). Christ does this by nourishing and cherishing the Body (Eph. 5:29; cf. Eph. 6:4 for "nurture" and I Thess. 2:7 for "cherish"). The sufficiency of the Body is from the Head.

D. *The Gifts to the Organism*

1. *The definition of gifts.* Except for one reference in I Peter 4:10, Paul is the only New Testament writer to use the word for grace-gift, *charisma*. His usage is wide, ranging from references to the gift of salvation (Rom. 6:23) to God's providential care (II Cor. 1:11). However, the most frequent occurrences refer to special gifts or abilities given to men by God. Thus, a *charisma* in this sense is a God-given ability for service.

2. *The description of the gifts.* This peculiarly Pauline

revelation is found in Romans 13, I Corinthians 12, and Ephesians 4.

a. Apostleship (Eph. 4:11; I Cor. 12:28). Apostleship has both a general and specific meaning. In the general sense it means messenger and is used, for instance, of Epaphroditus (Phil. 2:25). In the specialized sense it refers to the Twelve and a few others (e.g., Barnabas, Acts 14:14) to whom the gift was given and who were accredited by special signs.

b. Prophecy (Rom. 12:6; I Cor. 12:10; 14:1-40; Eph. 4:11). The exercise of the gift of prophecy included receiving a message from God by special revelation, being guided in declaring it, and having it authenticated by God Himself. It may have been rather widely distributed in New Testament times, though the record only mentions a few prophets specifically (Acts 11:27; 13:1; 21:9). The Corinthian church evidently had prophets in it (I Cor. 14).

c. Miracles (I Cor. 12:28). When Paul arranges the gifts in order of their relative importance this one appears as the first of the lesser ones.

d. Healing (I Cor. 12:9, 28, 30). Evidently this gift is a specific form of the gift of miracles.

e. Tongues (I Cor. 12:10). This was a God-given ability to speak in another language, either in a foreign, human language or an unknown ecstatic utterance. Abuse of this gift led Paul to list certain specific regulations to govern its exercise in the church. It was to be used only for edifying, only by two or three in a single meeting and then only if an interpreter were present, and never in preference to prophecy (I Cor. 14). The gift of interpretation is a corollary gift to this one.

f. Evangelism (Eph. 4:11). This gift involves two ideas—the kind of message preached and the places where it is preached. The message is the good news of salvation, and an evangelist's ministry is an itinerant one. For Paul the length of stay in one place on his itinerary sometimes lasted as long as two years (Acts 19:10). Paul evidently thought that one may do the work of an evangelist even though he does not possess the gift (II Tim. 4:5).

g. Pastor (Eph. 4:11). A pastor is one who leads, provides, cares for, and protects the flock of God. The full exercise of this gift will also include ruling and teaching.

h. Ministering (Rom. 12:7; I Cor. 12:28). This is the gift of helping in the broadest sense of the word. It especially includes ministering to physical and bodily needs of others.

i. Teaching (Rom. 12:7; I Cor. 12:28; Eph. 4:11). This is a gift which can be given alone or in connection with that of pastor. It concerns the imparting of truth to others.

j. Faith (I Cor. 12:8-10). This is the God-given ability to believe God's power to supply and guide.

k. Exhortation (Rom. 12:8). This is the talent to encourage, comfort, admonish, and entreat people.

l. Discerning spirits (I Cor. 12:10). This is the ability to distinguish between true and false sources of supernatural revelation given in oral form.

m. Showing mercy (Rom. 12:8). This is akin to the gift of ministering, for it involves succoring those who are sick and afflicted.

n. Giving (Rom. 12:8). The gift of giving concerns distributing one's own money to others. It is to be done with simplicity; i.e., with no thought of return or gain for self in any way.

o. Administration (Rom. 12:8; I Cor. 12:28). This is the ability to rule in the church.

3. *The design of the gifts.* The giving of gifts is with a view to fulfilling several purposes.

a. To promote the unity of the Body (I Cor. 12:12-26). Unity of the organism (not the organization) is accomplished as every part is functioning properly.

b. To promote the growth of the Body (Eph. 4:12-16).

Gifts, according to this passage, are given to equip (cf. Luke 6:40) the saints so that they in turn may give themselves to the work of ministering so that the Body as a result will be built up. This involves both quantity and quality.

4. *The development of gifts.* Although gifts are supernaturally bestowed, Paul indicates that they may be developed by the person to whom they are given. After listing some of the gifts in their order of importance he says that believers should covet the best gifts (I Cor. 12:31). This means that an individual may be ambitious to exercise certain gifts, which ambition can only be fulfilled by study and work. Paul himself, even though he was reared on the Old Testament, needed three years in Arabia to develop his gift of teaching.

In Romans 1:11 Paul indicates that he hoped to have a part in the developing of the gifts in the churches in Rome (cf. I Tim. 4:14; II Tim. 1:6). Quite clearly others may have a part in bringing gifts to maturity and full use (cf. Eph. 4:7-12). Thus, gifts may be developed as one is ambitious in relation to self and attentive to others.

Nowhere does Paul suggest that gifts are to be attached to a designated place. For instance, Paul does not equate the gift of pastor with the pastorate (as commonly done today). The pastor is one who shepherds—a gift which can be exercised in connection with the office of pastor or not. The gift is differentiated from the office. Neither does Paul suggest that there are special gifts for specific age groups. There is no gift of young people's work, for all ages need teachers, pastors, helpers, etc. (cf. Titus 2:1-8). The gift is the ability, according to Paul's thinking, and not the place or age group in which that ability is used.

Paul's doctrine of the Church as an organism contains the true idea of ecumenicity. His view of the oneness of all believers was deeply rooted, and that brought with it a firm sense of the necessity of the interdependence of Christians.

Much of the functioning of the organism is done through the visible organization, for they are interrelated ideas. For instance, gifts are exercised in the local assembly; nevertheless, in setting forth the doctrine, Paul keeps the organism paramount, for the gifts are given to the Body for the upbuilding of that Body. The Church as an organism, then, is basic to all that Paul says about the Church as an organization.

III. The Church Is an Organization

Paul's letters were written in the heat of the battle. Therefore, it is not unexpected to discover that for every single time he uses the word *church* in relation to the organism he uses it six times in relation to the organization. This is not to say that he thought the organization six times more important than the organism, but it is to say the church organization occupied a large place in his writing. In the theological substructure of his thinking, the large place he gives to the organism just discussed and the importance he placed on the revelation of the mystery of the Body can only lead to the conclusion that the organism occupied the basic place in his thinking. The organization occupies a large place in his writing simply because the majority of his writings were to local congregations, but the two concepts do not stand in opposition to each other, for the organism properly functioning will express itself in local organizations.

A. *The Officials in the Church*

1. *Elders.* Elders were taken over into the church from the synagogue organization (cf. Acts 11:30). They were considered essential for the proper functioning of a local testimony so much so that Paul saw to it that they were appointed in the churches he had established before returning to Antioch (Acts 14:23).[3] He recommended to Titus that they be ap-

[3] An extended note showing that Acts 14:23 does not indicate that elders were chosen by the votes of the people but that they were appointed can be

pointed in the churches in Crete (Titus 1:5). Their principal duties involved ruling (I Tim. 5:17), guarding the truth
(Titus 1:9), and the general oversight of the church (I Tim.
3:1). Some elders were also gifted in teaching (I Tim. 5:17),
but this was not a necessary *function* of an elder (though the
ability to teach was a qualification). In his Epistles Paul
usually mentions elders in the plural (Phil. 1:1; Titus 1:5),
but in I Timothy 3:1-7 the elder is spoken of in the singular
(note that deacons in the same passage are spoken of in the
plural, vv. 8-13). This may indicate that as time went on a
single elder led the congregation as a kind of pastor. The
qualifications for elders are clearly specified by Paul in two
passages (I Tim. 3:1-7; Titus 1:6-9). Nothing is said about
removing an elder from office once he had been chosen,
though one might infer that if he ceased to qualify he should
cease to function.

2. *Deacons.* The origin of deacons is not so clear as that
of elders. They were probably an innovation of the Christian Church, being at first helpers of the elders performing
functions which did not involve superintendence. They
were unofficial servants some of whom in process of time became the officially recognized diaconate. The general sense
of deacon as servant is found in the later of Paul's Epistles
(Col. 4:17; I Tim. 4:6), while in the same group of Epistles the office is mentioned (Phil. 1:1; I Tim. 3:8-10). The
standard of qualification for deacons (I Tim. 3:8-10) indicates that they performed a spiritual ministry, so that the
distinction between elders and deacons was not that the
elders had to do with spiritual things while the deacons concerned themselves with material matters (cf. Acts 11:30).
Rather the distinction was that the deacons were the subor-
dinates functioning under the general oversight of the elders.
Paul says nothing about the appointment of deacons though
the general indication of history is that the elders chose them.

profitably studied in W. Kelly, *Lectures on the Church of God* (London:
Morrish, 1918), pp. 217-23.

Did Paul recognize the office of deaconess? Phoebe's name is used in connection with the word *deacon* (Rom. 16:1), and certain women are mentioned together with the deacons in the passage concerning their qualifications (I Tim. 3:11). Whether these were official deaconesses or merely women servants (using the word *deacon* in the unofficial sense) is a question which perhaps can never be settled conclusively. It seems doubtful to this writer that Paul was using the word officially. Phoebe was a helper of the church but not a member of an order of deaconesses. The women mentioned in I Timothy 3:11 are probably the wives of deacons who helped them in their duties. Paul recognized the necessity for women helpers in the church, but that does not mean that there was an order of deaconesses.[4]

B. *The Ordinances of the Church*

1. *Baptism.* References to baptism are rare in the Pauline writings. We know that Paul was himself baptized (Acts 9:18) and that he baptized others (I Cor. 1:15 ff.). He evidently considered it an important ordinance to be experienced by every believer (Acts 16:31ff.; Eph. 5:26), and yet he clearly distinguished it from the Gospel itself (I Cor. 1:17, the *alla,* but, in the verse showing strong contrast). He practiced in one instance the rebaptism of those who had not received Christian baptism (Acts 19:1-7). Undoubtedly there was a close connection in his mind between the baptism of the Spirit and baptism with water. This is most clearly seen in Romans 6:1-10 where the accomplishments described can only be the work of the Spirit but where the background of the passage is clearly the ordinance and what it pictures. To rule the ordinance out of this passage is to be unrealistic in discerning both Paul's thought and that

[4]For further study on this question the reader may consult the author's *The Place of Women in the Church* (New York: Macmillan, 1958), pp. 85-91. Cf. also J. A. Robinson, "Deacon and Deaconess," *Encyclopaedia Biblica,* p. 1039, and H. P. Liddon, *Explanatory Analysis of St. Paul's First Epistle to Timothy* (London: Oxford, 1897), p. 34.

which would be conveyed to his readers. For Paul the ordinance apparently pictured the believer's association with Christ in death, burial, and résurrection.

2. *The Lord's Supper.* The Supper was for Paul primarily a memorial of the sacrificial death of the Lord (I Cor. 11:23-24). The observance of the ordinance involved a remembrance of love (vv. 24-25), a reiteration of the Gospel (v. 26a),[5] and a renewal of hope (v. 26b). The observance must be preceded by a self-examination. Failure to do that had resulted in the sickness and death of some of the Corinthian believers.

For Paul the Lord's Supper also had other significances. He calls it a *koinonia* or fellowship (I Cor. 10:16). Thus, spiritual fellowship with Christ is also part of the Supper. Too, the ordinance reminds all believers of their oneness in Christ (I Cor. 10:17). We are bound together because we are bound to Christ.

C. *The Order of the Church*

Detailed directions regarding the order and conduct of the meetings of the church are surprisingly few. Specific regulations concerning the use of the gift of tongues have been referred to. In general Paul urges the importance of reverence and proper decorum in the meetings of the congregation especially in the observance of the Lord's Supper (I Cor. 11). He also expected the churches to exercise their work of disciplining wayward members (I Cor. 5).

Leadership in the church was definitely placed in the hands of men. Paul's view about women in the church was that they should be subordinate and silent. Their subordination, which is based on the natural facts of creation, was to be exhibited in the church by the wearing of a veil. It was a matter of teaching a relationship which God established

---

[5]Whether this means that the elements of the Supper silently announce the facts of the Gospel or whether it refers to an oral explanation which accompanied the observance is difficult to decide.

in creation and not a matter of custom or local Corinthian peculiarity. In both I Corinthians 11 and I Timothy 2 Paul relates the subordination of women to the accounts of creation. This makes it a matter of doctrine and not custom.

Silence is also enjoined upon the women by Paul (I Cor. 11:5, 13; 14:34; I Tim. 2:12). She must not teach or speak in the public assembly of the church or even ask questions. Some have held that I Corinthians 11:5, 13 merely forbid a woman from praying or prophesying without a veil. This could not have been Paul's meaning, for in the next section of the same Epistle where he deals more specifically with the conduct of public worship he expressly forbids all speaking by women in the church (I Cor. 14:34). He could hardly have intended such a deliberate contradiction, which is the only conclusion if I Corinthians 11:5, 13 mean that if veiled a woman may pray *and* prophesy (for the one cannot be condoned without the other). Stevens has correctly noted in regard to I Corinthians 11:5, 13 and 14:34 that

> we observe that in the former passages Paul says nothing of how women may, *with propriety,* speak in public, but is merely denouncing the obvious impropriety of speaking without the veil. It is quite certain, as appears later when Paul takes up the subject of women's speaking in general, that for his mind the requirement to appear in the assembly only with veiled head would preclude, by its very significance, the public speaking in question.[6]

Again we notice that Paul's views are related to his literal interpretation of the accounts of creation in Genesis. They were not restricted to a particular situation in a local church in the first century. This was part of his theology.

[6]G. B. Stevens, *The Theology of the New Testament,* p. 461; cf. A. Plummer, *A Critical and Exegetical Commentary on the First Epistle of St. Paul to the Corinthians, International Critical Commentary* (Edinburgh: T. & T. Clark, 1914), pp. 324-25, who leans toward the same conclusion on the basis of the possibility that I Corinthians 11:5 is a hypothetical instance; that is, that a woman should pray or prophesy at all, and especially with her head uncovered, was such an unthinkable thing that it would never occur in the church.

In all of his teaching relative to the Church Paul's chief emphasis is on the unity of the Spirit which binds every believer to the Head and to other believers. The primitive church experienced its problems and divisions, but for all his teaching on church organization, Paul never campaigned for organizational unity. He firmly believed that the true unity of the Church was not outward but inward, and this is the spirit which permeates his ecclesiology.

Chapter 5

THE CHRISTIAN LIFE

EVEN THE MOST CASUAL READER of the Pauline Epistles realizes that the truth concerning the Christian life occupies a large place in those writings. This has led writers on Pauline theology to assert that Paul's doctrine of "in Christ" is his central one.[1] The case for such a conclusion is substantial, for many other doctrines are related to being "in Christ"; e.g., justification (Rom. 8:1), sanctification (Rom. 6:1-10), ethics (Col. 3:1), and eschatology (I Thess. 4:14-15). Perhaps it would be more accurate to say that the doctrine of God is the central doctrine of Pauline theology and that the doctrine of being "in Christ" is the focal point of all the teachings concerning the Christian life.

I. THE FOUNDATION OF CHRISTIAN LIVING

Paul was the chief exponent of the concept of being "in Christ" as far as making it normative in Christian thought and experience. The idea is found in the teaching of the Lord (John 14:20; 15:4), but generally speaking the Synoptics emphasize being "with (*meta*) Christ" while Paul speaks of being "in (*en*) Christ."

The term is far-reaching. The heavenly calling of Christians is "in Christ Jesus" (Phil. 3:14; cf. II Tim. 1:9). Their

[1]H. A. A. Kennedy, *The Theology of the Epistles* (London: Duckworth, 1919), p. 124; J. S. Stewart, *A Man in Christ* (London: Hodder and Stoughton, 1935), pp. 147-53.

election is in Him (Eph. 1:4). Forgiveness (Eph. 1:7; 4:32; Col. 1:14), redemption (Rom. 3:24; Eph. 1:7; Col. 1:14), freedom from condemnation (Rom. 8:1), freedom from the Law (Gal. 2:4), justification (Gal. 2:17), and life (Rom. 6:11, 23; 8:2) are all in Christ. Sanctification and Christian living are also related to being in Christ. In Him Christians are sanctified (I Cor. 1:2), rooted and built up (Col. 2:7), taught (Eph. 4:21), guarded (Phil. 4:7), and led in triumph (II Cor. 2:14). In Christ believers, both Jew and Gentile, are one body (Rom. 12:5; Eph. 2:13-22), and in Him they have boldness and access to God (Eph. 3:12). Bodily resurrection is also related to being in Christ (I Cor. 15:22).

Although Paul uses the term in many other passages with less doctrinal precision, considering all usages the term may be defined thus: in Christ is the redeemed man's new environment in the sphere of resurrection life. "He has been transplanted into a new soil and a new climate, and both soil and climate are Christ."[2]

Certain important distinctions are apparent in the concept. (1) This union with Christ is a gift of God and involves the baptizing work of the Holy Spirit. (2) The doctrine invalidates the idea that Jesus is merely an example. (3) The idea is mystical, but it is a mysticism of intimate communion with Christ open to all believers. (4) It is the basis for Christian ethics and the answer to the antinomian charge. If a Christian is really united to Christ He is identified with Christ's attitude toward sin, and this is the strongest reason for living the Christian life. This union also provides the power to live. Every indicative is a veiled imperative—you are a new man in Christ, live like one. This is the heart of all of Paul's teaching about the Christian life.

II. The Principle of Christian Living—Sanctification

Although Paul recognized the positional aspect of sancti-

[2]Stewart, *op. cit.*, p. 157.

fication (I Cor. 6:11), it is the progressive aspect of practical sanctification which is the subject of this section.

A. *The Divine Work in Sanctification*

God's work in practical sanctification involves placing the believer in Christ, the meaning of which has just been discussed. The means by which this is done is by the baptizing work of the Holy Spirit (I Cor. 12:13). Everywhere Paul's emphasis relative to the divine work in sanctification is on the work of the Holy Spirit in the believer's life. The basis of appeal to carnal believers is to recognize the indwelling of the Spirit and then to live as purchased ones (I Cor. 6:19-20). The fruit of the Holy Spirit is genuine sanctification, for it is He who empowers the believer to live (Gal. 5:16-26). All of the ministries of the Spirit mentioned under the doctrine of God demonstrate how vital His work is in producing a truly sanctified life.

B. *The Human Work in Sanctification*

Paul does not neglect to mention that there is a work to be done by the believer in sanctification. Presentation of the life is the starting point of all human effort (Rom. 12:1). This is a once-for-all offering of one's self without reservation. The corollary of that positive presentation is the negative breaking with sin (Rom. 6:1-13). It is a break which is based on realizing or reckoning that the believer, because of his union with Christ, has already crucified the flesh (cf. Gal. 5:24). The aorist tenses in Romans 6:1-10 and Galatians 5:24 conclusively show that the work of crucifixion of the flesh has been done completely for the Christian once for all. It is up to the individual to realize it and on the basis of that reckoning to make a presentation of himself. Prayer will have a large place in this, for it is through prayer that we learn what has been accomplished on our behalf (Eph. 1:15-22; Phil. 1:9-11; Col. 1:9-11), and it is on the basis of knowledge that an intelligent reckoning can be made (Rom. 6: 1-13).

However, the victory is not won by an initial presentation and break with sin. There is a battle to be fought, and Paul gives directions concerning that also. The battle to believe the truth concerning what God has declared to be true about the crucifixion of the flesh is a continuous one (Eph. 6:13; Rom. 8:13; I Tim. 6:12). The battle also includes a fleeing from sin and sinful situations (Rom. 13:14; I Cor. 10:14; II Tim. 2:22) and a following after good ideals in the company of good companions (I Cor. 15:33; I Tim. 6:11; II Tim. 2:22). For all the emphasis Paul placed on the work of God in sanctification, he did not neglect to spell out the human responsibility as well. Both aspects are necessary in victorious living.

III. The Practice of Christian Living—Separation

Being "in Christ" is the basis of sanctification. Sanctification in its outworking is separation from sin and unto Christ in all the relationships of life. It is living one's position in everything.

A. *In Relation to Self*

The practice of sanctification in relation to self means discipline (I Cor. 9:24-27). Discipline is required by the character of the enemies which the Christian faces in his race. The believer must live in the world without abusing it (I Cor. 7:31). The flesh, though crucified, is not eradicated, and the Devil and his hosts are constant and powerful foes of the Christian's warfare (Eph. 6:12-18). The rules to be followed in self-discipline are: condition the body (I Cor. 9:24a), control the body (I Cor. 6:12; 9:26), and capture the body (I Cor. 9:27; II Tim. 2:5). The reward is approval by Christ at His judgment seat (I Cor. 3:14; 9:27; II Cor. 5:10). Discipline is a good illustration of the combination of the divine and human in sanctification, for while it is an aspect of the fruit of the Spirit (Gal. 5:23) it is also the fruit of human effort.

B. *In Relation to the Family*

Order is the key thought in Paul's teaching concerning family relationships.

1. *Marriage.* Paul affirms that marriage is to be entered into only with believers (II Cor. 6:14). In I Corinthians 7 he seems definitely to give the preference to celibacy for two reasons: the Lord's coming is near, and the nature of Christian work demands one's full attention—something which cannot be given by a married person. The first reason could be called an interim ethic, but the second cannot and is just as valid a reason for not preferring marriage today as it was in Paul's time. This preference of Paul's does not indicate that he considered marriage wrong—rather he made it an individual matter (I Cor. 7:7).

2. *Divorce.* However, once marriage has been contracted between believers Paul allowed no divorce (I Cor. 7:10-11). In this he considered that he was following the Lord's teaching. In some circumstances when two unbelievers had married and one of them subsequently became a Christian a divorce was allowed (I Cor. 7:12-15).

3. *The Home.* Paul assigned the leadership of the Christian home to the husband (Eph. 5:22-33). His headship involves loving his wife with a divine love, expressing his love for his family by nourishing them into a maturing Christian experience, disciplining the children (Eph. 6:4), providing for the home (I Tim. 5:8), and, in general, being the presiding leader in the home (I Tim. 3:4). In turn the wife is to work at home (Titus 2:4-5), have a part in the rearing of the children (Eph. 6:1), and be in subjection to her husband (Eph. 5:23). The children expect to be governed (Eph. 6: 1-4; I Tim. 3:4); they should be grave in deportment

(I Tim. 3:4; Titus 1:6) and godly in conduct (I Tim. 5:4).
If the circumstances require it they should care for the material needs of a widowed mother or grandmother (I Tim. 5:
4). This evidently is a responsibility which a person has as
long as he has a living parent.

C. *In Relation to Governments*

The proper function of government is to promote good in
order that peaceable and godly lives may be lived (I Tim.
2:2; Rom. 13:3). For this reason believers should pray faithfully for those who rule (I Tim. 2:2), and be submissive to
rulers (Rom. 13:1-7). Submission is required for four reasons: government is ordained of God, any resistance to government is in reality to God, government is for the good,
and the conscience demands it. Submission will manifest
itself in paying dues and custom taxes and in fear and honor
of the rulers.

> There is nothing to show that the submission required
> by Paul includes active co-operation; it may even show
> itself in the form of passive resistance, and it does not at
> all exclude protestation in word and even resistance in
> deed, provided that to this latter there be joined calm
> acceptance of the punishment inflicted. . . .[3]

Paul does not equate government and the world, for, although there may be similarities, they belong to different
realms of authority. Paul also declares that the courts of
the governments should not be used by Christians for settling their disputes (I Cor. 6:1-8).

D. *In Relation to Work*

A Christian should not be a reactionary as far as his position in life is concerned (I Cor. 7:20-22). Performance of
his work should be as unto the Lord and not men (Eph. 6:

[3]F. L. Godet, *A Commentary on St. Paul's Epistle to the Romans* (Edinburgh: T. & T. Clark, n.d.), II, 308.

5-9; Col. 3:22-25). For employees this means doing the job in fear and trembling as doing the will of God, and for employers it means impartiality and just treatment of workers. Paul seemed to think that converted slaves could well be emancipated, though he did not crusade for it (Philemon 8-21).

E. *In Relation to the Spiritual Welfare of Others*

Paul always recognized and practiced the principle that the only thing that can benefit the lost man is salvation; therefore, the Christian life should be lived in relation to unsaved men so as to win them to Christ (Col. 4:5). This involved for Paul great strictness and discipline in living (I Cor. 9:19-27). Such evangelistic living is motivated at least in part by the fear of the Lord and by the hope of reward (II Cor. 5:10-11; I Thess. 2:19-20).

The Christian's relation to other believers should always be such as will help build them up in the faith. In principle it is simple; in practice it is complicated. The principle is ethical living and simply stated is: Do nothing which will put a cause for stumbling in the path of another Christian (I Cor. 8:13). Liberty which a stronger brother may have should always be exercised in love; therefore, love often brings restriction of liberty. Such limitation is not because the stronger brother thinks something is wrong but because it is wrong to the weaker brother; thus the restricting is out of love for the weaker brother (Rom. 14:13-19). Fear also motivates restricted living (Rom. 14:20-23), for Paul says it should be considered a little thing to give up something in the light of the awful consequences of offending a weaker brother.

When there is honest disagreement between believers the Pauline dictum is mutual consideration of one another (Rom. 14:1-12). Weaker and stronger brother alike should remember that God has received both (vv. 1-3), that both are the servants of God and not of one another (v. 4), that there can be conscientious differences (vv. 5-6), that all are under the lordship of Christ (vv. 7-9), and that each shall have to render an account to God in the judgment (vv. 10-12). For these reasons there should be mutual consideration between brethren who may honestly disagree about the propriety of certain actions in the Christian life.

The all-encompassing principle which guides all relationships of life is the imitation of Christ. Paul's emphasis is not on the imitation of the earthly life of Jesus but on glorifying God. This means imitating Christ. Since the glory of God is the manifestation of His attributes, and since Jesus of Nazareth perfectly showed forth the Father, glorifying God will imitate Christ. He is our pattern in matters of conduct (Rom: 15:1-3) and conforming to that pattern is the only way to glorify God in eating or drinking or whatsoever we do (I Cor. 10:31). This should be the aim of all Christian living.

Such considerate conduct assumes, of course, that the disagreeing parties are both attempting to do God's will. If there is any doubt, then one should give Christ the benefit of the doubt and not participate in a questionable activity. Self-discipline is also involved in our relations to others (I Cor. 9:19-21), and Christian liberty should never cater to license (Rom. 6:1).

Chapter 6

ESCHATOLOGY

I. The Future for the Church

WE HAVE ALREADY NOTICED that the doctrine of the Church occupies a major place in Pauline theology; therefore, it is not surprising to discover that the eschatology of the Church is also a prominent theme in Paul's teaching concerning future things.

A. The Last Days

In two places the apostle gives detailed characteristics of the last days for the Church (I Tim. 4:1-3; II Tim. 3:1-5).

1. *Declension in sound doctrine.* Before the Church is raptured there will be an increasing denial of sound doctrine so that men shall depart from the faith and be led away into demonism (I Tim. 4:1). They will have no conscience for the truth. The specific form of the error, misrepresentation of the person of Christ, is the subject of Johannine revelation.

2. *Declension in godly living.* This characteristic will take two forms—false asceticism and licentious living. The asceticism will forbid marriage and the eating of meats (I Tim. 4:3), and the license will take many forms (II Tim. 3:1-4). Briefly stated, God will be replaced by self so that love of self and love of money become the principal motivations of life. This will bring with it pride, blasphemy, parental disobedience, thanklessness, unholiness, perversion, enmity, slan-

dering, lack of self-control, savagery, opposition to all that is good, treachery, recklessness, highmindedness, and the love of pleasure. Even those who may want to resist will be swept along in the tide of gross sin in the last days.

3. *Increase in religion.* Along with the declension there will come an increase in religious interest, but in a religion that is powerless (II Tim. 3:5).

Though these characteristics have been and are found in the Church in all its history, they will increase in intensity as the age draws to a close. Thus Paul would say that we may expect to see an increase in religious interest and powerless preaching with its attendant loose living as the Church completes her mission on earth.

B. *The Translation of the Church*

In two places Paul speaks of the taking up of the Church into Heaven (I Cor. 15:51-57; I Thess. 4:13-18). It is an event which will involve the descent of the Lord from Heaven, the resurrection of the "dead in Christ," the translation of the living in Christ, and the meeting of these two groups with the Lord in the air. The aspect involving the change of the living believers Paul calls a mystery (I Cor. 15:51). The truth of resurrection was a subject of Old Testament revelation, but that there would be a group who would not see death was unknown until New Testament times.

This truth of the rapture of the Church had many practical ramifications for Paul. The fact that he believed it to be imminent affected the apostle's teaching concerning marriage (I Cor. 7:29-31). He believed even in his own day that the time was short; therefore, he not only gave the preference to celibacy but also exhorted those who were married to work for the Lord as if they did not have the responsibilities of marriage. The doctrine was also a source of comfort and assurance (I Thess. 4:18). The believers at Thessalonica had begun to wonder if their brethren who had died before the

Lord's coming would be able to take part in the kingdom reign of Christ. Paul assures them that Christ would include them (I Thess. 4:14—"with him") because they would be raised from the dead before the kingdom was ushered in. Paul also made this teaching a basis for steadfastness in the Lord's service (I Cor. 15:58). The truth of judgment to follow the Lord's return becomes an added incentive for faithfulness in living now (I Cor. 3:11-15; II Cor. 5:10-11).

C. *The Judgment of Believers*

The place of judgment of individuals in the Church was pictured by Paul as the *bema* (II Cor. 5:10). The basis of the judgment is the quality of works performed since conversion (I Cor. 3:11-13). Although there may be many varieties of works there are only two basic kinds—those which will pass the test of fire and those which will not. Works which are qualified will be rewarded; yet in no case is the individual's salvation in question, for even though his works are burned "he himself shall be saved" (I Cor. 3:15).

Paul describes these rewards under the figure of crowns. Specifically crowns will be given for converts (I Thess. 2:19), and for loving the appearing of the Lord (II Tim. 4:8). Other writers mention additional crowns, so this is not an exclusive Pauline revelation (cf. Jas. 1:12; I Pet. 5:4; Rev. 2:10).

II. THE FUTURE FOR ISRAEL

In the classic section in Romans (9-11) Paul deals with God's relationship to his kinsmen according to the flesh, the Jews. His discussion in chapter 9 proves that God was perfectly free as Creator to reject Israel. Even though He had elected them He did not lose the right to take severe measures against them. However, God did not reject them unjustly, for Paul shows that there was moral necessity for it. In the discussion in chapter 11 Paul returns to the original question,

"Has God cast away His people?" answering it with an emphatic no.

This answer is confirmed by two considerations: (1) the extent of Israel's rejection is only partial (vv. 1-10), and (2) the duration of it is only temporary (vv. 25-32). (The intervening section shows the relation of Israel's rejection to the Gentiles, vv. 11-24.) The partial nature of the rejection is illustrated by Paul's own case which proves that an individual Israelite can be saved. The gracious action of God in preserving to Himself a remnant is further proof that God has not cast away His people. Even though Paul later shows that Israel's future involves national restoration, these individual examples introduced at the beginning of the discussion are illustrations of the fact that rejection was only partial.

In the illustration of the olive tree Paul warns Gentiles against being proud of their present position. The olive tree represents the place of privilege which Israel first occupied. Then those natural branches were broken off and unnatural branches, Gentiles, were grafted into the root which remained. The root and fatness (v. 17) is a reference to the Abrahamic covenant, which promised blessing both to the nation Israel and to all nations. Paul admonishes Gentiles to learn the lessons of history and not to be boastful and proud of their present position, for God will not spare them if they act as the Jews did. God can easily graft in again the natural branches. Thus Paul makes it clear that the future restoration of the Jews is more probable than the salvation of Gentiles had been.

Not only is that restoration highly probable but it is certain, for Israel's rejection is not permanent (vv. 25-32). It is temporary because it is only "until" a certain event. Since there is no other possible way to understand "until" (v. 25), it is clear that the rejection must end eventually. The event which marks the end of Israel's rejection is the coming in of the fullness of the Gentiles. Since this is a mystery it was not the subject of Old Testament revelation and means the completion of the full number of Gentiles who are to be saved in this age. It goes without saying that individual Jews are also being saved today, but the Church is predominately called from among Gentiles (Acts 15:14). Therefore, Paul's point is that when the Church is complete God will again begin to deal with the nation Israel.

A second reason why Israel's rejection is not permanent is that "all Israel shall be saved" (v. 26). Amillennialists are divided on the meaning of "Israel" in this verse, some holding that it refers to the Church and others that it means Jews who are individually saved today. Premillennialists believe that it refers to Jews who will be saved when the Redeemer comes out of Zion, that is, at the second coming of Christ. By any interpretation that makes Israel mean Jews it is quite clear that their rejection cannot be permanent since salvation will come to them at the return of Christ. At that same time the new covenant will be established (v. 27) and God will have mercy on His people (vv. 31-32). Thus Israel's future rests secure on the promises and nature of God.

III. The Future for the World

The eschatology of Paul is, comparatively speaking, lacking in much detail with respect to this topic which is primarily a subject of Johannine theology. What Paul does reveal could be summed up in the word *judgment*. Judgment upon the world at the return of Christ will be "in flaming fire taking vengeance on them that know not God and that obey not the gospel of our Lord Jesus Christ" (II Thess. 1:8). The result of this is the everlasting destruction of unbelievers from the presence of the Lord (II Thess. 1:9). The practical ramification of this assured fact that judgment will come upon believers is patience in the midst of persecution now. Believers who were suffering then could be assured that the wicked at whose hands the persecutions came would some day themselves be punished at the coming of the Lord.

The last days of the history of the world before the coming will also see the rise of the great deceiver, the man of sin (II Thess. 2:1-12). His appearance was associated with the Day of the Lord (II Thess. 2:2-3, A.S.V.). Paul had explicitly taught the Thessalonians that as believers they were not appointed unto the wrath of that day (I Thess. 5:1-10), but some had been deceived into thinking that the personal persecution they were experiencing meant that they were already in the Day of the Lord. Paul says that this could not be, for the Day of the Lord will not come until first there be an *apostasia,* a falling away or departure,[1] and the revelation of the man of sin. The revelation of the man of sin is further dependent on the removal of "he who restrains" (v. 7). When the restrainer is removed the man of sin will be revealed.[2] His coming is after the working of Satan with all power, signs, lying wonders, and deceit. Among other things he will sit in the temple of God demanding to be worshiped. But his doom is sure, for the Lord's coming in judgment will include the destruction of this archenemy of God. Further judgment falls on unbelievers during the reign of the man of sin in that God will send them "strong delusion" so that they will not believe the truth (vv. 11-12).

It is remarkable that whether Paul is speaking of the return of the Lord for the Church or for judgment on the world

[1] Whether the word *apostasia* means falling away, apostasy, or catching away, departure (thus referring to the rapture of the Church) may be studied with profit. Cf. E. Schuyler English, *Re-Thinking the Rapture* (Travelers Rest, S. C.: Southern Bible Book House, 1954), pp. 85-91, and Kenneth S. Wuest, "The Rapture—Precisely When?" *Bibliotheca Sacra,* January, 1957, pp. 60-69.

[2] Whoever the restrainer is, He must be more powerful than Satan, who empowers the man of sin. Only a person of the Godhead would so qualify, and since each and all of the persons of the Godhead indwell the believer (Eph. 4:6; Gal. 2:20; I Cor. 6:19), the removal of the restrainer requires the removal of believers whom He indwells. Thus the rapture of the Church must precede this tribulation period when the man of sin holds sway.

the ethical value of the doctrines are constantly being reiterated. Undoubtedly the nearness of the coming of Christ was "one of the most momentous and inspiring influences for holiness in the primitive Church. It was a call to watchfulness and prayer, a call to strenuous effort and solemn preparation."[3] Too, it preserved the elasticity of Christianity, for the apostles, under the influence of the doctrine, "never realized that they were building up a Church to last through the ages. . . . They never wrote or legislated except so far as existing needs demanded. . . . They never administered or planned with a view to the remote future."[4] The eschatology of the early Church, as especially reflected in the writings of Paul, did more than any other doctrine in giving impulse and vitality to the life of the primitive community.

IV. THE FUTURE OF THE BODY

"No other conception of his Eschatology has received such elaborate treatment at the hands of St. Paul as that of the Resurrection."[5] Due to Platonic influences the conception of life after death was not new to the educated Greek mind, and by the middle of the first century the idea had filtered down to the lower classes. However, the Greek conception of life after death or immortality was not the same as the Christian doctrine of resurrection. Immortality was a spiritual thing, for there was no place for the idea of a bodily resurrection in Greek thought. To the Greek, matter was essentially evil; thus physical death which released a man from his body was a liberation; hence, resurrection of the body would be a return to bondage. Those who accepted the bodily resurrection of Christ considered it an abnormal case which was in no wise a pattern for the Christian. Even

[3]H. A. A. Kennedy, *St. Paul's Conceptions of the Last Things* (London: Hodder and Stoughton, 1904), p. 221.
[4]W. Sanday and A. C. Headlam, *A Critical and Exegetical Commentary on the Epistle to the Romans* (New York: Charles Scribner's Sons, 1895), p. 380.
[5]Kennedy, *op. cit.*, p. 222.

in Judaism the doctrine of resurrection was not clearly defined, though it is stated in the Old Testament.[6] Thus Paul's teaching was far advanced over anything in Judaism and distinctive from anything in Hellenism.

In the classic passage on resurrection, I Corinthians 15, Paul writes of the meaning of resurrection (vv. 1-34) and the manner of it (vv. 35-58). Christ's resurrection, he writes, was no abnormal exception, but is the basis of the Gospel and the assurance of all resurrection. Christ's resurrection was testified to by many witnesses including Paul himself, who saw Jesus alive on the Damascus road. If, then, Christ be risen how can there be those who deny the fact of the resurrection of the dead? Conversely, if the dead do not rise then Christ is not risen, for He cannot be an exception (v. 13), the apostles were false witnesses of God (v. 15), faith is fruitless (v. 17), we are still in our sins (v. 17), those who have died in the faith have perished for they too are yet in their sins (v. 18), and there is not even any hope in this life (v. 19). Thus resurrection must mean the same for both Christ and the Christian; if Christ be raised the Christian's resurrection is also assured; and if there is no resurrection for the Christian then Christ could not have been raised. Resurrection cannot mean one thing in the case of Christ and another in the case of the Christian.

In describing the manner of the resurrection of the body Paul characteristically dwells on some points which we might pass over and scarcely touches others which would appeal to us. He begins with the well-known analogy of sowing seed, a popular symbol in the mystery religions and in Stoicism.[7] This is an analogy and must not be unduly pressed; nevertheless, even though the seed does not actually die, the living stalk will not be put forth by the seed until its present exist-

[6]Cf. Kennedy, *op. cit.*, pp. 223-29, and H. Buis, *The Doctrine of Eternal Punishment* (Philadelphia: Presbyterian and Reformed Publishing Co., 1957), pp. 1-32.
[7]Kennedy, *op. cit.*, pp. 241-42; cf. John 12:24.

ence dissolves or disappears. The seed must die to its existing condition in order for life to burst forth. All this is accomplished by the power of God. Thus in the illustration
of the seed Paul teaches correspondence between the present
life and the resurrection life, for the harvested grain, though
not identical with the grain sown, is of the same kind. In
other words, the resurrection must be bodily, "for God giveth
it a body as it hath pleased him, and to every seed his own
body" (v. 38).

A second illustration emphasizes difference in the resurrection body. Just as there are different kinds of flesh and
differences between terrestrial and celestial bodies, so the
resurrection body is different from the earthly one. It is
"spiritual" in contrast to "natural" (v. 44). A spiritual body
is not a disembodied spirit but a new kind of humanity, and
even in our earthly frame of reference we realize that the
word *body* is not restricted to one kind of body. Likewise in
our concept of the resurrection body we must incorporate
the idea of spiritual body so that it means neither a disembodied spirit nor flesh and blood. It is in reality a body but
of a different kind, for flesh and blood as we know it on
earth "cannot inherit the kingdom of God" (v. 50). This
kind of body is characterized as incorruptible, glorious,
powerful, spiritual, and heavenly.

In concluding this discussion Paul shows that there are
two routes to obtaining this resurrection body. The one is
the route of death—corruption putting on incorruption, and
the other is the route of translation—mortality putting on immortality (vv. 53-54). Those who see corruption are those
who die, and those who are mortal are those who are alive;
both groups, however, are changed instantly at the Lord's
coming and receive resurrection bodies. Then is death swallowed up in victory. The fact that all would not die and see
corruption but that there would be this group who would be
living at the Lord's coming to be changed from mortality

to immortality was a mystery (v. 51). Therefore, Paul could not be speaking of the second advent and the general resurrection, for those things were not unknown in Old Testament times and therefore were not mysteries; he must be speaking of the rapture of the Church, a mystery unknown to Old Testament saints.

Whatever questions Paul leaves unanswered, one fact is outstanding in his teaching on resurrection. He believed most emphatically in a bodily resurrection. It is the body which is sown in death and like the seed which brings forth that which corresponds to what was sown it is a body which God gives that is raised. It is a spiritual body, to be sure, but nonetheless an actual entity just as real as the body in which our Lord was raised (cf. Phil. 3:21). If He was seen after His resurrection so shall we be, and this could only be true of bodily resurrection. This clearly is Paul's concept of the resurrection.

As all of Paul's theology, his eschatology is theocentric. The entire Pauline system seems to be rooted and grounded in the apostle's conception of God. The future for the Church is in the hands of her sovereign Head, who will return personally to take her to be with Himself. That Israel will have a future is guaranteed by the "gifts and calling of God [which are] without repentance" (Rom. 11:29). The world will be judged because "it is a righteous thing with God to recompense tribulation to them that trouble you" (II Thess. 1:6); and the assurance of resurrection rests on the power of God who gives the body and who according to His mighty power raised Jesus from the dead (I Cor. 15:38; Eph. 1:19-20). In every area of eschatology Paul's thought reflects his basic conception of the sovereign God. The consummation of all things depends on this God who in the forging of His majestic plan made no miscalculations and who in the execution of it leaves no gaps or imperfections.

These, then, are the major themes of Pauline theology.

In surveying them one is constrained to the conclusion that as far as the fundamental principle in the thought of Paul is concerned "his whole mind was built on the foundation: *God is.*"[8] That God was to Paul an absolute sovereign, and in the revelation of Himself He has revealed the nature of man. In Pauline theology man's sinful nature, his need of salvation, and God's provision of redemption all stem from the fact that God has chosen in His grace to reveal these things and send the Saviour. The Church is governed by that Redeemer, and the Christian life is the ethical outworking in every area of living of the change which God has worked in the believer's heart. The features of the final consummation are also related to the purposes of God. The motif by which this foundational principle is displayed is Christological. It is Jesus Christ who is the epitome of the revelation of God; it is Christ who became the Redeemer from sin; it is He who is the Head of the Church and the Judge of the end time.

Paul's thought pattern in which his theology was expressed has several apparent features. The mystical element is prominent. The race condemned in Adam, the believer's position in Christ, the identification of the believer with Christ's death and resurrection all illustrate this mode of thought which may be called mystical. Furthermore, Paul's thought often moved in the sphere of legal relations (Rom. 3:21-26; 7:1-6; Gal. 4:1-7; cf. Rom. 8:15-17). Parallelism, too, found an important place in the apostle's mode of thinking and expression. Notable examples are found in Romans (1:18-32; cf. 2:1—3:20; 5:12-21) and I Corinthians (15:35-49). However, the outstanding feature is the vibrantly ethical character of all his thought and writing. His letters throb with apostolic commands, missionary zeal, pastoral counsel and comfort, earnest Christian morality, and sublimest heights of in-

[8]W. Ramsay, *The Teaching of Paul in Terms of the Present Day* (London: Hodder and Stoughton, n.d.), p. 65.

spiring expression. Whatever be the means—righteous anger, suppressed pain, wounded love, fatherly pleading, or soft entreaty—Paul's end was the same: that his readers would practice their position in Christ. The foundation of Pauline theology is God; the motif is Christ; but the expression is the great heart of the apostle himself.

Part V

THE THEOLOGY OF HEBREWS

Chapter 1

HISTORICAL BACKGROUND

THERE ARE UNUSUAL PROBLEMS which are peculiar to the Book of Hebrews. Some of them will never be solved, but all of them need to be thought about. The mental exercise of considering the various pros and cons of the problems connected with the book will contribute to the total picture the student has as he comes to study its theology. Whether solutions are found or not, there is no substitute for the benefit derived from giving consideration to the questions.

I. THE NATURE OF THE BOOK

The first problem concerns whether the Book of Hebrews is an essay or a letter. In favor of the former is the lack of a particular address at the opening of the book and the general plan of the body of the text. It appears to be more homiletical than epistolary (cf. chapter 7). However, it can be pointed out that other books in the New Testament which are definitely letters have no address (e.g., I John), and that even though the plan appears to be sermonic, nevertheless, it is a sermon with a particular group or community in mind. The book is definitely not a theoretical essay to be read just anywhere; it is a letter addressed to a particular community of people. While "the subjects themselves are of universal interest, the discussion is directed by special circumstances."[1] Therefore, one prefers to say that we are dealing with a letter.

II. THE DESTINATION OF THE LETTER

Scholars are much divided on this question, and it probably can never be decided with certainty. The less traditional view is that Rome was the original destination of the letter. It is first quoted explicitly by Clement of Rome (cir. 95). "Those of Italy" (13:24) does not really help solve the problem, for it can be translated "those in Italy" (cf. Luke 11: 13; Matt. 24:17; Col. 4:16) —meaning the writer was there too, or it may mean "those from Italy"—those who were with the writer elsewhere and who were sending their greetings back home. The more traditional view assigns Jerusalem or Palestine as the destination. This view is not without difficulties: (1) the use of the Septuagint in Old Testament quotations seems hardly consistent with Hebrew readers; (2) the readers of this Epistle were not poor (6:10; 10:34) as the saints in Jerusalem were. All things considered, this writer leans toward Rome as the destination, but whichever it was, the author of Hebrews definitely had a specific church or several house-churches in mind when he wrote.

III. THE CHARACTER OF THE RECIPIENTS

Two problems arise in connection with this question. The first is the racial background of these readers. Were they Jewish or Gentile or a mixture of both? Some hold that they were of Gentile background because of the quotations from the Septuagint and the reference in 6:1-2 to things taught which Jews would have had no need to learn.[2] A less common view is that the readers were a group of Jews and Gentiles, neither group being predominant. If this were the

[1] B. F. Westcott, *The Epistle to the Hebrews* (London: Macmillan, 1892), p. xxviii.
[2] J. Moffatt, *A Critical and Exegetical Commentary on the Epistle to the Hebrews*, International Critical Commentary (New York: Scribner's, 1924), p. 74.

case one might expect to find more mention of relationships between the two groups. The traditional view holds that the readers were predominantly Jewish in their background.[3] The title of the Epistle, the references to the prophets and angels as active agents in God's dealings with Israel, and the numerous references in the present tense to Levitical worship support this view. Indeed, "not a word suggests any alternative to Christianity except the ancestral faith of Israel."[4]

The second problem involved in this matter concerns the spiritual condition of the recipients. Because of the nature of the warnings in the Epistle some hold that the readers were professors and not possessors of Christianity.[5] One sometimes wonders if this view is an expediency for interpretation of one passage, 6:4-6, and not the result of the picture given by the entire book. These readers are called holy brethren (3:1) who have suffered for their faith (10:32), some of them even being in bonds (13:3). Undoubtedly as in every church group there were professing Christians, but the group viewed as a whole was certainly considered by the writer to be composed of those who had believed unto salvation. Their problem was not caused by mere profession but by declension from the truth possessed.

IV. THE AUTHOR

The history of discussion of the problem of authorship is lengthy and involved. There are admittedly many resemblances between the theology and style of Paul and that of Hebrews. There are also many dissimilarities. Luke, Apollos, Barnabas, Aquilla and Priscilla have also been named as candidates for author, and the arguments pro and con can be

[3]G. B. Stevens, *New Testament Theology* (Edinburgh: T. & T. Clark, 1899), p. 486; W. Manson, *The Epistle to the Hebrews*, p. 24.
[4]F. V. Filson, "The Epistle to the Hebrews," *Journal of Bible and Religion*, January 1954, p. 22.
[5]W. R. Newell, *Hebrews Verse by Verse* (Chicago: Moody Press, 1947), p. 186.

found in the commentaries. The only sure conclusion is that spoken by Origen: "Who wrote the Epistle to the Hebrews, the truth of the matter God only knows." Yet it is equally true that

> in spite of its divergences from the standard of Pauline authorship, the book has manifest Pauline affinities, and can hardly have originated beyond the Pauline circle, to which it is referred, not only by the author's friendship with Timothy (xiii. 23), but also by many unquestionable echoes of the Pauline theology . . .[6]

V. The Date

The traditional date (and more recent scholarship is returning to this view) is early—between 64 and 67. The lack of mention of the destruction of Jerusalem in the book and the fact that it is quoted authoritatively by Clement of Rome in 95 argue against a late date. There is an interesting conjecture based on chapter 3 and Psalm 95 which draws an analogy between the forty years' wandering of the children of Israel in the wilderness and the present status of the Hebrews who were approaching the fortieth anniversary of the death of Christ. This, of course, supports a date just prior to 70.

VI. The Doctrinal Circumstances of the Readers

A. *The General Circumstances*

Although a great deal is revealed about the historical, physical, and spiritual circumstances of the Hebrews, it is their doctrinal situation which forms a vital part of the background for the study of the theology of the book. We know, for instance, that these people were in a position to be generous (6:10), that some of them had been exposed to persecution (10:32; 12:3; 13:3), that they were second genera-

---

[6]W. R. Smith and H. von Soden, "Hebrews" *Encyclopaedia Biblica* (New York: Macmillan, 1914), p. 1993.

tion Christians (2:3; 13:7), and that they had failed to grow spiritually in proportion to the time that they had been believers (5:12; 6:1; 10:25).

B. *The Specific Circumstances*

But the doctrinal circumstance in which these people found themselves was one of religious drift. They had made their confession of Christ; now they were drifting from those moorings, and were being exhorted to hold fast to their original confession. This circumstance of drifting is vividly underscored by the writer's use of nautical terms in the Epistle. In 2:1 he exhorts them to be careful lest they drift away, loose their moorings, and drift out to sea. In 3:6 he encourages them to hold fast or be firmly moored. In 6:19 he declares that our hope is an anchor for the soul, sure and steadfast. In 10:38 the readers are warned against drawing back—literally, shortening their sail. In 11:27 Moses is held up as an example for one who endured or who held steadily on course. In 13:9 is the warning against being carried away or swept about with the current or tide. The spiritual tide for these people was at a low ebb, for it was going out away from Christ and carrying them along with it. Against this they are warned.

C. *The Causes and Cures*

With equal clarity the author sets forth the reasons for this drifting.

1. *Formalism.* There is always present in religious life the danger of regarding religion as the fulfillment of certain outward acts. This the Hebrews had done, dwelling in the shadows rather than upon the substance (10:1-4). The cure for this is the realization that the essence of worship is a meeting with God directly.

2. *Familiarity.* These people were evidently Christians of long standing, but spiritually and intellectually they had

grown sluggish (2:3; 5:11-12; 6:12). They had lost their first love and familiarity with their faith was breeding contempt. The cure for this is to see the splendor and grandeur of one's faith. It involves taking earnest heed of the things once known (2:1) and pondering daily the wonders of the Saviour (12:3). The romance of orthodoxy is cultivated only by going to Bethlehem, Calvary, and the Tomb. Stagnation is overcome only by pressing on, for there is no such thing on earth as a finished Christian. Knowing Christ is not a finished proposition like knowing a geometric theorem.

3. *Persecution.* Some of the readers had evidently been subjected to persecution, and this had dulled the zeal of others. The Epistle was written about the same time as thousands of Christians were perishing under Nero's persecution, and even though these people had not yet themselves been persecuted unto death, the increasing danger was hindering their spiritual growth. For this the writer prescribes patience (12:1, 13) —the kind which is produced by remembering their own past (6:10; 10:32; 13:7), by remembering the examples of faith in the Old Testament (11), and by remembering the sufferings of their Lord (12:2; 13:12).

4. *Compromise.* Into the lives of some had crept the subtlety of compromise. For some it meant dabbling in strange doctrines (13:9) while for others it was not a matter of doctrines but of lowering the ethical standard (10:33). They needed to remember that the truth is the same (13:8) yet never becomes monotonous.

If we were to seek in the Epistle a summary statement of the cure for religious drift it would be found in the writer's summons to a renewed commitment in 13:13: "Let us go forth therefore unto him without the camp, bearing his reproach." Outside the camp means not only outside Judaism's ritual but also outside Judaism's safety. The camp in the wilderness was an oasis of safety, while the way to Canaan was full of unknown and dangerous pitfalls. Some wanted to stay in the camp instead of proceeding to the promised land. So it was with God's people under the New Covenant. Remaining inside a static camp is more attractive than moving out into the world, calling others to follow Him, and moving on in one's own spiritual life and growth. The call is to an aggressive and advancing faith in the midst of a Christ-rejecting world.

Drifting was the peril in which these people were engulfed. The causes are all too commonly prevalent in the life of the Church in every day and country, but the cure is just as effective now as it was then.

Chapter 2

THEOLOGY PROPER AND CHRISTOLOGY

ONE'S CONCEPTION OF GOD will color his entire theology. Undoubtedly the Christology of Hebrews is one of the central theological themes of the book. But before looking at the author's development of that doctrine, we must first examine briefly what he says about the other persons of the Godhead.

I. THE IDEA OF GOD

A. *He Is a Living God* (3:12; 9:14; 10:31; 12:22)

The construction in all four references is anarthrous, emphasizing the character of God as one who is living. People may back off from Him, serve Him, fall into His hands, or come unto His city.

B. *He Is Enthroned in the Highest* (1:3; 8:1)

In both references "Majesty" seems to be a synonymous name for God, and as such He is enthroned in Heaven.

C. *He Is Holy Energy* (12:29; 4:12-13; 12:14)

Fire is not used in the figure as a picture of the way God manifests Himself, but to describe His very nature. As such He burns up all that is unworthy in those who serve Him.

D. *He Is Lord* (8:2, 11)

The Old Testament idea expressed by *Adonai,* a possessive plural, is reiterated here. Majesty and ownership are the two ideas conveyed by this word.

E. *He Is Absolutely Righteous*

As the writer to the Hebrews employs this concept it includes the ideas of punishment (2:2), reward (6:7, 10), and faithfulness (10:23; 11:11).

The foregoing all express Old Testament concepts of God and show how deeply the writer's own idea was rooted there.

F. *He Is a God of Peace* (13:20)

He becomes the author and giver of peace when the way of access to Him is opened through the blood. The unapproachable God—generally speaking—of the Old Testament has opened the way through the gift of His Son and brought peace to man.

G. *He Is Love* (12:5 ff.)

This aspect of God's character is spoken of in connection with the believer's chastening.

II. THE HOLY SPIRIT

A. *His Deity*

The deity of the Holy Spirit is seen in the following ways:

1. *He is called God.* In 4:4 ff. the same words attributed to God are those which were ascribed to the Spirit in 3:7 ff. Thus the Holy Spirit must be God.

2. *He performs the works of God.* The Spirit was the one who gave the Scriptures (3:7; 9:8; 10:15) and He indwells believers (6:4).

3. *It is possible to blaspheme the Spirit* (10:29).

B. *His Work*

1. *He gives gifts* (2:4). First generation Christians were given gifts from the Holy Spirit (this is a subjective genitive) which enabled them to perform extraordinary acts.

2. *He is the Author of Scripture* (3:7; 9:8; 10:15). This is the most frequently mentioned work of the Holy Spirit in Hebrews, and it is characteristic of the book that the origin of Scripture is ascribed to the divine author and not the human authors.

3. *He indwells believers* (6:4). Since the word *partaker* is the same as used in 12:8 it means more than simply "going along with." It "marks more than the simple fact of participation (c. vii. 13; I Cor. x. 17). It brings out the fact of a personal character gained; and that gained in a vital development."[1] To partake of the Spirit is to possess Him.

4. *He gives grace* (10:29). Grace finds expression through the Spirit.[2]

Certain general observations may be made concerning this doctrine. (1) Quite obviously from these seven references in the entire book, the Holy Spirit is in the background in Hebrews, and the Son is in the foreground. (2) Conviction of sin which elsewhere in the New Testament is particularly ascribed to the Spirit is in Hebrews made a matter of relationship of the sinner to a living God. This is true of both unbelievers (3:12; 10:31) and believers (9:14; 12: 22). (3) Sanctification which is generally thought of in relation to the Spirit is in Hebrews primarily the separation unto God effected by the death of Christ (10:10, 14; 13:12).

III. The Christology of Hebrews

The Christology of Hebrews—one of the central themes

---

[1]B. F. Westcott, *The Epistle to the Hebrews* (London: The Macmillan Co., 1892), p. 149.

[2]Some would add a fifth work of the Spirit, namely, the part He played in the death of Christ (9:14). At best, however, it is a debatable reference to the Spirit, for it very likely refers to Christ's human spirit (cf. Westcott, *op. cit.*, pp. 261-62).

of the book—is more incidentally than systematically developed as a result of the warning of the book against drifting and the statement of the glories of the New Covenant. The writer's concern about their drifting from Christ, the mediator of the New Covenant, would naturally bring, in the course of his message, a thorough, if unsystematic, statement of the doctrine of Christ.

A. *The Names and Titles of Christ*

1. *His names.*

a. Christ. This is the most frequently used name of the Lord in Hebrews (as in Paul's writings). When used without the article it is a proper name (3:6; 9:11, 24), while the presence of the article generally incorporates the idea of His office as Messiah (3:14; 5:5; 6:1; 9:14, 28; 11:26).

b. Jesus. The human name is used eight times in the Epistle (2:9; 3:1; 6:20; 7:22; 10:19; 12:2, 24; 13:12), and in each case it furnishes the key to the argument of the passage in which it stands. For instance, in 2:9 ff. we are told that man's lost dominion will be regained in Jesus the Son of Man. In other instances it is related to His priesthood and the necessity for perfect and glorified humanity.

c. Other names of Christ used in Hebrews in common with the rest of the New Testament are Lord Jesus (13:20), Jesus Christ (10:10; 13:8, 21), Jesus the Son of God (4:14), and Lord (2:3; 7:14).

d. Especially distinctive of this Epistle, however, are three names of Christ. (1) Son (1:2, 5, 8; 3:6; 5:5, 8; 7:28). With the exception of 1:8 the form is always without the article in order to fix the reader's attention on the nature, not the personality, of the Son. The writer is displaying one whose character is a Son. (2) Son of God (6:6; 7:3; 10:29). This is a formal designation of the second Person. (3) Priest and high priest (5:6; 7:3, 11, 17, 21; 8:4; 10:21; 2:17; 3:1; 4:14-15; 5:10; 6:20; 7:26; 8:1; 9:11). The frequency of this name stems from the systematic treatment of the doctrine of the priesthood of Christ.

2. *Titles.* The distinctive titles of Hebrews are all soteriological. They are: mediator of the New Covenant (8:6; 9:15; 12:24); ground of eternal salvation (5:9); author of eternal salvation (2:10); forerunner (6:20); apostle and high priest of our confession (3:1); great shepherd of the sheep (13:20) and firstborn (1:6).

B. *The Pre-existence of Christ*

The doctrine of pre-existence is related to that of the deity of Christ, which in turn is vitally connected with the doctrine of priesthood, which is so important in this Epistle. Therefore, the proof of pre-existence finds an important place in the writer's theology.

1. *Proved by Christ's works.* Before the incarnation Christ was working; therefore, He was pre-existent. He was the one who made the ages (1:2) and who is the continuous support of all things (1:3).

2. *Proved by Christ's eternal generation* (1:5-6; 5:5; cf. 7:3). This is the really conclusive argument for pre-existence. There is no question about the meaning of generation in these texts; the question concerns the meaning of "today." In the second Psalm, from which the quotations are taken, the begetting is connected with the day of the decree. Thus if it be granted that the decree is eternal it must follow that the begetting of the Son was also eternal. However, it is argued from 5:5-6 that eternal generation is not in view but rather appointment to sonship by resurrection, since verse 6 concerns the Melchizedek priesthood. However, the emphasis of the passage is on the one who appoints, God, for He, God, who declared the eternal generation of the Son (v. 5) is the same one who appointed that Son as priest (v. 6).

3. *Proved by Christ's heavenly origin* (10:5-7). The pas-

sage makes little sense unless it is a pre-existent one who came into the world and for whom a body was prepared.

Whatever we may think about these texts, it is apparent that the author considered the Son to be pre-existent or eternally generated. The only way to escape this conclusion is arbitrarily to avoid the meaning of "today" in 1:5 and 5:5. But in such a course of action the Biblical theologian would be unfaithful to his task.

C. *The Deity of Christ*

If pre-existence is the first step, deity is the second step which leads to the important doctrine of the priesthood of Christ. The proofs for Christ's deity are incidentally, rather than systematically, presented, but the overwhelming number of them shows how deeply rooted was the concept in the writer's mind.

1. *Proved by His names.* These names have already been discussed, but it must be remembered that they constitute a proof of deity. Notice especially the names *Son of God, firstborn, Lord, author of eternal salvation,* and *great shepherd of the sheep.*

2. *Proved by His attributes and characteristics.*

a. Effulgence of glory (1:3). The Son is said to be in His essential nature the brightness of God not in the sense of a reflection but of a shining forth, which means that He has it within Himself to shine forth. The glory of God is the manifestation of God's attributes, and since Christ manifests them in and of Himself, He must be God.

b. Image (1:3). The Son is the express image of God's essence; thus He is God.

c. Omnipotence (1:3, 13). All things are supported by Him—something no mere man can do.

d. Impeccability (4:15; 7:26). Christ was holy, sinless, stainless, and separate from contact with sinners. He had no sin nature (4:15—apart from sin) and in that He possessed a different human nature from that which we possess. That does not mean that His temptations were unreal; indeed they were more real, for He could have turned stones into bread, for instance, which is something we cannot do. He was tempted because of His likeness to us in becoming flesh, but not in every particular in which we are tested. In the things of Christ's humanity where He seems to be closest to us He is actually farthest from us. In things of Christ's deity where He seems to be farthest from us, He is closest to us. He was absolutely holy and thus incapable of sin.

e. Immutability and eternity (1:12; 13:8). All change but He is the same forever.

3. *Proved by His works.* Works are also attributed to the Son which can only be done by God; therefore, He must be God. For instance, He is the Creator (1:2, 10; 11:3) and upholder of all things (1:3, 12); He is the author of salvation for men (2:10; 5:9; 7:25; 9:12); He is the deliverer from the power of death (2:14-15); He overcame the Devil (2:14-15); and He is the one who sanctifies (2:11; 9:13-14; 13:12).

4. *Proved by the worship given to Him.* Both men and angels worship the Son (1:6; 13:20-21), proving He is God.

Some observations should be made concerning these proofs of the deity of the Son. (1) They are inclusive in their number. All the standard proofs are found in the book. (2) They are conclusive because they are based on many references which state things that can only be true of God. (3) They are scattered throughout the entire book. Therefore, these facts show not only the deity of Christ but the primary place that doctrine had in the mind of the writer.

D. *The Humanity of Jesus*

For a book which is generally thought of as stressing the deity of Christ there is a great deal said about His humanity. It is also interesting (especially if the writer were not an eyewitness) how many references there are in the Epistle to events in the earthly life of Christ. His incarnation (2:14, 17), ancestry (7:14), persecution (12:3), agony in Gethsemane (5:7), crucifixion (13:12), resurrection (13:20), and ascension (1:2-3) are all referred to.

1. *His human nature was real.* The reality of the humanity of Christ is displayed by the author in his many references to human traits which were exhibited in Christ. He was dependent on God (2:13); He exhibited mercy and faithfulness (2:17); He was humble (5:5); He was reverent (5:7); He prayed in dependence on God (5:7); He was obedient (5:8; 10:7); He developed into maturity (5:8); He partook of flesh and blood (2:14); and He was the epitome of the life of faith (12:2). In all of these characteristics He reflects real humanity.

2. *His human nature was shared in common with man.* Because He was human He shared certain things with all of mankind. Our frail nature He took upon Himself (4:15). This subjected Him to sufferings (5:8; 12:3; 13:12), sorrow (5:7; 4:15; 12:2), temptations (2:18; 4:15), and death (2:14). Only grace can account for His taking the nature of man and sharing the resultant consequences.

3. *His human nature was perfect.* Christ was human but not as we are, for His humanity was perfect. The writer is careful to state this and relate it to His essential nature (7:26; 4:15). Furthermore, the Lord's perfect human nature was demonstrated so through His suffering and discipline (2:10; 5:7; 7:28).

E. *The Superiority of Christ*

"All that the author says about Christ has as its presupposition His Divine Sonship."[3] This is underscored by showing His specific superiority. This is a necessary part of the writer's argument in showing the superiority of the better

[3]H. A. A. Kennedy, *The Theology of the Epistles* (London: Duckworth, 1919), p. 202.

covenant, for the supremacy of the covenant involved the supremacy of its mediator:

> The author, however, is not content with a general ex-hibition of Christ's sovereignty as Revealer of God. For his concern is to show how the later revelation over-shadows and antiquates the earlier. Therefore he draws a contrast in detail between the new and final Mediator between God and men, and those temporary mediators to whom his readers were inclined to attach undue im-portance.[4]

First he shows how Christ is superior to the prophets of the Old Testament (1:1-3). It is not that they are depre-cated, for God did speak through them, but there were two defects. Revelation through the prophets was neither final (for it was always progressing throughout the periods of Israel's history) nor full (for only Christ is the effulgence of God's glory).

Second, he shows the superiority of the Son over angels (1:4—2:18). Again there is no disparagement of angels, but the writer simply points out the differences. Angels will wor-ship the Son (1:5-6); therefore, He must be superior. An-gels were concerned with the giving of the Law, but Christ brought grace to men (2:1-4). Angels could never bring to men, as the Son did, the new relationship of brethren (2: 5-8), the new release from the fear of death (2:14-16), or the new redemption from sin (2:17-18).

Third, he shows the superiority of Christ to Moses (3:1—4:13). The difference is the difference between building and Builder, between servant and Son, member and Master, the provisional and permanent. High honor is accorded to Moses but he is thrown into the shadows by the light of the Son.

Finally, the author contrasts Christ with the priests of the Old Testament. Again he does not minimize their valuable

Ibid., p. 203.

function, but they too were deficient in comparison with God's priest after the order of Melchizedek. They were mortal and sinful, their sanctuary was inadequate, and their sacrifices were insufficient.

In all of these contrasts the writer is seeking to fortify his readers' loyalty to Christ the Mediator of the New Covenant.

F. *The Offices of Christ*

The principal attention of the book is given to the priestly office of Christ which will be discussed in full later. The prophetic and kingly offices are mentioned but briefly. As prophet (1:2) the Son speaks in this present period of history. As King He shall be worshiped by the angels when He comes again (1:6).

F. *The Exaltation of Christ*

Again the chief emphasis of the Epistle in this area is related to the priesthood of Christ in the stress the writer places on the present session of the Lord at the right hand of God (1:3; 8:1; 10:12; 12:2). The resurrection is mentioned specifically in only one place (13:20) although it is obviously implied in all the passages dealing with the present session of the Lord. The ascension is mentioned with some frequency because it is the gateway to the present high priestly ministry (4:14; 6:20; 9:11, 24). It involved passing through the lower heavens into Heaven itself (4:14).

Since Biblical Theology is concerned with discovering the thought of the writer concerned, it must be apparent that the writer of Hebrews held the same "higher Christology"—as it has been called—as Paul and John. That is, he believed that the Lord was both human and divine and had no hesitancy about applying the titles *God* and *Lord* to Jesus—titles which were perfectly familiar to him as designations of deity.

However others may attempt to do away with this conclusion[5] this was the evident thought of the author; and to discover that, not the opinion of interpreters, is the task of Biblical Theology.

[5]As Beyschlag, *New Testament Theology* (Edinburgh: T. & T. Clark, 1899), II, 313-15.

Chapter 3

THE PRIESTHOOD OF CHRIST

THE DOCTRINES OF CHRISTOLOGY and high priesthood are vitally interrelated in the Epistle to the Hebrews. Nowhere else in the New Testament is the title *priest* or *high priest* applied to Christ (though the idea is certainly present in such passages as John 17 and Revelation 1). The doctrine of the priesthood of Christ is the outstanding doctrine of the Epistle, and it is undoubtedly that which most people reading the book think of first. In the historical circumstances which called forth the Epistle it was the most important doctrine about which the author wrote, for its truth was unrealized, if not new, to the believers to whom he wrote. Though they had trusted the atoning work of Christ, the full realization of the priestly nature of that work and of the present ministry of the priest had not dawned on their consciousnesses. This is almost a paradox, for it should have been this very aspect of the truth of the work of Jesus Christ which appealed to these believers particularly, for with their background in the Old Testament they had been accustomed to think of priesthood and priestly functions. And yet these were the very things that they had failed to see in their Saviour.

The teaching concerning the person of the high priest is found mainly in the section from 4:14 to 7:28. However, references to His work are scattered throughout the whole Epistle. In this entire section it is obvious that the Jewish sacrificial arrangements furnish the background for the presentation of the work of Christ.

> The Jewish sacrificial system belonged to the world of picture and symbol; Christ's sacrifice belongs to the world of eternal spiritual reality. The words by which it is described are Jewish, but the writer takes all possible pains to make his readers understand that they are used in a higher than the Jewish meaning. He sees in the death of Christ a wealth of divine truth at which the Old Testament sacrifices could only vaguely hint.[1]

I. THE QUALIFICATIONS FOR THE OFFICE OF HIGH PRIEST (5:1-10)

A. *He Had To Be a Man* (v. 1)

Christ's incarnation qualified Him to serve, for in it He took upon Himself the nature of man.

B. *He Had To Be Compassionate* (v. 2)

Although the Mosaic Law did not specifically state this qualification it is inherent in the priest's duty to judge the people in matters concerning sin. In this the priest had to have gentle consideration because he was compassed about with weakness.

C. *He Had To Be Chosen by God* (vv. 4-6)

Written in the days when the high priests were chosen carelessly for political considerations, this was a striking statement. Christ qualified because the God who eternally begat Him also chose Him a priest forever. The quotation from Psalm 2 attests to the authority, not to the time, of the calling by God of Christ to be a priest.

D. *He Had To Be Prepared* (vv. 7-8)

Since men suffer, they need a sympathizing high priest, and since sympathy can only be genuinely exercised by one

[1] G. B. Stevens, *The Theology of the New Testament* (London: Richard B. Dickinson, 1894), p. 512.

who has suffered himself, our Lord had to learn of suffering and obedience. There is no record of Christ ever laughing, though in these verses is one of the several mentions of His weeping.

II. THE ORDER OF THE PRIESTHOOD OF CHRIST

A. *The Point of the Melchizedek Priesthood*

The point is simply that this priesthood of Christ is a Melchizedekan one, not an Aaronic one. The writer of Hebrews offers no proof for this except the quotation of Psalm 110. (This shows again the high concept he had of the inspiration and authority of the Word.) For these Jewish readers this was sufficient evidence. This fact enables him to say that Christ is another kind of priest (7:15). The emphasis is on the personality of the priest and not on the functions performed. This revelation of a different order of priesthood has two ramifications: (1) it explains why only certain things are said about Melchizedek, i.e., so that Christ could be compared accurately to him; and (2) it obliterates the artificial distinctions usually raised concerning the Aaronic and Melchizedekan priesthoods. It is not that Christ was a priest in His person after the order of Melchizedek and in His work after the order of Aaron. He was never a priest in any sense after the Aaronic order nor could He be. Some of the things He did were foreshadowed in the Aaronic arrangements, so that some of the features of the Aaronic order are legitimate types of the priestly functions of Christ, but that is quite a different thing from saying that Christ is a priest after the order of Aaron.

B. *The Portraiture of Melchizedek* (7:1-3; Gen. 14)

The writer sets forth certain facts concerning Melchizedek's life and then says that he was "made like unto the Son of God" (v. 3). The grammatical form of "made like" is not an adjective as if Melchizedek were like Christ in His being (which would lend support to the idea that he was a theophany), but a participle which means that the likeness is in the Biblical writer's statement. The comparison is between Christ and the limited revelation given concerning Melchizedek, the specifics of which concern the manner of Melchizedek's appearing in the priesthood and not the manner or nature of his birth or life. The portraiture is a limited one in order that the resemblance may be extensive.

C. *The Particulars of the Melchizedek Priesthood*

In the likening of Melchizedek to Christ, certain particulars concerning the Melchizedekan priesthood stand out.

1. *It was royal.* The line of priests which came from Aaron were only priests, but Melchizedek was a king as well as a priest.

2. *It was individual.* As far as the record goes Melchizedek appears without mention of father and mother. Ancestry was unnecessary to justify his claims to be a priest, for his appointment was independent of human relationships. It was not so with the Aaronic priests who rested on their ancestry (Ezra 2:61 ff., Neh. 7:64).

3. *It was timeless.* Again the record mentions no beginning or end of Melchizedek's life, previewing Him who abideth a priest continually after the order of Melchizedek.

4. *It was inclusive.* Melchizedek was a priest of the Most High God, a name of God which associates Him with all peoples. Evidently he was one of the last such priests, for he was a contemporary of Abraham, who fathered the exclusive Aaronic priesthood which ministered to one nation only.

In all these particulars Jesus is also a priest, for He too is a king, His priesthood stands on His individual merits, it is eternal, and it affects all who will come unto God by Him.

D. *The Pre-eminence of the Melchizedek Priesthood*

Having established the order to which Christ belongs, the

writer proceeds to prove that the Melchizedek priesthood is the superior order.

1. *The proof of superiority.* The proof is twofold. Because Melchizedek blessed Abraham he assumed the part of the superior (7:7). It is noteworthy that this happened at the height of Abraham's career. Because Melchizedek took tithes from Abraham his priesthood is superior to the Aaronic order. The picture the author draws in this proof is a remarkable one:

> He beholds generation after generation of the Levitical priests during the whole period of the Mosaic economy passing before Him, and exercising the privileges of their divinely-appointed order. Each generation is maintained by its tithe; and as, man after man, each member of the priesthood dies, another steps into his place, claims his rights, and is honoured with the cheerful submission of the people to his claims. But in the midst of all this change, exalted above all this frailty, he beholds another figure, a venerable priest of an altogether different kind . . . the Melchizedek who is the shadow of the coming High-priest of God's final dispensation of grace, floating as it were in a heavenly, not an earthly, atmosphere, and receiving tithes from the father of the faithful of all ages. . . .[2]

2. *The points of superiority.*

a. The priesthood is new and better (7:15; cf. 7:7, 19, 22; 8:6). If the writer can make his readers see this, he can then make them see the change that has been wrought in the Mosaic Law.

b. The priesthood is indissoluble (7:16). The Mosaic priesthood depended on natural fleshly generation to sustain it; the Melchizedek priesthood of Christ is based on an indissoluble life.

c. The priesthood is inviolable (7:24). Literally, the

[2] G. Milligan, *The Theology of the Epistle to the Hebrews* (Edinburgh: T. & T. Clark, 1899), p. 118.

word *inviolable* means that no one can step across into Christ's priesthood. Because He is complete in Himself He is also able to save completely (v. 25).

d. The priesthood is eternal (7:20-28). With an oath God has affirmed it (vv. 20-22), and by the resurrection assured it (vv. 23-24).

e. The priesthood is based on a better covenant (8:6; 6: 13). The Aaronic priesthood was related to a covenant dependent on conditions; the work of Christ is unconditional.

f. The priesthood is related to a better realm. The Old Testament and all of its services belonged to the realm of the typical; the New Testament with its high priest belongs to the realm of reality (2:10; 4:14; 6:20; 8:1-5). The Aaronic priests ministered in an earthly sanctuary on earth; Christ ministers in the heavenly sanctuary.

III. The New Covenant

The idea of covenant is frequently mentioned in the Epistle. The Old Covenant with Israel, the Mosaic Law, figures in the discussion concerning the tabernacle (9:1-10). The New Covenant with Israel prophesied by Jeremiah (31:31-34) is prominent in the discussion of chapter 8. A better covenant is spoken of in 8:6 and 7:22 and the everlasting covenant in 13:20. Of the New Covenant Jesus is the Mediator (9:15; 12:24) because of the shedding of His blood by which He ratified it (9:16-20).

The principal point of the writer is plain: these Jewish believers were to look no longer to the Mosaic covenant with its services and priesthood, for now they had something better in Christ. What the old had to do repeatedly and could never do finally Jesus had done once and for all. His death, the necessary basis for the establishing of the new covenant, had brought in better promises than they had ever had in Judaism.

This much is clear. What is debated is the author's purpose in quoting Jeremiah 31 in chapter 8. The amillennialist says that this proves that he expected the Church to fulfill these promises made originally to Israel, thereby obviating the need for a future millennial age. Some premillennialists see the Church entering into the blessings of the New Covenant with Israel. Other premillennialists say that there is only one New Covenant and that with Israel, but the Church's promises are based on the *blood* of the New Covenant but not on the New Covenant itself. This interpretation would not find too many difficulties in Hebrews but strains the interpretation of II Corinthians 3. The other premillennial interpretation recognizes a New Covenant with Israel which will yet have its fulfillment in the millennium and a New Covenant with the Church, both of which are based on the sacrifice of Christ. The New Covenant with the Church is that better covenant of which the author speaks. In any case, the prophecy of Jeremiah is quoted in chapter 8 in order to emphasize that even the Old Testament predicted the end of the Mosaic covenant. The author's point of quoting is plainly stated in his conclusion: "In that he saith, A new, he hath made the first old" (v. 13). In the fact that God through Jeremiah had said that a New Covenant coming He made the Mosaic Law old even before the time of Christ. The New Covenant under which the Church is blessed is not the same as that which Jeremiah promised, for that is yet to be fulfilled to the house of Israel and the house of Judah as prophesied.

IV. THE HIGH PRIESTLY WORK OF CHRIST

It has already been pointed out that Christ, being a priest after the order of Melchizedek, could never be related to the Aaronic order. Even that which He did was done as a Melchizedekan priest. Nevertheless, priestly functions of the Aaronic could and do foreshadow in type those things which

---

[3]For further discussion and references see the author's *The Basis of the Premillennial Faith* (New York: Loizeaux, 1953), pp. 105-25.

Christ, the Melchizedekan priest, also performed. Christ can and does fulfill Aaronic types, but He as fulfiller has no other relationship to that order. Even in fulfilling the typical features of the work of the Aaronic priests, Christ's work was different for He did not offer anything for Himself and His offering of Himself was once for all.

A. *The Background of the High Priestly Work*

In the background of 8:1—9:18 the writer views the Jewish high priest at the moment of his greatest glory when he appeared for all the people on the Day of Atonement. This was the great day accompanied by the only fast prescribed by law for Israel on which a certain ritual was carefully followed as set down in the Old Testament and added to somewhat by traditions practiced at the time of Christ (Lev. 16). In the ritual as practiced then the high priest began his rites of personal purification and preparation seven days before Atonement. Twice during that period he was sprinkled with the ashes of the red heifer (cf. 9:13). On the great day he donned his white linen garments as he approached the presence of God in the Holiest. Then followed the ritual of killing a bullock for his own sins and those of all the priests, sprinkling incense to save him from death, sprinkling the blood on and before the mercy seat, killing a goat for the people and sprinkling its blood as before, confessing sin over the head of the live goat which was then sent into the wilderness, and offering the burnt offerings for himself and all the people.[4] This is the background against which this section of Hebrews stands, and glorious as the Day of Atonement was in the lives of God's ancient people, that glory had faded in the light of the better covenant founded on better promises and mediated by a better sacrifice.

[4]The detail of the ritual should be studied from Leviticus 16 and a work such as A. Edersheim, *The Temple, Its Ministry and Services* (London: Religious Tract Society, 1908), pp. 302-29.

B. *The Base of the High Priestly Work*

The work of the Aaronic priest was carried on in the old tabernacle (9:1-5) in which there was inadequate access, the veil shutting God in and the people out. Separation and limitation are the writer's chief points in mentioning the furniture of the tabernacle in this passage. The arrangement under the Old Covenant even shut out the Lord Himself, for His tribe disqualified Him (8:4-5). If the Mosaic Law is in force today then Jesus Christ cannot be our high priest (7:11-14). His base of operations has to be in another place and under another covenant.

Our Lord ministers in the new tabernacle (8:1-5). This concept of the heavenly tabernacle is difficult to grasp since our minds are limited by conceptions of time and space. The true tabernacle is real and perfect—Heaven itself—and that in which Christ ministers today. Reality must be divorced from materiality in this concept.

C. *The Basis of the High Priestly Work*

The high priestly work of Christ is based on His death.

1. *The relation of the death of Christ to His present work.* The writer of Hebrews reiterates the completed once-for-all character of the death of Christ (7:27; 9:12, 25-26; 10:12) and declares this to be the basis of the present ministry (8: 3-5). Christ's offering was once at Calvary (note the aorist in 8:3), and on the basis of that He exercises His present ministry in Heaven. Milligan erroneously insists that Christ continues to present His life to the Father and explains that the reason the offering can never be repeated is simply because it has never come to an end. His reasoning is based on the misconception of the offering, for it was an offering of death, not an offering of His life. As Melchizedekan priest His work of offering Himself was completed when He died,

although it is true that His work of sustaining His people continues in Heaven today.[5]

2. *The relation of the blood of Christ to His sacrifice.* The sacrifice was a sacrifice of blood (9:7, 12), which was shed at Calvary and not taken into Heaven.

> The use of *dia* [in 9:12] as marking the means but not defining the mode (*meta*) is significant when taken in connection with v. 7 (*ou choris*). The earthly High-priest took with him the material blood: Christ "through His own blood" entered into the Presence of God, but we are not justified in introducing any material inter-pretations of the manner in which He made it effica-cious.[6]

3. *The relation of the body of Christ to His sacrifice.* The body which the Lord took was the instrument for fulfilling God's will (10:5-10). The action on His part was that of a voluntary slave.

D. *The Benefits of the Death of Christ*

Throughout the book are scattered references to the bene-fits of the work of Christ.

1. *He delivers from an evil conscience* (10:22).
2. *He purifies from the stains of guilt* (9:22; 10:22).
3. *He sanctifies* (10:10, 14; 13:12).
4. *He perfects* (10:14; 11:39-40; 12:21).

> He who is *teleios* [perfect] has reached the end which is in each case set before him, maturity of growth, com-plete development of powers, full enjoyment of privi-leges, perfect possession of knowledge.[7]

When the writer declares that the Christian is "perfect" he is expressing the Pauline idea of being righteous in Christ.

5. *He gives the privilege of access* (4:16; 7:25; 10:19-20; 11:6).

[5]Cf. Milligan, *op. cit.*, pp. 140-43.
[6]B. F. Westcott, *The Epistle to the Hebrews*, pp. 258-59.
[7]*Ibid.*, p. 65.

6. *He enables us to serve* (9:14).

7. *He enables us to worship* (13:15-16).

The priesthood of Christ is the central doctrine of Hebrews. The Christology is subordinate because preparatory. The doctrine of the Christian life is a result of the work of the priest in bringing believers into the relationships of the better covenant. The apprehension of the truth of a high priest whose one sacrifice and continuing ministry is the essence of Christianity was the necessary antidote for the ills of these readers.

Chapter 4

THE CHRISTIAN LIFE

A DISTINGUISHING CHARACTERISTIC OF HEBREWS is the prominence which it gives to the Christian life as a practical outworking of the better covenant relationship. Indeed, the writer describes this entire work as an exhortation (13:22). The work of the high priest as mediator of the New Covenant should issue in a Christian walk that is characterized by certain distinctives.

I. IT IS A LIFE OF FAITH (11:1-40)

A. *The Description of Faith* (11:1)

Faith as described by the author gives substance to things hoped for and demonstrably provable reality to things unseen. Faith does not create things in the unseen world of experience, but faith assures the reality of their existence. The Christian life is lived in the assurance of the reality of those things which are even outside the range of the believer's present experience.

B. *The Different Kinds of Faith*

The author speaks of different kinds of faith or of faith which effects different results.

1. *Intellectual faith* (11:6). Faith in the existence of God is basic to everything else. Without this no one can go on to experience the accomplishments of faith.

2. *Saving faith.* Saving faith is illustrated by the writer in the actions of Abel (v. 4), Abraham (v. 8), Rahab (v. 31), and Moses (v. 28). Today it is effected by the proper relationship to Christ (3:1; 5:9; 10:23). The writer makes synonymous disobedience and unbelief in the Epistle (3:12, 18-19; 4:6, 11; 5:9; 10:26).

3. *Ethical faith.* Saving faith results in the Christian's life in proper ethical conduct. This is illustrated by most of chapter 11, and those who serve as illustrations show clearly that (1) such faith produces actions of a manly character, (2) it is costly (cf. 13:13), and (3) it is the essence of the Christian life. Growing unto perfection must involve becoming more childlike in faith.

Faith is the path that leads to a life of rest (3:7–4:13), for the believing Christian is the yielded Christian, and the yielded life is the restful life. Only the sin of unbelief can rob of rest.

II. It Is a Life of Growth

Attention has already been drawn to the teaching of the Epistle against drifting in general. In addition the writer speaks of specific things which are to be left behind and certain things which are to be gained in the process of normal Christian growth.

A. *Certain Things Are To Be Left Behind* (6:1-3)

In the process of growth it is not a question of forgetting certain things but of assuming them as settled and then going on. Rudiments are not to be despised but there must be a progressive building on those rudiments. The author mentions six things specifically which are rudimentary—repentance and faith, baptisms and laying on of hands, and resurrection and eternal judgment. Important as these doctrines are, they are part of the foundation of the Christian life, and one takes the foundation for granted after it has been laid and does not keep going back to it relaying it again and again.

B. *Certain Things Are to Be Gained* (5:11-14)

As life grows the believer should develop a sensitive hearing of things hard to be interpreted (v. 11). Too, he should show ability in teaching instead of having to be taught all the time (v. 12). He should display skill in discussing the larger problems of Christian thought (v. 13). This maturity should manifest itself in the proper use of all of the believer's faculties—especially the ability to discriminate between that which is good and that which is evil for the soul (vv. 13-14). These are the marks of progress.

III. It Is a Life of no Retreat (6:4-6)

It is not the task of Biblical Theology to state all the views of a given passage but to endeavor to express the thought of the author. If the background of the Epistle is as has been suggested, the author is still speaking to Jewish believers. There may have been a few professing people in the group or groups, but they were the exception, for the great majority were true believers. He certainly does not say that a person can be saved, lost, and saved again. If he could be lost it would be impossible to be saved again. That is clear. Neither is he speaking hypothetically; this is a severe warning concerning a very real danger. Therefore, the author, writing to believers who were drifting, argues in this passage concerning (1) the impossibility of renewal (2) in view of their spiritual position and privilege (3) in the event a lapse could occur (4) for the reasons stated. In other words, he warns these people that they must go on in the Christian life because they cannot retreat. If you cannot go back, you must go on. Let us examine the argument further as to why retreat is impossible.

A. *Because of the Spiritual Privileges You Have, You Cannot Retreat*

The spiritual position of these people is described in clear terms. They had been once for all enlightened (cf. 10:32 where the same word is used). The use of *hapax* and the aorist tense both point to their time of conversion and not merely being under the influence of the Gospel. They had tasted of the heavenly gift (cf. 2:9 where the same word is used of Christ's tasting, not nibbling, death). They had partaken of the Holy Spirit (cf. 12:8 where the same word is used of experiencing, not "going along with" chastisement). They had tasted of the Word of God and the knowledge of things to come. These are Christians the writer addresses, and because they have embraced Christianity it is impossible to go back.

B. *Because You Cannot Fall Away, You Cannot Retreat*

The participle, "falling away," is unqualified in verse 6, but it is undoubtedly conditional (as Matt. 16:26; Luke 9: 25). Although this passage strictly does not say anything about the possibility of falling away, the author makes it clear elsewhere in the Epistle that it is an impossibility (cf., e.g., 7:25). You cannot fall away, retreat is impossible, therefore "let us go on unto perfection."

C. *Because You Cannot Recrucify Christ, You Cannot Retreat*

There is no second Cross or second Cross experience, for that would mean that Christ would be recrucified, which is impossible. There is no such thing as being saved a second time (though it might be convenient sometimes!); therefore, you cannot retreat but must progress.

Each of these three reasons for the impossibility of retreat point to the solemn conclusion that progress must be displayed in the believer's life. The warning is a sober one: if it were possible to fall away, which it is not, then you could not possibly start the Christian life over; therefore, be warned as to how you are presently living it, for you must go on if you cannot retreat.

IV. It Is a Life of Training (12:3-13)

Christian experience includes discipline, or child training, as a normal accompaniment.

A. *The Reasons for Discipline*

Discipline is necessary for training, and since the normal Christian life is a life of growth, discipline must be involved. Further, discipline is a proof of a normal Christian relationship, showing that God our Father loves us.

B. *The Results of Discipline*

The writer lists two things that should result from discipline properly received: reverence (v. 9) and righteousness (v. 11).

C. *The Reactions to Discipline*

He warns against fainting under discipline, against forgetting the necessity of it, against despising it, and exhorts that the believer be exercised by it. Only that will make a real Christian leader (vv. 12-13), and these Hebrew Christians had too long been followers.

V. It Is a Life of Sanctification

In the Epistle sanctification is related to the work of Christ primarily and not to the Holy Spirit (10:10, 14; 13:12). It is a requirement of a true Christian life (12:14-17), being a lifetime practice of personal holiness. In order to effect that kind of life the writer delineates certain standards.

A. *It Involves Running Away from Certain Things* (12: 14-17)

The practice of sanctification includes running from backsliding, bitterness, fornication, and a flippant attitude toward spiritual blessings.

B. *It Involves Putting Off Weights* (12:1)

A weight is anything superfluous which hinders in the running of the Christian race. It is not necessarily something wrong in itself, but it becomes wrong because it hinders. "Lay aside such" is the exhortation of the writer.

C. *It Involves Putting Off Unbelief* (12:1)

Again the importance of faith in the Christian life is emphasized when unbelief is pictured as an engulfing, entangling hindrance to progress in the life. It is a single basic sin though it may express itself in many ways.

D. *It Involves Looking at the Examples of Faith* (11:1-40)

Practical sanctification is encouraged by observing others whose lives pleased God. Young, old, those whose circumstances were for them, and those whose were against them are all found in chapter 11, and all these conquered by faith.

VI. It Is a Life of Service

Service is one of the reasons why God saves men; therefore, the believer serves (9:14; 10:2; 12:28). The writer of Hebrews, like the apostle John, sees service as the exercise and exhibition of love.

A. *In Relation to Social Duties* (13:1-6)

The serving believer will show brother love (v. 1), stranger love (v. 2), compassionate love with those in bonds (v. 3), faithful love in marriage (v. 4), and contented love for the Lord who will never leave him (vv. 5-6).

B. *In Relation to Religious Duties* (13:7-19)

The loving servant will occupy himself with the person

and work of Christ as he is led into that through the ministry of church leaders (vv. 7-9). He will follow Christ to the place of separation without the camp (vv. 10-14); he will offer sacrifices of praise and money (vv. 15-16); and he will pray for the servants of the Lord (vv. 18-19).

VII. It Is a Life of Corporate Fellowship in the Church

The doctrine of the Church is developed in the Epistle along practical rather than didactic lines. Believers are exhorted not to forget the importance of their regular meetings (10:25), for the need for mutual support will increase as the end approaches. This idea of corporate fellowship is also expressed in the figure which the writer employs (3: 6) of the house over which Christ is the head. Clearly, however, the author conceived of difference in office within the fellowship, for he speaks of those who rule and those who are ruled (13:17). Even the examples of those who had led the church in days past is still to be revered (13:7).

Nothing is said concerning the Lord's Supper although baptism was evidently a prerequisite to membership in the group (3:1; 4:14; 6:1; 10:23).[1] The future hope of the Church is in Heaven where evidently she will be distinguishable from other groups which will be there too (12:23).

In conclusion one observes that the theology of Hebrews is essentially the theology of the priesthood of Christ in relation to the better convenantal promises for the Christian in this age. The writer hoped that understanding the truth of wha. nis readers had in Christ would be the tonic which would cure their ills and stop their drifting course of life. The logical order of the development of the theology is very convincing. First, the writer introduces Christ in all of the essential dignity of His person overshadowing all others.

[1]Cf. B. F. Westcott, *op. cit.*, p. 323, for evidence that "confession" has to do with the confession of the convert at his baptism.

Then he develops the theme of His priesthood, and finally, he shows the ethical and moral implications of the work of Christ as they should be displayed in the lives of believers. The Christology of Hebrews is preparatory; the priesthood is central; the Christian life is consequent.

Part VI

THE THEOLOGY OF PETER AND JUDE

Chapter 1

THE THEOLOGY OF PETER

I. Preliminary Considerations

A. *Sources of Petrine Theology*

THE WHOLE OF PETRINE THEOLOGY finds source material in many places in the New Testament. Although Peter's activity began when he was called to follow the Lord, Petrine theology did not begin to be revealed until after Pentecost. Therefore, speeches and remarks of Peter in the Gospels do not contribute to the source material of his theology.

1. *Discourses in the Acts.* Any discussion of the theology of Peter must include references to the Petrine discourses in Acts. All of these occur in the first half of that book and are to be dated in the first half of the first century.

2. *The Epistles of Peter.* The two letters of Peter are the primary source material. Whatever interrelation there may be between II Peter and Jude, they must not be considered together in a Biblical Theology study, for they do not represent the doctrine of the same author. It is generally considered that the Gospel of Mark reflects the teaching of Peter. However, that Gospel belongs to the Synoptic theology and not to this division.

How are these two sources, the Acts and the Epistles, related? Biblical Theology can have several emphases. It may emphasize the chronological development of doctrinal revelation, or it may emphasize the theological pattern of thought in the minds of various writers of Scripture. To substantiate a chronological development in Petrine theology would necessitate showing differences between the speeches of Peter found in Acts (spoken early in his ministry) and the writing of the Epistles (written late in his ministry). This is impossible to do, for there is no such development. Therefore, it is the viewpoint of the man which should have our attention. If this be so, the Epistles will have to be the basis for Petrine theology simply because Peter's speeches in Acts have been recorded by another who.had his own theological purpose in mind in the selection of the material. While we should freely use the relevant material in Acts, it is supplementary to the source material of the Epistles.

B. *Introduction to the Epistles*

The genuineness and authority of the First Epistle was universally recognized by the early Church.[1] It was obviously written by an eyewitness to the earthly life of Christ (2:19-24; 3:18; 4:1, 14; 5:1). Even those who do not accept the genuineness of the Second Epistle admit that its testimony (3:1) dates the First Epistle very early (probably 64-65). The matter of the place of writing of the First Epistle is not so simple. Though it is said to be Babylon (5:13) the meaning of Babylon is not clear. Since it really makes very little difference to Petrine theology, the various views need only be mentioned. Some hold Babylon to refer to the city of that name in Egypt, but the view lacks positive evidence to support it. Others hold that it refers to Babylon on the Euphrates.[2] This is the most natural way to take the word, and it is known that it was an important center of Jewish dispersion, and a center plagued by persecution. There is no evidence, however, to connect Peter with this city, though it is certainly possible that he may have gone there. Others

[1] Eusebius, *Ecclesiastical History*, IV, xiv.
[2] So Calvin, Hort, Alford, and Meyer.

hold that the reference is to mystical Babylon, i.e., Rome.[3] This is supported by tradition[4] and was universally held until the time of the Reformation. There is a great deal of strong evidence that Peter was in Rome[5] which may give weight to this view, though it in no way supports the claims of the Roman Catholic Church concerning the papacy. It is argued too that within the verse (5:13) itself there is evidence for assuming the mystical sense of Babylon. "She who is elect together with you" is claimed to be a metaphorical expression meaning the church. "Mark my son" is undoubtedly a reference to the well-known Mark who was to Peter a spiritual son. Since two expressions in the verse are figurative, why should not Babylon be also?

The authenticity of the Second Epistle is widely disputed. The external evidence in support of the Petrine authorship leaves much to be desired, but even those fathers who expressed doubts about it did so with less frequency and vehemence than the modern critics suggest.[6] Internal evidence is likewise controverted; nevertheless, certain internal considerations support the Petrine authorship strongly. For instance, the use of the name Simon in 1:1 would hardly have been a wise choice for a forger who would want to imitate as closely as possible. If the Epistle were a forgery, what motivated the forger is an unanswerable question. It contains no heresy, tells nothing new about Peter, contains no anachronisms, and puts nothing into his mouth which is contrary to history (as the noncanonical works about Peter do). If it were a forgery it is one without an object, without the customary marks of a forgery, and without resemblance to undoubted

---

[3] So Robertson, Blenkin.

[4] Eusebius, *op. cit.*, II, xv.

[5] Ignatius, Papias, I Clement, Hegesippus, Clement of Alexandria, Origen, Dionysius, Tertullian, and Jerome attest to it. The evidence is conveniently summarized in G. W. Blenkin, *The First Epistle General of Peter, Cambridge Greek Testament* (Cambridge: University Press, 1914), pp. xvii-xix.

[6] C. Bigg, *A Critical and Exegetical Commentary on the Epistles of St. Peter and St. Jude, International Critical Commentary* (Edinburgh: T. & T. Clark, 1902), pp. 199-215.

forgeries.[7] We accept it as a genuine work of the apostle
Peter written in 66 or 67.

C. *The Apostle Peter*

It is always important in Biblical Theology to review
something of the life of the writer involved. Peter was the
son of Jonas (Matt. 16:17) and brother of Andrew, their
home being in Capernaum. Though married at the time
(Mark 1:30), he was called by Jesus to be a disciple (Mark
1:16; Luke 5:1-11). About six months later a second call to
apostleship came (Mark 3:14). Clement of Alexandria
called him one of "the elect of the elect" because he belonged
to the innermost circle of three and witnessed events the
others did not, such as the raising of Jairus' daughter, the
transfiguration, Gethsemane, the empty tomb, etc. He was
the leader of the Twelve, acting continually as their spokes-
man. He took the place of leadership after the ascension of
Christ by presiding at the choosing of Judas' successor,
preaching at Pentecost, and being the focal point of attack
by the Jewish leaders. He attended the council in Jerusalem in 49, went to Antioch (Gal. 2:11), and visited other
places, including perhaps Rome. Before Pentecost he was
like a pendulum, always swinging from one extreme to another; after Pentecost he was Peter, a rock.

D. *The Persecution Referred to in the First Epistle*

Prominent in the background of I Peter is the thought
of persecution and trial (1:6-7; 2:11-20; 3:13-17; 4:3-5, 12-
19; 5:8-10). Some believe that these were official persecutions of the Roman Empire against the Christians,[8] and it is
certainly true that the Church was never free of such until
the time of Constantine. However, the persecution of Nero,
which would have to be in the background of First Peter if

[7]Cf. Theodor Zahn, *Introduction to the New Testament* (Grand Rapids: Kregel, 1953), II, 262-93.
[8]W. M. Ramsay, *The Church in the Roman Empire Before A.D. 70* (London: Hodder & Stoughton, 1894), p. 281.

this is official persecution, was largely confined to the city of Rome itself and could hardly qualify as that which plagued the believers of the dispersion.[9] Official persecution was an isolated matter at that time.

From the Epistle itself we glean certain characteristics about the kind of persecution the Christians were undergoing. For one thing it was of "diverse sorts" (1:6). That phrase lends little support to the idea of an official persecution by edict of Rome. Again, Peter says that the believers should silence the opposition by their good deeds (2:15) which indicates a more personal kind of persecution. The picture in the book itself seems to be of sporadic, unofficial, social persecution incident to the normal practices of Christianity.

E. *Characteristics of Petrine Theology*

Petrine theology is fundamentally Christological. This exhibits itself in two principal ways. It is didactically and experientially Christological. In the area of teaching Peter reflects in many instances the Lord's own teaching. Plumptre has compiled a list of cross-references which show the extent of this.[10] Many of these echoes are from the ministry of Christ during His earthly life and came to Peter in the normal course of his association with his Lord. One basic doctrine in Petrine theology, however, did not come from the period of humiliation. Peter beheld the Lord repeatedly after the resurrection; he saw the empty tomb; he gazed upon the scars of Calvary; and he witnessed the ascension into Heaven. From this post-resurrection association came the emphasis on the resurrection in Peter's theology.

But Petrine theology is also experientially Christological. That is, it is a theology of practical exhortation and comfort for the daily needs of believers. This also stems from Peter's

[9]E. Gibbon, *The Decline and Fall of the Roman Empire*, I, 460.
[10]E. H. Plumptre, *The General Epistle of St. Peter and St. Jude, Cambridge Bible for Schools and Colleges* (Cambridge: University Press, 1893), pp. 65-67.

background, for was he not the one who from the highest place of spiritual privilege fell so miserably that upon his restoration he could strengthen his brethren? He also had witnessed the life of his Master who went about doing good (Acts 10:38). Peter's walk with that One who gave comfort, help, healing, and hope to people is sharply reflected in the experiential side of his Christologically centered theology.

Let it not be assumed that the didactic and experiential are unrelated in Peter's thought. For example, the doctrine of the Fatherhood of God should produce holy living (I Peter 1:14-16). The facts of the life of Christ should serve as an example for patience in times of trial (2:21-25). The doctrine of future rewards should constrain the leaders of the church to govern properly (5:1-4). The two areas of doctrine and practice are inseparably interrelated, their focal point being the teaching and life of the One in whom Peter's thought centered.

II. The Doctrine of Christ

To say that Petrine theology is Christocentric does not mean that his writings contain nothing about the Father or Holy Spirit, but since the primary emphasis is on the revelation of God through the Son, the doctrine of Christ must be given prominence in the development of the theology of Peter. Further, in order to try to catch Peter's perspective, it seems natural to include the saving work of Christ in this section rather than in a separate division on soteriology.

A. *His Names and Descriptions*

1. *Jesus.* In the early days of his ministry Peter frequently used the name *Jesus* or *Jesus of Nazareth* (Acts 1:16; 2:22, 32, 36; 3:13; 10:38) simply because he desired to identify Jesus with the Old Testament concept of Messiah. The theme of his early sermons was that Jesus whom they knew

was the Messiah of Israel (Acts 2:36; 3:18). He also identified Jesus as the Lord early in his ministry (Acts 1:21; 2:36;
10:36; 11:17) so that we may say that whatever else Peter had
to learn later, he had from the very beginning an exalted
view of the person of Jesus Christ.

2. *Christ.* The principal designation of the Lord in the
First Epistle is the simple Christ (1:11, 19; 2:21; 3:15-16, 18;
4:1, 13-14; 5:1, 10, 14). Next most frequently is used the
simplest of the solemn compound names, Jesus Christ (1:1-
3, 7, 13; 2:5; 3:21; 4:11). The Second Epistle is lacking in
these simple designations, Peter preferring to use compound
names of the Lord (1:8, 14, 16; 2:20; 3:18). Again this
shows the high estimate which Peter, the companion of the
Lord, put upon His person. He was to Peter the divine Son
of God, and

> so far as appears it did not occur to anyone in the primi-
> tive Christian community to put a lower estimate upon
> His personality than that; and writer vies with writer
> only in his attempt to give his faith in his divine Re-
> deemer clear and emphatic expression.[11]

3. *Spotless and pre-existent Lamb* (I Pet. 1:19-20). In this
passage Peter designates the Lord as the Lamb without spot
(inherent blame) and blemish (external defilement). He
also predicates of Him existence before the foundation of the
world. This must be real pre-existence because of the presence of the participle *manifested* in the same verse. The pre-
existence and manifestation are of the same subject, and if
the latter is real and not ideal so is the former.[12]

4. *Precious cornerstone* (I Pet. 2:6-7). Peter seemed to
have learned well the lesson of the difference between Judaism and Christianity, for he used Psalm 118:22 not only here

---

[11]B. B. Warfield, *The Lord of Glory* (New York: American Tract Society,
1907), p. 275.
[12]As G. B. Stevens, *Theology of the New Testament* (Edinburgh: T. & T.
Clark, 1899), p. 299, and *contra* Weiss, *Biblical Theology of the New Testament* (Edinburgh: T. & T. Clark, 1882), I, 226-27.

but also in the message recorded in Acts 4:11. He whom the Jews had rejected was now the precious cornerstone of the Church.

5. *Rock of stumbling* (I Pet. 2:8). To those who did not receive Him, Jesus of Nazareth was a stone of stumbling and a rock of offense. In God's wise purposes He so ordained it that Jesus would be put in the way, though God assumes no responsibility for anyone falling over Him.

6. *Shepherd and Bishop of our souls* (I Pet. 2:25). After speaking of the sufferings which a believer may have to endure, Peter concludes with this title of comfort. Called unto Christ means called unto One who cares for and sustains His sheep in every trial.

In Peter's use of names and designations for Christ one thing is outstanding. The thought with which his mind was saturated throughout all his ministry was that Jesus of Nazareth was the Messiah. The use of the names *Jesus, Christ,* and compounds has shown that. In addition, these descriptive phrases just cited—the Lamb, Cornerstone, Shepherd— are from an Old Testament mold. The Messianic teaching was deeply rooted in his thinking, and this Jesus was that Messiah.

B. *His Messiahship*

"Peter is unique in his Messianic teaching."[13] The manifestation of this we have seen in the preceding section, but the basis of that which is displayed in his Epistles is in Peter's early sermons in Acts. (Since these sermons have been discussed under the theology of Acts only the principal points will be listed here.)

1. *Messiah must be raised from the dead (which necessarily includes the fact that He would have to die).* This is the principal contribution to Peter's Messianic doctrine from the sermon preached on Pentecost (Acts 2:14-36). A risen

[13]James M. Gray, "Peter," *International Standard Bible Encyclopaedia* (Grand Rapids: Eerdmans, 1943), IV, 2350.

Messiah meant a crucified Messiah, and that Messiah is Jesus.

2. *The fulfillment of Israel's promises awaits the personal return of Messiah, which awaits the national repentance of Israel.* This is the substance of Peter's sermon preached after the healing of the lame man at the temple (Acts 3:12-26). When Israel repents the Lord will return and fulfill all of God's promises concerning the millennial times of refreshing. This is still a true statement today, though when Peter preached it was as if he were putting the Stone of stumbling in the way of the entire nation, which stumbled and became disobedient—all in perfect accord with the eternal purposes of God.

C. *His Life*

1. *It was an example* (I Pet. 2:21-23). The chief point made of the life of Christ as an example for believers is the patient endurance which He exhibited throughout His life (note the imperfects in v. 23). All attacks on Him were undeserved, for He did not even commit one act of sin (note the aorist in v. 22). To this kind of patient endurance even when suffering wrongfully the Christian is called, and in the context Peter is especially speaking to Christian slaves who were finding it difficult to work for unbelieving masters.

2. *It was a confirmation* (II Pet. 1:15-19). To confirm the truth of the everlasting kingdom which the Christian will enter (v. 11) Peter refers to the incident of the transfiguration in the life of Christ of which he was an eyewitness. The result of that event is that prophecy concerning the kingdom is made more sure (v. 19), and the effect of it should be taking heed in the heart.

D. *His Pre-incarnate Activity* (I Pet. 3:18-22)

The principal views concerning this passage are: (1) Christ preaches now through apostles and prophets to sin ners who are imprisoned; (2) Christ descended into hades between His death and resurrection to offer a second chance to those imprisoned there; (3) Christ descended into hades to make a judicial declaration of His victory on the Cross to wicked spirits, who may be (a) wicked angels confined, or (b) spirits of wicked dead men; (4) Christ preached by the Spirit to the men of Noah's day, and because they were disobedient to His message they are now imprisoned spirits awaiting judgment.[14] It is the last view which the writer prefers and which would justify the title of this section. While all the arguments pro and con for each view cannot be presented, it may be noted briefly that the first necessitates too figurative an interpretation, the second involves the unscriptural idea of a second chance, the third has little point and is open to the charge that Christ was taunting those in hades, but the fourth satisfies grammar and context (cf. Heb. 12:23, where "spirits" is used of men). Undoubtedly the Lord preached in the Spirit in other periods of Old Testament history, but the days of Noah are cited because of their extreme wickedness and similarity to the times of persecution which the believers of Peter's day were experiencing. If this be the true meaning of the passage the Lord is seen to be active in His preincarnate days.

E. *His Salvation*

Although soteriology might well be made an entirely separate division of Petrine theology, it is placed under Christology in order to reflect better the Petrine thought pattern.

1. *The person.* The Saviour was the spotless, undefiled One (I Pet. 1:19) who could not have died for His own sins since He, being the Just One, did not commit sin (I Pet. 2:22; 3:18). As shown previously, He was the divine One who died for sins.

[14]Cf. William Kelly, *The Preaching to the Spirits in Prison* (London: F. C. Race, n.d.), pp. 1-139.

2. *The preplanning.* Salvation was not an afterthought but a forethought in the mind of God. It was the aim of the diligent searching study of the prophets (I Pet. 1:10-12) that they might know at what season and with what characteristics Christ would come. The entire program was foreordained by God before the foundation of the world (I Pet. 1:20).

3. *The purpose.* His death was a real substitution for sin. This is seen (a) in the use of the figure of a lamb (I Pet. 1: 19) which would bring to the readers' minds the substitutionary aspect of the Levitical sacrifices; (b) by the direct statement of I Peter 2:24, "who his own self bare our sins in his body upon the tree"; and (c) by the meaning of *huper* (for) in I Peter 3:18, where it means "in substitution for" as it does in Philemon 13, a nonatonement passage.

Further, it was a conclusive substitution for sin, for Christ died once for all (I Pet. 3:18, *hapax*, not *pote*).

Too, it was an effective substitution for sin, for it brought redemption (I Pet. 1:18). The word for redemption used is *lutroo*, which means to set free by payment of a ransom.[15] Thus, Christ's work on the Cross was completely effective in setting the sinner free.

4. *The proofs.* The proofs of the efficacy of the work of Christ on the Cross are: first, the resurrection (I Pet. 1:3, 21; Acts 2:32); and second, the exaltation of Christ to glory (I Pet. 1:21; Acts 2:33). A possible third proof is based upon a difficult passage (I Pet. 3:18). Usually this is taken as a reference to Christ being made alive by the Spirit in resurrection. The difficulty with the view is the use of the aorist participle "being made alive." Unless this be an exception, the aorist participle does not express time subsequent to that of the main verb, "died" (ASV). Therefore, Peter does not seem to be speaking of the resurrection subsequent to Christ's death. If one does not make a grammatical exception here,

---

[15]A. T. Robertson, *Word Pictures in the New Testament* (New York: Harper, 1930), VI, 90; A. Deissmann, *Light from the Ancient East* (New York: Hodder and Stoughton, n.d.), p. 333.

the reference seems to be to an exaltation on the Cross. Probably it may be linked with the cry of victory, "It is finished," uttered when Christ died. If so, then this, too, is a proof of the efficacy of the work of the Son on the Cross.

5. *The provisions.* First Peter was written that believers might know the "true grace of God" (5:12), and in it Peter mentions many of the benefits of that knowledge of personal salvation. For instance, it brings hope (1:3-4) of Heaven which is described in three negatives—uncorrupt, unpolluted, unfading. This inheritance has already been put in safekeeping for the Christian and it continues there ("reserved" is a perfect passive participle). Again, salvation provides safekeeping for the inheritor (1:5). Faith on man's part is necessary in order to be conscious of the power of God, but the keeping is ultimately and continuously (present tense) the work of God's power. Further, salvation brings rejoicing even in the midst of persecution and trial (1:6). Actually the basis of salvation, the suffering of Christ, is to be the believer's example in persecution (I Pet. 1:6-7; 2:20-25; 4:1 ff.; 4:12-13). Salvation also provides a new position (I Pet. 2:9-10), for whereas the former position was one without mercy and not as a people even, it is now one of being a people[16] of God, particularly possessed by Him. Finally, being saved is made the incentive for holy living (I Pet. 1: 14-18; 2:24).

6. *The people.* The lesson about who could be saved was one that Peter learned on Simon's housetop (Acts 10). That he had learned well the fact that God intended to bring Gentiles unto Himself as well as Jews is evinced by what he had to say about it at the Jerusalem council (Acts 15:11; cf. II Pet. 1:1).

7. *The possession.* Salvation is possessed by faith (I Pet. 1:5, 9, 21; 2:7; II Pet. 1:5; Acts 10:43; 15:9).

---

[16]While there are parallels in these verses between Israel and the Church, nowhere are they equated. Indeed, the absence of the article before "people" guards the distinction, for it is said that Christians are *a* people of God, not *the* new Israel of God.

III. THE DOCTRINE OF THE SCRIPTURES

Although the central feature of Petrine theology is the doctrine of Christ, the doctrine of the Scriptures also plays an important role. "Considering their limitations as to space, Peter's Epistles are notable for the emphasis they lay upon the character and authority of the Holy Scriptures."[17]

A. *Petrine Appellations*

Peter uses a number of descriptive phrases for the Scriptures which show something of his estimation of them.

1. *The prophetic word* (II Pet. 1:19). The attributive position of the adjective makes the translation "prophetic word" preferable to "word of prophecy"[18] and conveys the idea that Peter is describing the entire Old Testament as prophetic. The reason for this description is Peter's emphasis on Christ; or as another has put it:

> This, on account of the unity of its origin and its one all-pervading theme—Christ's sufferings and glories (I Peter 1:11) —is spoken of as one word, one scheme or body of prophecy.[19]

2. *The living and abiding Word of God* (I Pet. 1:23-25). In this appellation we discover several things about Peter's conception of the Word. It finds its origin in God. Its living character gives it animation, but that animation resides in the message preached (note *rhema,* spoken word, in v. 25), rather than in the letters and words on the page (though they are indispensable for the accurate conveying of the message). The Word also has eternal character for it abides forever.

3. *The Word as guileless milk* (I Pet. 2:2). Although there is no specific word or phrase for the Word in this verse,

[17]Gray, *op. cit.*, p. 2351.
[18]Cf. H. E. Dana and Julius R. Mantey, *A Manual Grammar of the Greek New Testament* (New York: Macmillan, 1927), p. 118.
[19]J. Lillie, *Lectures on the First and Second Epistles of Peter* (London: Hodder & Stoughton, 1870), pp. 413-14.

the thought is obviously of the Scriptures as guileless milk. Peter is not calling part of the Word milk in contrast to meat as Paul does in I Corinthians 3:2, but he is saying that all of the Word should be as pure milk which appeals to the reason. This involves putting away the things mentioned in the preceding verse. Thus to Peter the Word was pure and authoritative.

4. *The Scriptures.* Peter used this phrase in three places (Acts 1:16; I Pet. 2:6; II Pet. 1:20). He evidently understood and used it in the sense commonly held by Jews at that time; i.e., as standing for the very Word of God, His decrees, to or from which no one would dare add or subtract, and for which one would willingly die.[20]

B. *Revelation*

Peter mentions several means of revelation or of God's ways of communicating to man.

1. *Prophecy.* This was the primary channel of revelation (I Pet. 1:11); i.e., God's revealing things before they happened. Note that these prophecies were written, not spoken.

2. *History.* Historical portions of the Old Testament taught Peter about God's dealings with man and therefore of His purposes in the future (II Pet. 2:4-9).

3. *The life of Christ.* This too was a source of the revelation of God (Acts 2:22, 32; I Pet. 1:3; 3:18-22; II Pet. 1:15-18).

4. *The New Testament.* Peter apparently gained knowledge of the mind of God through the writings of Paul (II Pet. 3:15-16).

5. *Direct guidance.* As all authors of Scripture Peter was himself a channel of revelation as he wrote under the guidance of the Holy Spirit (cf. II Pet. 1:21; 3:1-2).

C. *Inspiration*

1. *The agent of inspiration.* Early in his ministry Peter expressed the generally held concept that the Holy Spirit

[20] J. Orr, "The Bible," *International Standard Bible Encyclopaedia*, I, 461.

was the one who inspired the writers of the Old Testament (Acts 1:16). That this was an apostolic concept is affirmed in Acts 4:24-25.

2. *The means of inspiration.* Peter's chief contribution to the doctrine of inspiration is the classic passage in II Peter 1:20-21. These verses teach that God originated Scripture, for "no prophecy of Scripture comes into being of one's own unfolding." However, God did not dictate the Scriptures, for *men* spoke as they were *borne along* by the Spirit. The Word is a divine-human production. The human part in the production is also emphasized in I Peter 1:10-11—the "searching" and "showing" implying a good deal of hard work on the part of the prophets.

3. *The extent of inspiration.* It has already been shown that Peter looked upon all of the Old Testament as inspired. Further, he included the Pauline Epistles as Scripture (II Pet. 3:16), and the use of the word *Scriptures* with the meaning that it had at that time could only indicate that he considered Paul's writings inspired like the Old Testament. Other New Testament writings are not mentioned by name, but there is specific reference to the words of other apostles as being on the same plane of authority as the words of Old Testament prophets (II Pet. 3:2).

Thus, though not systematically presented, Peter's doctrine of inspiration is one of the most completely presented of all the writers of the New Testament. It goes without saying that his high view of inspiration carried with it a correspondingly high esteem of the authority of the Scriptures. Remarkably developed as this doctrine is, it nevertheless seems to stand in a secondary relationship to Christology, and in many respects Peter's presentation of the doctrine of the Scriptures may be viewed as an offshoot of his central doctrine of Christ. The origin of the doctrine is undoubtedly related to his background in Judaism, but its presentation is a product of his Christology.

IV. THE CHRISTIAN LIFE

Much of what Peter has to say in his Epistles concerns Christian living. This too is a direct result of his Christology, for every major passage in the Epistle concerning the Christian life is based upon the sacrifice of Christ (I Pet. 1; 2:21; 3; 4:1; cf. 2:18 ff.; 5:5-11; II Pet. 1). Peter's thought runs like this: because we have a Saviour who has done everything for us in His sacrifice, we should respond with a walk that is pleasing to Him in all the relationships of life.

A. *The Christian's Relationship to Governments* (I Pet. 2: 13-17)

Three of the specific relationships of life can be summed up in the single word *obedience*. Christians should obey governments and masters, and wives should obey their husbands (2:13, 18; 3:1). In relation to governments obedience is a voluntary matter based on one's position as a servant of God (v. 16). It should extend to every ordinance of man (v. 13). The reasons for obedience are three: first, rulers are the God-appointed method of governing human affairs; second, it is the will of God that we obey in order to muzzle the blameworthy ignorance of men who would malign Christianity if we did not obey; and third, the Lord's own example was one of obedience during His life.

Peter also allows for an exception to the general rule of obedience. It is bound up in the words *servants of God* (v. 16). Primarily and fundamentally the Christian is God's servant and should a governmental decree come between God and His servant the relationship to God supercedes the relationship to man (cf. Acts 4:20). But normally, the believer is responsible to obey.

B. *The Relationship of Servants and Masters* (I Pet. 2:18-25)

Again the principle is obedience on the part of servants in

relation to their masters. This includes both good and perverse masters, for obedience finds favor with God. In case this seems grievous Peter reminds his readers of the example of Christ who, when He was buffeted (cf. v. 20 with Matt. 26:67; Mark 14:65), suffered without complaint. The follower of Christ should, like his Lord, commit his case to the One who judges righteously.

C. *The Relationship of Husbands and Wives* (I Pet. 3:1-7)

1. *The principles* (vv. 1-2, 7). For the wife the principle is again obedience. This should be coupled with purity and fear (v. 2). For the husband the principle is honor (for the "likewise" refers back to 2:17). This is based upon the fact that, although both husband and wife are weak, the wife is the weaker vessel. Such a relationship of honor brings with it a life of answered prayer as the two who sustain this close relationship agree in their prayer life.

2. *The purpose* (vv. 1-2). One would gather from this passage that the greater number of spiritually mixed marriages in New Testament times involved an unsaved husband rather than an unsaved wife. It is also evident that the proper relationship in such cases was considered highly important, considering how much space is devoted to it by several New Testament writers. Christian wives should be obedient to their unsaved husbands in order to win them to the Saviour. It is the obedience which is to be the winsome testimony, not a vocal witness (note the literal translation of v. 1: "they also may without a word be won by the manner of life of the wives"). These unbelieving husbands, Peter says, do not need more preaching from their wives; they need to see Christianity lived through the obedience of the wife.

3. *The procedure* (vv. 3-4). Carrying out these ideas of obedience, subjection, and reverence will involve the outward appearance as well as the inner character of the woman. Undoubtedly the stress is on the inner nature being

characterized by meekness and quietness, but outward appearance is also involved. Braiding of the hair in elaborate knots, undue use of gold ornaments, and excessive display of clothing are inconsistent with a meek and quiet spirit. Since Peter is writing under the inspiration of the Holy Spirit, it must be recognized that this is still God's procedure for winning the unsaved partner.

4. *The pattern* (vv. 5-6). The pattern for this type of conduct on the part of Christian women is found in the women of the Old Testament. They were separated unto God, found their hope in Him, and like Sarah were submissive to their husbands. God's ideals for women were the same in both Testaments, and they remain unchanged today.

D. *The Christian's Relationship to Persecution*

Mention has already been made of the fact that the persecution in the background of the Petrine writings is not official but personal and social. In such trial the believer's reaction could be such as to bring disgrace on the name of Christ. If the Christian suffers as an evil-doer thereby bringing shame on himself and dishonor to Christ (I Pet. 4:16) he deserves the unbeliever's accusations (I Pet. 2:12). In such cases judgment needs to come to the house of God (I Pet. 4:17). However, the believer's reaction should be that which honors Christ. Such conduct involves committing oneself to God (I Pet. 4:19), patient endurance (I Pet. 2: 20), remembering the example of Christ (I Pet. 2:23), and exuberant rejoicing (I Pet. 1:6; 4:13). This is acceptable with God.

The result of suffering is twofold. First, it brings a partnership with the sufferings of Christ (I Pet. 4:13-14) —not the vicarious atoning sufferings but the trials which came to Him as the Holy One who lived in a sinful world which hated Him. So the believer living a holy life will be despised by the world and thus share in the sufferings of Christ. Second, suffering brings a proving of the faith of the Christian (I Pet. 1:7). It shows that a believer can be trusted, and this brings glory to God.

E. *The Christian's Relationship to All Manner of Living*

1. *The adversaries in Christian living.* The antagonism of the world in its hatred for the believer is patent in Peter's Epistles. The flesh, too, wars against the soul in its endeavor to live for Christ (I Pet. 2:11). The Devil is specifically called an adversary or accuser (I Pet. 5:8) and his tactics involve stalking the Christian in order to swallow his testimony. Against him the believer must be sober and alert in his resistance.

2. *The aim of all Christian living.* The single aim of the Christian life is holiness (I Pet. 1:14-16). The standard or pattern is God Himself; the extent is all manner of life; and the requirement is being unfashionable in respect to the old life.

3. *The attitudes in Christian living.*

a. Yieldedness. Basic to all successful Christian living must be the attitude of dedication of life. A concrete proof that the life has been dedicated will be persecution by the world (I Pet. 4:1).

b. Humility (I Pet. 5:5-6).

c. Sobriety (I Pet. 1:13; 5:8). Constant watchfulness in an alert but unexcited state is also necessary for victorious living.

4. *The actions of Christian living.*

a. In relation to self. Growth is the keynote of Christian living (II Pet. 1:5-11; 3:18). To faith at least seven virtues are to be added as evidence of progress in the Christian life. They are temperance, virtue, knowledge, patience, godliness, brotherly kindness, and love. The end of such constant growth is an abundant entrance into the kingdom; i.e., an entrance with rewards.

b. In relation to the brethren. Certain actions in relation to fellow-believers are becoming to the Christian life. They are: love (I Pet. 4:8), sympathy (3:8), tenderheartedness (3:8), humblemindedness (3:8), and hospitality (4:9). Christian love should be fervent (at a high pitch, 4:8), unfeigned (without unreal pretense, 1:22), and from the heart (1:22). Christian love is affection without affectation.

c. In relation to all men. The word which summarizes the believer's relation to all men is the word *honor* (I Pet. 2:17).

Though sketchy, this gives some idea of the areas of thought and lines of development in Petrine theology concerning the Christian life. Again let it be emphasized that all this teaching was definitely associated in Peter's mind with Christology, for every major passage concerning the Christian life is based on the doctrine of the sacrifice of Christ.

V. The Doctrine of the Church

It is surprising to learn that the word *church* does not appear anywhere in Peter's Epistles or in his discourses in Acts; nevertheless, certain features of ecclesiology are clearly present.

A. *The Universal Church*

The Church conceived of as the universal Body of Christ is discernible in Peter's thought. Peter learned the lesson of the unity of all believers whether Jew or Gentile (Acts 10; 15) in the universal Church. His figurative titles also support the doctrine of the universal Church (I Pet. 2:5, 9). "This spiritual house is not the local church nor even a group of saints, but the Mystical Body of Christ, the Church Universal, for Peter is addressing believers in five Roman provinces."[21] Likewise when Peter speaks of the gifts given

[21]K. S. Wuest, *First Peter in the Greek New Testament* (Grand Rapids: Eerdmans, 1945), p. 53.

to all men to be exercised among the saints he does not limit the giving or the exercise to any one local group (I Pet. 4:10-11, the only place *charisma,* gift, is used outside the Pauline Epistles).

B. *The Local Church*

1. *Church government.* Little is said about the organization of the local church. The elders were evidently the most prominent group of officials in the church (I Pet. 5:1-4). Their duties were to tend, feed, guide, and guard the flock in the spirit of being examples, not lords. Thus, two principles are quite clear: elders are not to lord, and laymen are not to lead. If all recognize and fulfill all their duties there would be no disputes. Elders apparently received some pay for their work (v. 2), though their greater reward will be the crown of glory which the Lord will give (v. 4).

A group that are called "younger" are also mentioned by Peter (I Pet. 5:5). These may simply be younger people or they could conceivably be organizations of youth.[22] In either case they were to be in subjection to the elders.

It is doubtful that the word *deacon* is used by Peter in reference to an official group in the church. It is used in the non-technical sense of ministering or serving (I Pet. 1:12; 4: 10-11), and even though some churches did have at this time official groups of deacons (cf. Phil. 1:1), evidently all did not.

2. *Church ordinances.* The ordinance of baptism was recognized and practiced by Peter as an important feature of church life. The record of its prominence in the early chapters of Acts has already been discussed. That this importance did not lessen as time went on is evident from I Peter 3:21. Although Peter states that there is no saving efficacy to baptism, he is speaking of water baptism as the sign of the resurrection life received in the heart by faith.[23]

The love feasts which accompanied the Lord's Supper are

[22]*Ibid.,* p. 126.
[23]Cf. Blenkin, *op. cit.,* pp. 78-80.

mentioned in II Peter 2:13 without elaboration. Extra-Biblical evidence pictures them as a time when the Christian group gathered for prayer, Scripture reading, the fellowship meal, a collection for widows and orphans, the reading and writing of communications with other churches, and the observance of the Lord's Supper.[24]

VI. ESCHATOLOGY

A. *The Coming of Christ*

There is a distinction in Peter's thought relative to the events involved in the coming of Christ, but he does not speak in terms of rapture and return, though that is what it amounts to. The First Epistle emphasizes the coming of Christ in relation to His own (the rapture), and the Second in relation to the wicked (the return).

Though Peter does not call it the rapture, he speaks of accompaniments of that event when Christ comes for His own. For instance, it is then that believers will be rewarded (I Pet. 1:7). Salvation will be consummated, and God glorified in His saints (I Pet. 1:12; 2:12; 5:1). In light of that event Christians are to have a sense of urgency in Christian service (I Pet. 4:7).

Rewards are also associated with the coming of Christ for His saints. Individual reward will be given for steadfastness of faith (I Pet. 1:7). The coming of Christ will consummate salvation which in itself is a reward as the full revelation of the grace of God is seen (I Pet. 1:13). Faithful elders are particularly promised a crown of glory at His coming (I Pet. 5:1), and all believers will of course be rewarded by being able to see Him whom they love (I Pet. 1:8).

In relation to Christ's second advent which particularly concerns the wicked, Peter speaks at greater length. For one thing, he is emphatic about the certainty of His coming, and

[24]W. Lock, "Love-Feasts," *Hasting's Bible Dictionary* (Edinburgh: T. & T. Clark, 1899), III, 157-58.

for Peter that certainty was based on the confirmatory experience of being an eyewitness of the transfiguration (II Pet. 1:16-18). Peter's own assurance stands in sharp contrast to the scoffers' willful ignorance of the fact of His coming (II Pet. 3:1-7). For another thing, Peter associates judgment with His coming (II Pet. 1:16; 2:1, 3-4; 3:7). In his early messages recorded in Acts he also connected the kingdom promises to Israel with the coming of Christ (Acts 3:17-26).

B. *The False Teachers* (II Pet. 2:1-22)

The burden of Peter in his Second Epistle concerns apostasy in the church. In some respects this is related to ecclesiology and in other respects to eschatology. Peter's word is predictive, while Jude's is historical.

In conduct (vv. 1-3) the apostates will be secretive, heretical, Christ-denying, infectious, lascivious, blasphemous, covetous, and self-seeking. Their condemnation (vv. 4-9) is certain, God having long before placed them in the category of being under judgment; and it is assured by historical examples of past judgments of God upon sin. The characteristics of the false teachers (vv. 10-22) include licentiousness, haughtiness, brutishness, recklessness, sensuality, hypocrisy, infamy, emptiness, instability, boastfulness, seductiveness, deceit, powerlessness, and ignorance. From the picture Peter draws we can gather that these teachers will clothe their false teaching with sound words, combining truth with their error so as to engender disbelief of the truth. Discrediting the redemptive work of Christ is also part of their program which brings with it the inevitable consequences of immoral, sinful lives (II Pet. 2:10, 14, 18). Peter holds out no hope that the presence of false teachers in the church can be avoided. They shall come and be active until destroyed by the judgment of God. In the meantime believers are to be warned against the dangers of their teaching.

C. *The Day of the Lord*

Peter introduces the Day of the Lord without any preliminaries or qualifying phrases because it was unnecessary to explain the concept to his readers. Their understanding of the meaning of the phrase associated it with the coming and reign of Messiah,[25] and since Peter did not qualify it in any way, that is undoubtedly the meaning he intended to attach to it. Although a study of what the entire Bible has to say about the Day of the Lord would yield a much longer list, Peter only picks out two events in connecton with that day—the coming of Christ and the destruction of the heavens and earth (II Pet. 3:10). He implies that these events are separated by some time, for the destruction occurs within the period ("in which"). Specific mention of the millennium is not found here though it is allowed for by the "in which."

D. *The Day of God*

Many understand no difference between the Day of the Lord and the Day of God because apparently Peter connects the destruction of the earth with either phrase (II Pet. 3: 12).[26] However, a correct translation of verse 12 will bring out the force of the preposition *dia*, on account of. The meaning is that the coming of the Day of God is on account of the dissolution of the elements. Thus the destruction is in the Day of the Lord and as a preparation for the Day of God, which follows. In other words, the Day of God is the eternal state (cf. v. 18, where the equivalent phrase "day of eternity" is used). The chief characteristic of that Day of God is that righteousness dwells (makes its home) in it. For this, the believer looks and longs.

It is not difficult to see how Peter's eschatology is also

[25] G. N. H. Peters, *The Theocratic Kingdom of Our Lord Jesus, the Christ* (Grand Rapids: Kregel, 1952), II, 409.
[26] Cf. C. Bigg, *Critical and Exegetical Commentary on the Epistles of St. Peter and St. Jude, International Critical Commentary* (Edinburgh: T. & T. Clark, 1902), p. 296.

Christological. The coming of Christ, the nonredemptive teaching of the false teachers, the Day of the Lord, and the Day of God all focus on the Saviour. Peter's last exhortation links eschatology with Christology, for, he says that knowing these future things ought to cause one to grow in grace and knowledge of Jesus Christ. This is typical of all Petrine theology.

Chapter 2

THE THEOLOGY OF JUDE

C HRONOLOGY AND SUBJECT MATTER link Peter's Second Epistle and the book of Jude. Authorship distinguishes them. From the viewpoint of progress of doctrine, then, the theology of Peter and Jude must be treated as a unit; from the viewpoint of agent of revelation there must be some distinction. Therefore, we have placed the theology of Peter and Jude under the same division but separated them within that division.

I. HISTORICAL BACKGROUND

Little is known of the writer of this short Epistle. He was the brother of James, half-brother of our Lord, an unbeliever until after the resurrection (Matt. 13:55; Mark 6:3; John 7: 5; Acts 1:14). The home of Joseph and Mary would have surrounded him with a pious atmosphere in which God was feared and His Word learned. His relationship to Jesus gave him some advantage when he finally believed.

There is no clue in the Epistle itself as to whom it was particularly directed. It is not unlikely that the readers were Palestinian Christians, both Jew and Gentile. The peril of false teachers of which Peter had spoken was an actuality when Jude wrote, and his urgent letter was written in light of that crisis. Apostate conditions were evidently much more serious when Jude wrote, making it more probable that

II Peter was written before Jude. Jude seems to assume the writing of Peter in verses 17-18. The interrelationship of the two letters is apparent but more easily accounted for if Jude, the shorter Epistle by a less well-known person, was written after II Peter.[1]

II. THE LORDSHIP OF CHRIST

Even though the contents of Jude principally concern the false teachers, one agrees with Stevens, who says that the doctrine of the lordship of Christ is "the principal doctrinal assumption of the letter."[2] Concerning this, Jude has certain basic ideas in the theological substructure of his thinking.

A. *Christ Is God and Absolute Master* (v. 4)

Although there is dispute among the commentators concerning whether "Master" refers to God or to Christ, there is no question as to the meaning of *despotēs,* the word translated Lord or Master. It means one who has absolute, unrestricted authority. Probably Trench is correct in saying that it "is to Christ, but to Christ as God, that the title is ascribed."[3] Jesus Christ is a despot, i.e. one who possesses absolute and unlimited authority. This was basic to Jude's theology.

B. *Since Christ Is Master, the Christian Is His Slave* (v. 1)

Doulos, slave, is the strictly correlative idea to *despotēs,* Master. "He who addresses another as *despota* puts an emphasis of submission into his speech which *kurie* would not have possessed."[4] If Christ is our Master there is no other position for a Christian to take except that of slave.

---

[1] See R. C. H. Lenski, *The Interpretation of the Epistles of St. Peter, St. John, and St. Jude* (Columbus, Ohio: Lutheran Book Concern, 1938), pp. 597-602; for the opposite view cf. M. R. James, *The Second Epistle General of Peter and the General Epistle of Jude, Cambridge Greek Testament* (Cambridge: University Press, 1912), pp. x-xvi.

[2] *The Theology of the New Testament,* p. 318.

[3] R. C. Trench, *Synonyms of the New Testament* (London: Kegan, Paul, Trench, & Co., 1886), p. 98.

[4] *Ibid.,* p. 96.

C. *Christ Is Also Lord* (v. 21)

Kurios, Lord, is a less authoritarian word than despot. In a Greek household the man was a despot in respect to his slaves and a *kurios* in respect to his wife and children. Thus *kurios,* Lord, includes the idea of desiring the good of his subjects. A despot may do that too, but it is not inherent in the meaning of the word. Notice that Jude's use of Lord is in connection with His mercy.

III. The Salvation of Christ

For a short letter there seems to be a remarkable emphasis on salvation especially when the purpose of the letter relates to another subject. And yet it is not so remarkable, for to write about the common salvation was the original intention of Jude (v. 3).

A. *The Past Aspect of Salvation*

Concerning that which is related to the past aspect of salvation Jude speaks of election, retribution, human responsibility, and faith. Election is referred to in verses 1, 4, and 5. Retribution is seen in the fact that the apostates were "written before" to judgment (v. 4). The writing in which they were written before may be the prophecy of Enoch, and even though there is no direct reference to a decree there is no doubt in Jude's mind that the apostates on the scene in his day were foreordained to doom. Human responsibility is exemplified in the unbelieving Israelites in the wilderness and in the ungodly apostates in the church of Jude's time. Faith as the foundation on which the Christian life is built is spoken of in verse 20. Stevens[5] takes the faith of verse 3 as the subjective human experience, but it is probably a reference to the objective body of truth.

B. *The Present Aspect of Salvation*

Even though the Christian is kept by God (v. 1) he is to

[5]*Op. cit.,* p. 312.

keep himself in the Christian life (v. 21). This involves the continuous doing of three things: building, praying, looking (vv. 20-21, where the three present participles explain the single command *keep*). Christian growth, Spirit-directed prayer, and an expectant attitude toward Christ's coming are the essentials of the present experience of salvation.

C. *The Future Aspect of Salvation*

What God has begun He will also consummate (v. 24). He will keep us from stumbling and present us faultless in respect to His own glory with an exulting joy. The glory of God is the absolute standard for our future glorification, and its attainment is certain through the power of God.

IV. THE LIBERTINES

A. *Their identifications*

"Libertines" is a good name for the apostates which Jude describes as invading the church, for they were evidently people who were more interested in living false doctrine than teaching it. They had turned the grace of God into a shocking unbridled lust in their lives. Their denial of the Lord was more in life than doctrine, and as far as Jude's opinion is concerned, they are not saved people (v. 19).

B. *Their Characteristics*

It is most remarkable to find these unbelievers actually associating themselves with the church in their love feasts (v. 12). They stood apart, however, from the rest of the group (v. 12) and refused to place themselves under the leadership of the recognized shepherds of the group (v. 12). Defiance is their keynote (cf. v. 8); their own lusts, their motivation (v. 16); their own advantage, their goal (v. 16).

C. *The Christian's Reaction to Them*

Although the text is somewhat uncertain in verses 22-23,

it seems as if there are three possible attitudes a believer may have toward libertines, depending on the circumstances. On those who separate themselves the believer is to have mercy, for in their wavering they need to be treated with great kindness. Others are to be snatched from the fire of the situation in which they are presently living. On still others, who have evidently gone much deeper into sin, the Christian is to show fearful mercy lest he should be led to think too lightly of the sin from which he is trying to snatch them. The remarkable thing about this advice is that Jude does not recommend denunciation in any of these instances. It is especially remarkable that Jude

> after all the strong language which he has used in describing the wickedness of those who are corrupt in the Christian community, does *not,* in this advice as to different methods which are to be used in dealing with those who are going or have gone astray, recommend denunciation.[6]

Sometimes it may be necessary, but often it does more harm than good.

D. *Their Judgment*

Judgment is certain. Enoch prophesied of it (vv. 14-15), and what came upon unbelieving Israelites, the angels who sinned, and Sodom and Gomorrha assures it (vv. 5-7). The pattern of past judgments affirms that the judgment on the libertines will be with eternal fire (v. 7). Jude also emphasizes again and again that it is deserved judgment (cf. v. 15).

V. BIBLIOLOGY

The problem of Jude's quotation of noncanonical sources has often obscured his references to canonical books. In his

---

[6] A. Plummer, *The General Epistles of St. James and St. Jude, The Expositor's Bible* (Grand Rapids: Eerdmans, 1943), VI, 666.

short Epistle he refers to five or six incidents recorded in the Old Testament. These are: the exodus from Egypt (v. 5), the destruction of Sodom and Gomorrah (v. 7), the story of Cain (v. 11), the account of Balaam (v. 11), and the gain-saying of Korah (v. 11). The account of the angels who kept not their first estate may be a sixth reference (Gen. 6: 1-4). These references show the influence of a godly Jewish home where the children were taught the Old Testament Scriptures. In this respect James and Jude are. similar.

Jude also includes references and allusions to the non-canonical books, Assumption of Moses and the Book of Enoch (vv. 6, 9, 13-15). This too shows the influence of Jude's Jewish background, for these books were a valued part of the Hebrew literary inheritance, and undoubtedly Jude was brought up to respect them. Sometimes it is assumed from these quotations that the entire doctrine of the inspiration of the canonical Old Testament books is undermined; but Jude's quoting

> does not warrant us to affirm that he indorsed the book. Paul cites from three Greek poets: from Aratus (Acts 17:28), from Menander (I Cor. 15:33) . . . and from Epimenides (Titus 1:12). Does anyone imagine that Paul indorses all that these poets wrote? . . . So Jude cites a passage from a non-canonical book, not because he accepts the whole book as true, but this particular prediction he receives as from God.[7]

VI. THE DOCTRINE OF ANGELS

Again, for a short letter it is surprising to find so much said about the angels, though most of the references are incidental to the purpose. It is apparent that Jude everywhere assumes the existence of all classes of angels—the good angels, the evil angels, an archangel, and Satan. He infers that Satan is the highest of God's creatures, for Michael the arch-

[7]W. G. Moorehead, "Jude, The Epistle of," *International Standard Bible Encyclopaedia*, III, 1771.

angel had to resort to the Lord to rebuke Satan. In the case of the death of Moses angels were concerned about his body (cf. Luke 16:22). It is also clear that Jude had the same idea about the respect due to angels who are present in the assembly of believers as Paul had (v. 8; cf. I Cor. 11:10). He uses an *a fortiori* argument in verse 8: the libertines have an attitude toward and use language against good angels which Michael the archangel would not dare use of evil angels. Jude also affirms that angels will accompany the Lord at His coming (v. 14).

The principal reference to angels, however, is to those who kept not their first estate (v. 6). The verse is reminiscent of an account in the book of Enoch which is an expansion of the story in Genesis 6:1-4. Satan evidently persuaded some of the angels who originally fell with him to cohabit with women on the earth, and these God confined immediately because of the gross nature of that sin. The other fallen angels who did not participate in this sin are still free to roam the earth as demons carrying out Satan's designs. The Septuagint has the word *angels* in Genesis 6, and this was the uniform interpretation of Judaism and the early Church (with the exception of Julius Africanus in the entire ante-Nicene period). The Lord's word concerning angels neither marrying nor being given in marriage in the resurrection (Matt. 22:30) does not contradict this interpretation of Genesis 6:1-4, for the Lord's point is simply that with resurrection bodies there will be no procreation of human babies just as angels cannot produce angelic offspring. But He does not say that angels could not have cohabited with women to produce abnormal, yet human, offspring. At any rate, in Jude's mind the angel interpretation of Genesis 6 would undoubtedly be the only one he knew, and since we study the theology of Jude it must be admitted that the reference in his Epistle is to that event. This natural emphasis on angelology again reflects the background of the author.

In summary the theology of Jude may be said to be simple like James's, saturated with a knowledge of the Old Testament, and emphasizing the lordship of Christ with its concomitant, proper Christian conduct. All the elements of apostolic theology are present even in this short example of Jude's theology which we have—the principles of grace and faith, salvation through Christ, holy Christian living, the coming of Christ and judgment. The letter was born in the midst of trouble in the Church, but not the theology, for that was evidently fixed in the writer's mind long before the letter was written.

Part VII

THE THEOLOGY OF JOHN

Chapter 1

INTRODUCTION

BIBLICAL THEOLOGY investigates the "historically conditioned progress of revelation." As pointed out in the
introduction, this means that the study is concerned with the
persons through whom revelation was given (the historical
conditioning) and with the periods in which it came (progress of doctrine). In the Old Testament generally the periods are more prominent; while in New Testament Biblical Theology the other is true. In the case of Johannine theology there is a remarkable combination of the two factors,
for we are dealing with a distinctive person[1] whose character
stamps his writings, which were written during the last period in the progress of revelation. Because of this

> the doctrinal teaching of John, the Apostle of Love,
> occupies not merely the last but also the highest place
> in the succession of Apostolic testimonies . . . As in the
> natural, so also in the spiritual domain, that which is
> noblest comes most slowly to perfection. Already have
> Peter and Paul deposed their written testimony, and left
> the scene of their earthly activity, before the testimony
> of John is heard. . . . No wonder that the Church of all
> ages has attached the highest value to the testimony of
> the bosom friend of the Lord, the venerable and pro-

---

[1] "The apostle John was an intuitionist and a mystic. He does not argue;
he sees. . . . What men need is not more light, but an eye." G. B. Stevens,
Theology of the New Testament (Edinburgh: T. & T. Clark, 1899), p. 566.

found Apostle John. While the Petrine bears a Jewish-Christian, the Pauline a Gentile-Christian character, we here see the whole opposition between the Gospel and Judaism on the one hand, and heathenism on the other, recede entirely into the background; and Christianity is regarded, in the fullest sense of the word, as the absolute religion. Thus, the highest point is attained; and, at the same time, the future development of Church and theology is sketched in broad outlines. The Petrine type is regarded by preference in the Roman Catholic, the Pauline in the Protestant development of Church and doctrine; the Johannine theology seems emphatically destined to become the theology of the future.[2]

There are two principal ways of treating Johannine theology. One considers all of John's writings as a unit;[3] the other separates the Gospel and deals with it from the viewpoint of the theology of Jesus rather than the theology of John.[4] This latter course is preferable if one's basic concept of New Testament Biblical Theology is that the teachings of Jesus are its focal point from which other types of apostolic teaching emanate and evolve. To treat all of John's writings as a unit is more desirable if one prefers to emphasize the individuality of the Johannine type of thought, and even Stevens in his *Theology of the New Testament,* which does not follow this method of treatment, admits that "the whole Gospel, as truly as the first Epistle, embodies the theology of John and exemplifies the Johannine style, terminology, and mode of conceiving Christian truth."[5]

Undoubtedly there are advantages and disadvantages to either plan, and one must choose according to his basic concept of Biblical Theology. To this writer it seems impera-

[2]J. J. Van Oosterzee, *The Theology of the New Testament* (New York: Dodd & Mead, 1871), pp. 372-73.

[3]As Weiss, Sheldon, and Stevens in his *The Johannine Theology* (London: Dickinson, 1894).

[4]As Van Oosterzee, Beyschlag, and Stevens in his *The Theology of the New Testament.*

[5]P. 175.

tive to treat Johannine theology as a distinctive and climactic unit, making it necessary to consider all of his writings together. The chief disadvantage of this method is that it excludes Johannine Christological discourses from the theology of Jesus, but since, as we have already seen in the Synoptic theology, the theology of Jesus was preserved in the historically conditioned writings of men, this is not a serious disadvantage. The advantages are considerable, and the result of the application of this method should best set forth the "historically conditioned progress of revelation as deposited in the Bible."

Chapter 2

HISTORICAL AND CRITICAL
BACKGROUND

THIS DISCUSSION of certain introductory matters is always necessary in every section of Biblical Theology. Some are historical and furnish the background picture for the writings involved, while others are critical. To these matters we now turn our attention.

I. THE LIFE OF JOHN

To understand the theology one must know something of the human instrument through whom it came. The life of John naturally divides itself into two periods. The first concludes with his departure from Jerusalem sometime after the ascension of Christ, and the second continues from that time to his death. The source material for the facts for the first is Biblical and for the second is extra-Biblical.

Nothing definite is known about the birth of John except that he was evidently much younger than Jesus and that he may have been born in Bethsaida (John 1:44). He was the son of Zebedee and Salome, and had a younger brother, James. He evidently came from a fairly well-to-do family, for they had servants (Mark 1:20), his mother helped support Christ and his band (Mark 15:40-41), and John himself was personally acquainted with the high priest who was always chosen from the upper classes (John 18:15). His home environment in Galilee would have given John a Greek mixture in his outlook. Probably he never attended rabbinical schools (Acts 4:13), but he would have had the thorough religious training of a Jewish household which observed the liturgical ritual of Judaism. At least he shows detailed acquaintance with it in his writings.

Though artists have generally pictured John as an effeminate person, his character was much different from that. Galileans were by nature industrious, hardy men of action (cf. John 6:14-15). John, who was known as a son of thunder (Mark 3:17), was no exception. Glimpses of him in the other Gospels reveal him acting in bigotry (Mark 9:38; Luke 9:49), vindictiveness (Luke 9:54), and intrigue (Matt. 20: 20; Mark 9:35). The power of Christ made over John as much as it did Peter, for by nature he was a typical Galilean, but by new nature he became the Apostle of Love.

How long John remained in Jerusalem after Pentecost is not known. He was part of the delegation which went to Samaria after the preaching of Philip there, but he evidently was not in Jerusalem when Paul first visited the city (Gal. 1:18-19) though he may have been there later as one of the apostles mentioned at the council (Acts 15:6). However, that eventually he went to Ephesus is the reliable evidence of tradition. The tradition is also supported by the inference of the Apocalypse that it was written by someone who was a leader in Asia Minor and specifically Ephesus, the first church mentioned. The extra-Biblical literature is replete with the accounts of John's activities, the most famous stories being (1) Cerinthus in the bath house, (2) the young lad who became a bandit, and (3) the repeated admonition to love one another.[1]

As the Apostle of Love, John is well-known, but he was also a man who even in his later years was sternly intolerant

---

[1]The evidence and these stories are conveniently collected in A. Plummer, *The Gospel According to St. John, Cambridge Greek Testament* (Cambridge: University Press, 1891), pp. xvii-xviii.

of heresy. Both aspects of the man—the love and the stern-
ness—are seen, for instance, in the same Epistle, I John. Perhaps the best way to describe his character would be with
the word *intense*. In actions, in love for the brethren, in
condemnation of Christ-rejectors he was the Apostle of Intensity. This was the instrument through which Johannine
theology came.

II. Matters of Introduction

While this is mainly in the area of New Testament introduction, certain matters of introduction must be touched
upon in Biblical Theology. For instance, if one does not
divorce the sayings of Christ as recorded in the Fourth Gospel from Johannine theology, then the problem of the authorship of the Gospel becomes important. For fuller treatment of these subjects the student should consult the literature of New Testament introduction.

A. *Authorship of the Gospel*

Older liberalism held that the Gospel of John was spuri-
ous, being a product of a Hellenizing type of thought and belonging to the second century. More recent liberalism holds
that the Gospel was an edition of genuine memoranda of
John by some unknown editor or disciple of John.[2] Neo-
orthodoxy thinks that John did not write it, though the
truths contained are of the most vital kind. Conservatism
has held that the Gospel was by John the son of Zebedee.

External evidence for the Johannine authorship is abundant and uniform after A.D. 170. Before that time allusions
are more scarce but not entirely absent. An unusual source
of external evidence in the case of John's Gospel comes from
the early heretical sects. After citing this evidence Lightfoot
concludes:

Differing in almost every other particular, heterodoxy

[2] G. Appleton, *John's Witness to Jesus* (New York: Association Press, 1955),
p. 9.

> unites in bearing testimony to St. John's Gospel. . . .
> More than enough of the unorthodox literature can be
> tested to throw back the date of the general acceptance
> outside the church of St. John's Gospel as genuine to a
> very early period in the second century.[3]

The argument for the Johannine authorship based on internal evidence of the Gospel itself is standard and well
known. It is like three concentric circles. (1) The largest
circle proves that the author was a Palestinian Jew. This is
shown by his use of the Old Testament (cf. John 6:45; 13:
18; 19:37), by his knowledge of Jewish ideas, traditions, ex-
pectations (cf. John 1:19-49; 2:6, 13; 3:25; 4:25; 5:1; 6:14-15;
7:26 ff.; 10:22; 11:55; 12:13; 13:1; 18:28; 19:31, 42), and by
his knowledge of Palestine (1:44, 46; 2:1; 4:47; 5:2; 9:7; 10:
23; 11:54). (2) The middle circle proves that the author was
an eyewitness. This is done by pointing to the exactness of
detail of time, place, and incidents in the Gospel (cf. John
1:29, 35, 43; 2:6; 4:40, 43; 5:5; 12:1, 6, 12; 13:26; 19:14, 20,
23, 34, 39; 20:7; 21:6), and by pointing to the character
sketches (e.g., Andrew, Philip, Thomas, Nathanael, the woman of Samaria, Nicodemus) which are distinctive to John. (3)
The third circle concludes that the author was John. This is
done first by a process of elimination of the others who belonged to the inner circle of disciples and then by citing
confirmatory evidence.

However, the question is raised as to whether the John
who wrote both the Gospel and Epistles was really John the
son of Zebedee or John the elder of Ephesus. Early Church
literature mentions a presbyter John in Ephesus, which has
led some to conclude that John the son of Zebedee was a
different person from the John of Ephesus and that it was the
latter who wrote these books.[4] The arguments for the com-

[3]J. B. Lightfoot, *Biblical Essays* (London: Macmillan, 1893), p. 121.
[4]Irenaeus in Eusebius, *Ecclesiastical History*, V, viii and xx; Papias in
ibid., III, xxxix; Polycrates in *ibid.*, V. xxiv; Muratori on the canon.

mon authorship of the Gospel and Epistle are conclusive,[5] and any inevitable and expected differences are swallowed up by the overwhelming number of resemblances. Therefore, the question is, Was the author John the apostle or John the elder?

Some of the reasons for not identifying John the apostle with John the elder are: (1) an unlettered man (Acts 4:13) could not have written anything so profound as the Fourth Gospel; (2) a fisherman's son would not have known the high priest; (3) an apostle would not designate himself as a presbyter as the writer of the Epistles does (4) since the writer of the Fourth Gospel used Mark it could not have been John, because an apostle would not use the work of one who was not an apostle. Answers to these arguments are not difficult to find. (1) The meaning of "unlettered" is reckoned from the viewpoint of formal training in rabbinic schools and does not mean unlearned; (2) all fishermen cannot be assumed to be from the lower classes; (3) the apostle Peter calls himself a presbyter (I Pet. 5:1), so why should not John? (4) Matthew, an apostle, used Mark, according to the critics, but that is never used as an argument against the Matthean authorship of the first Gospel. Furthermore, if John the elder is the author of the Gospel, and therefore the beloved disciple, it becomes very difficult to explain why such an important person as the son of Zebedee is never mentioned in that Gospel. Taken at face value the evidence points to one writer of Gospel and Epistles, John the apostle, the son of Zebedee, who is one and the same as John the elder who spent his later years in Ephesus.

B. *Date and Place of the Writing of the Gospel*

Tradition is unanimous in assigning Ephesus as the place of the writing of the Gospel. The elders of the Asian churches

[5]The evidence is built on the parallel passages (e.g., John 1:1; I John 1:1), common phrases (e.g., "only begotten," "born of God"), common constructions (use of conjunctions instead of subordinate clauses), and common themes *agapē*, love; *phōs*, light; *zōē*, life; *menō*, abide).

had probably requested that the things which John had been giving them orally be put in writing before he died. It is evident in the book that the author is looking back (7:39; 21:19), and it is not unlikely it was published between 85 and 90 (though the writing may have been done before that time).[6]

C. *Date and Place of the Writing of the First Epistle*

The message of I John seems to presuppose a knowledge of the contents of the Gospel, and since there is no mention of the persecution under Domitian in 95, it was probably written about A.D. 90. There is no address or salutation, which points to its being a homily rather than a personal letter. Probably it was written from Ephesus to all the churches in Asia Minor.

D. *Matters Concerning II John*

Again the student is referred to other books whose province it is to discuss these matters fully,[7] but for the sake of this work the position is taken that the Second Epistle was written very shortly after the First to an unknown lady and her children who resided in the neighborhood of Ephesus.

E. *Matters Concerning III John*

This Epistle can also be dated at about the same time as the others; i.e., 90. Undoubtedly it was written from Ephesus

---

[6]Note the dilemma of the critics who argue for a date between 110 and 165 and who assume that John did not write it. If the Gospel was published between 110 and 140, why did not the hundreds of living Christians who had known John during his later years denounce it as a forgery? Or at least why did not someone mention that it did not come from John himself? If it was not published until 140-165 how could it have been universally accepted by 170 as it was? Moreover, the discovery of the Rylands fragment of John's Gospel (generally dated during the second quarter of the second century) has tended to push the date of composition back into the first century.

[7]Plummer has a good summary of views on "elect lady" in *The Epistles of St. John, Cambridge Greek Testament* (Cambridge: University Press, 1886), p. lxxvii.

(for it "has the tone of being written from head-quarters"[8]) to a church under John's supervision.

III. EPHESUS

No historical background for Johannine theology would be complete without a picture of Ephesus.

A. *The City of Ephesus*

Ephesus lies advantageously in the midst of a fertile plain near the mouth of the Cayster River. It was a center of trade both of the eastern Aegean area and that which passes through Ephesus from the east. Marseilles, Corinth, Ephesus, and Tarsus were principal centers of trade in that day. The city was the capital of the province of Asia Minor and the Roman proconsul resided there. In addition, the people had a measure of self-government, for they were allowed to have assemblies (Acts 19:39).

B. *The Church of Ephesus*

As far as the Biblical record reveals, the church at Ephesus was founded by Paul about 55. It received from him a circular letter about eight years later. For some time Timothy was the pastor of the congregation (I Tim. 1:3). Actually before John came to Ephesus many had labored there (Aquila and Priscilla, Acts 18:19; Paul, Acts 19:8-10; Trophimus, Acts 21:29; the family of Onesiphorus, II Tim. 1:16-18; and Timothy, II Tim. 4:9). After the destruction of Jerusalem in 70 it is quite likely that many Christians fled to Ephesus so that between the time of the fall of Jerusalem and the rise of Rome it may be said that Ephesus was the center of the Christian world. "To touch Ephesus was to touch the world."

C. *The Morals of Ephesus*

1. *Diana worship.* The temple of Diana, one of the seven

Ibid., p. lxxx.

wonders of the ancient world, was like a magnet drawing people to a cesspool in Ephesus. Its proverbial magnificence was deserved, for it was built with 127 columns 60 feet high, surrounding an area 425 by 220 feet (about the size of a football field enlarged both ways by one-third). The wealthy vied to lavish gifts on the temple so that much treasure was kept there. It was also, in the name of religion, a house of prostitution. And yet in spite of the iniquitous idolatry of the place, it was a Mecca or Rome of religious worship, and the people of the city itself delighted to call themselves temple-sweepers of the great Diana (Acts 19:35).

2. *Magic.* Superstition invariably accompanies idolatry, and so it was in Ephesus. Around the statue of Diana were written unintelligible sayings which were supposed to be magical in their effect. Magic charms and magic sayings were made and sold to the worshipers. So universal was the grip of this idea of magic that even the Christians banked on its powers after they were converted (Acts 19:13-20; I John 5:21). The sale of horoscopes and lucky charms in our day only feebly compares to the traffic in magic in Ephesus.

D. *The Gnosticism of Ephesus*

Gnosticism is in reality a philosophy of existence or being. It involves speculations concerning the origin of matter with resultant ideas about how human beings can be free from matter. *Gnōsis* was considered superior to the *philosophia* of the heathen, and it stood in sharp contrast with the *pistis,* faith, of the Christian. Most of its elements were Greek, though they were mixed with Oriental dualism too. The intellect was supreme; faith and conduct were definitely inferior and secondary considerations. This is what John battles against in the First Epistle.

In particular, gnosticism held that knowledge was superior to virtue, that the facts of Scripture should not be treated literally and in this nonliteral sense could only be understood by a select few, that evil in the world makes it impossible for God to be its creator, that the Incarnation is incredible because deity could not unite itself with material body, and that there was no resurrection of the flesh.

Such doctrine resulted in docetism, asceticism, and antinomianism. Extreme docetism held that Jesus was not human at all but was merely a prolonged theophany, while moderate docetism considered Jesus the natural son of Joseph and Mary upon whom came the Christ at His baptism. Both forms are attacked by John (I John 2:22; 4:2-3; 5:5-6). Asceticism was practiced by some gnostics because they considered matter evil. Antinomianism was the conduct of others since they thought knowledge was superior to virtue (cf. I John 1:8; 4:20). John's answer to gnosticism is the Incarnation. An actual Incarnation gives a real example (I John 2:6) which should result in proper ethical conduct. Philosophic arrogance (as in liberalism), any attempt to disentangle eternal truth from its historical shell (as in Barthianism), and neglect of the Jesus of history and His example (as sometime in fundamentalism) are all echoes of contemporary gnosticism. They make the study of Johannine theology particularly relevant in our day.

IV. Outstanding Features of Johannine Theology

When one thinks of Pauline theology, certain things, like his doctrine of "in Christ," naturally stand out. The theology of James brings to mind either justification and works or the doctrine of the Word. Likewise, Johannine theology has certain distinctive and distinguishing features.

A. *Its Antecedent Is Paulinism*

Usually we do not think of a relationship between John and Paul, and yet chronologically and theologically Paul was antecedent to John. Geographically, too, there is relationship, for John labored in the same territory where Paul had laid foundations. It is not difficult to discover that some of the principal features of Paulinism are taken up by John not in the sense of borrowing but in the sense of building upon them as the historical antecedents which they were. For instance, John carries forth the Pauline contrast between Moses and Christ (John 1:17; 10:34; 15:25), and the Fourth Gospel is the only one which does not contain discourses forecasting the future for the Jews. John also gives large place to faith (what new Christian has not been exhorted to count the occurrences of "believe" in the Gospel?). Again, although I Corinthians 13 is always thought of as the love chapter, why should not John 13 or the entire First Epistle be so considered also? Paul's great mystical theme of being "in Christ" finds correspondence in John (John 14:20; I John 3:24). Thus, though there is not personal antecedence in the sense of borrowing from Paul, there is historical antecedence so that whatever John learned from Paul came through his own mind bearing a distinctively Johannine stamp.

B. *It Has Its Foundations in the Old Testament*

This involves a paradox, for while John shows his love for the Old Testament and uses it to point to Christ, at the same time he displays open hostility toward Judaism. Of course, the hostility was because the Jews rejected that to which their own Scriptures should have led them. Thus, John's use of the Old Testament in the Gospel (for there is only one direct reference in the Epistles) is to draw from it types and prophecies of Messiah. There are general statements that should point a man to Christ (1:45; 4:22; 5:39, 46). There are direct references to the Old Testament which show John's belief in it as the inspired Word of God (Abraham, 8:56; serpent, 3:14; bridegroom, 3:29; manna, 6:49; lamb, 1:29; 19:36; the Psalms, 2:17; 10:34; 13:18;

19:24, 36; prophets, 6:45; Isaiah, 12:38, 40; Zechariah, 12:
15; 19:37; Micah, 7:42). Mention is also made of events in
the life of Christ which fulfill Old Testament prophecies (12:
14-15; 17:12; 19:24, 28, 36-37; 20:9). "Without the basis
of the Old Testament, without the fullest acceptance of the
unchanging divinity of the Old Testament, the Gospel of
St. John is an insoluble riddle."[9]

C. *It Is Ethical*

This trait of Johannine theology is nowhere clearer demonstrated than in the First Epistle. Since the detail will be dealt with later, suffice it to mention only certain general features of John's emphasis on ethics.

1. *Proper ethical conduct is based on the pattern of the earthly life of Christ* (I John 2:6).

2. *This is in turn related to the doctrine of the Incarnation* (I John 4:1 ff.). If the Incarnation is not real, then there is no real basis for ethics.

3. *Proper Christian conduct is primarily demonstrated by love for the brethren* (I John 2:7-11; 4:11-12).

4. *The result is a life of habitual righteousness* (I John 3: 4-18). One may say even more summarily that John's thesis concerning ethics has two main points: ethical conduct is based on sound doctrine and results in the imitation of Christ.

D. *It Is Antithetical*

Antithesis is another characteristic of Johannine theology —not antithesis in the sense of contradictions but of contrasts.

1. *The antithesis of the Christian and the world.* Undoubtedly this is one of the most pronounced in John's thought. The world and the Christian stand apart from each other not in any metaphysical dualistic sense but more in an ethical sense. Such statements as those in John 3:16 and

[9]B. F. Westcott, *The Gospel of St. John* (London: John Murray, 1908), I, cxxxix-cxl.

I John 2:2 guard against the idea that the world is intrinsically evil. Nevertheless, the cosmos hated Christ and His disciples, is under the headship of the Devil, is transient (John 7:7; 8:23; 14:17, 30; 15:19; 17:14; I John 3:13; 5:19); therefore, it must not receive the love of the Christian (I John 2:15-16).

2. *The antithesis of light and darkness.* John uses both light and darkness as symbols for knowledge, but these symbols are antithetical in two areas. They are used to express the idea of God Himself (I John 1:5), and they represent spheres of life (I John 1:7). This latter idea is associated with love and hatred of the brethren (I John 2:10-11).

3. *The antithesis of death and life.* This is much the same as the preceding contrast, for John associated life with fullness of right ethical action and death with the lack of it (I John 3:14; John 8:51).

E. *It Is Contemplative*

John is not an apologete or a polemicist; he is more of a mystic in the proper Christian sense. The truths of Christianity are set forth in their own beauties so that others may see and believe. Even in proving that Jesus is the Messiah he employs miracle-signs (2:11; 4:54), and throughout his use of symbols is graphic (10:1; 15:1).

Though he is referring to the Fourth Gospel only, Plummer has observed characteristics which apply equally well to all of Johannine theology:

> These characteristics combined form a book [or, just as well, a theology] which stands alone in Christian literature, as its author stands alone among Christian teachers; the work of one who for threescore years and ten laboured as an Apostle. Called to follow the Baptist when only a lad, and by him soon transferred to the Christ, he may be said to have been the first who from his youth up was a Christian. Who, therefore, could so

fitly grasp and state in their true proportions and with fitting impressiveness the great verities of the Christian faith? He had had no deep-seated prejudices to uproot, like his friend Peter and others who were called late in life. He had had no sudden wrench to make from the past, like Paul. He had not had the trying excitement of wandering abroad over the face of the earth, like most of the Twelve. He had remained at his post at Ephesus, directing, teaching, meditating; until at last when the fruit was ripe it was given to the Church in the fulness of beauty which it is still our privilege to possess and learn to love.[10]

[10]A. Plummer, *The Gospel of St. John*, pp. xlviii-xlix.

Chapter 3

THEOLOGY PROPER

JOHANNINE THEOLOGY, unlike Pauline theology, can be catalogued under relatively few categories. If the Apocalypse is excluded, John's thought focuses on two principal themes—God and salvation—and most Biblical Theologies, with slight variations, deal with the Johannine system in this way. When the Revelation is included, of course a third category, eschatology, must be added. As the viewpoint of Matthew's theology may be epitomized as theocratic, James's bibliological, Paul's theological, so John's viewpoint may be said to be theological or Christological. Schmid explains:

> He takes the principle of all life as his groundwork, and then descends to all the matters presented to him by experience. But in his view the theological standpoint is identical with the Christological, because this very principle of life is in Christ, and the Father is known through the Son . . . The divine nature as it is in Christ is not, in the first place, considered in its communication to men; but eternal life in Christ is first regarded *per se,* although he goes on to represent its communication to the world.[1]

Life *per se* is the first main section of Johannine theology—the doctrine of God; the second is the communication of the life—the doctrine of salvation; and to these may be added

[1]C. F. Schmid, *Biblical Theology of the New Testament* (Edinburgh: T. & T. Clark, 1877), pp. 523-24.

the judgment as revealed in the Apocalypse of the One who is life. In these three principal areas all of Johannine theology is found.

I. THE DOCTRINE OF GOD

A. *The Nature of God*

For the most part John, like the other writers of Scripture, leaves the reader to form his own conclusions as to the nature of God from statements made concerning God's actions. However, John, unlike the other writers of Scripture, does speak of God's nature in three statements—God is spirit, God is light, and God is love. These statements do not reflect properties of God (i.e., God is spiritual or loving) but state essential aspects of His nature.

1. *His metaphysical nature—God is spirit* (John 4:24). Negatively, the statement of the Lord to the Samaritan woman does not refer to personality but to nature. Neither does the text say that God is a spirit but that He is spirit. Nor is it a reference to the spirit of God but to God's own nature.

Positively, the statement includes several definite ideas. (1) God is not limited to space, for spirit is not confined. This was of course the question which the Lord was discussing with the Samaritan woman. She was concerned about place, but in His answer the Lord pointed out that since God is not limited to space He can be worshiped anywhere. (2) God is not limited to time, for since spirit is not material it cannot be subject to the restrictions of time. (3) God is understood by spiritual and inward not carnal and outward perception. The Jews thought they knew God through their forms of religious worship; whereas He is revealed in a spiritual manner and especially through Christ, for even the revelation of God through Christ must be spiritually perceived.

The principal resultant idea from this revelation of the nature of God is related to worship. Since God is spirit man must worship Him in spirit and in truth. Such worship rules out local claims (John 4:21) concerning places and forms, and it sets aside the ritualistic worship of Judaism as well as the false worship of the Samaritans. Worshipers of that sort are sought by the God whose nature is spirit.

2. *His moral nature—God is light* (I John 1:5). Negatively, John again is not speaking of personality but of essential nature. (In each of these phrases the construction is anarthrous.) The idea is that God is such a one who is light. The statement could not be more simple or more profound. As above, it is not that God is a light among others but He is light in His being.

Positively, "God is light" includes the ideas of holiness, for in Him is no darkness; revealedness, because when the light shines there can be no shadows (this does not necessarily imply revelation but simply revealedness); and infinitude, for light is not bound except by darkness and in God there is no darkness.

The principal resultant idea is related to ethics. God's being light is made the basis for Christian ethics in the First Epistle. The believer is not expected to become light, else he would be as God, but he is exhorted to walk in the light; that is, to respond to its revelations with conduct pleasing to God. God *is* light, but we are to walk *in* the light.

3. *His personal nature—God is love* (I John 4:8). Negatively, the phrase does not say merely that love is of God, but that God is in His essential nature love (again the construction is anarthrous). Further, the phrase does not imply that God's being love is occasioned by anything. In other words, He is love apart from any opportunity to express it.

Positively, this love is the original love (I John 4:10) because the source of it is God (I John 4:19). It seems to be best illustrated by the earthly picture of the love within a family (I John 4:7; cf. Eph. 3:15; 5:25).

It is this expression of love within the family which is the resultant idea from "God is love." John's reasoning is very simple: God is love; therefore, what God begets loves; thus, Christians should show that they are begotten of God by loving one another. This idea seemed to captivate John as he grew older as being the central feature of Christianity, for in no book of the New Testament does the word *love* appear as often as it does in I John 3:1—5:12. In the heart of that section, 4:11-21, John lists the important practical ramifications of our loving one another because God is love. Love fulfills our duty (v. 11); love can be realized in its most complete form when we love others (v. 12b); love causes us to know the indwelling of the Holy Spirit (vv. 13-15b); love gives us boldness in the day of judgment (v. 17); love casts out fear (v. 18); and love proves our profession of Christianity (vv. 19-21). It is easy to say "I love God," but it is often much more difficult to prove it by loving the brethren. This, however, is the expected result of the fact that we know God, who is love.

B. *The Fatherhood of God*

The idea of the Fatherhood of God reaches its most complete development in the writings of John. In the Old Testament the phrase is limited in use to describe God's relationship to Israel, His people (Exod. 4:22; Deut. 32:6) and to Messiah, His Son (Ps. 2:6). The principal idea connected with it is that of authority with its consequence, obedience. In the Synoptics that same general conception also prevails. However, in John's writings the phrase does not have Messianic or national connotations as much as personal ramifications in describing man's relation to God through Christ, the revealer of God. This we now examine in more detail.

1. *In relation to Christ.* Primarily John uses two terms, *the Father,* and *my Father.* Generally the latter is used in revealing the Son as the one who fulfilled and properly interpreted true Judaism (John 2:16; 5:17; 6:32; 8:19, 49, 54; 10:

37; 15:1, 8, 23-24). It is also used in revealing certain facts about the Son Himself (John 6:39-40; 10:18, 29; 14:2, 7, 20-21, 23; 15:15; 20:17). The phrase *the Father* shows God as One who is revealed by the Son (John 1:18; 6:46; 10:29), as the One who sent the Son (5:23, 36-37; 6:44; 10:36; 20:21; I John 4:14), and as the One who helped the Son accomplish His mission (5:19; 6:37; 10:15, 38; 14:10-11, 31; 16:32). In these usages the Messianic concept is entirely lacking.

2. *In relation to the believer.* John also speaks of the Fatherhood of God as relates to the believer in Christ. Again the relationship is personal and based on the new birth and rooted in God's love toward mankind. There is no idea of universal Fatherhood. Indeed, just the opposite is true, for nowhere else, with the exception of Paul, is there the stress on spiritual rebirth as the prerequisite for sonship as in Johannine theology. To those who have become sons by being rightly related to His Son there come certain blessings and requirements. (1) The Father wants to be worshiped by believers (4:24). (2) It is to the Father that we are to direct our prayers (15:16). (3) The Father's love toward His children is like that which He has for His only begotten Son (17:23). (4) The promise of the indwelling of Father and Son is given to those who love Him (14:23). (5) This relationship carries with it the privilege of fellowship with the Father (I John 1:3). The intimacies of the family relationship is John's particular contribution to the doctrine of the Father of believers.

3. *In relation to the Holy Spirit.* It is only John who speaks of that relationship of the Holy Spirit to the other persons of the Trinity which theologians have called procession (15:26). Like all attempts to describe eternal relations within the Godhead in temporal terms, the term *procession* does not fully satisfy, for there must not be any thought of inferiority or chronological order in the term. The Spirit's eternal relationship to the Father and the Son is one of pro-

cession (note the present tense which indicates the eternity of the relation).

In respect to the new relationship that the eternal Spirit would have to the believer, the Lord said that the Father would send Him (14:16, 26). It is not as if nothing had previously been known of the Holy Spirit, for He was actively ministering in Old Testament times; nevertheless, Jesus spoke of a different relationship which He would have when the Father would send Him. That difference is succinctly stated in John 14:17: "for he dwelleth with (*para*) you, and shall be in (*en*) you." Universal, permanent indwelling of all believers was the new relationship which the Spirit would have after the Son returned to the Father.

II. The Doctrine of Christ

If John's central purpose is theological and Christological, then it is natural to find a large amount of revelation concerning Christ. In this section we are treating the person of Christ apart from His work.

A. *The Designations of the Lord*

1. *Jesus.* As in the other Gospels "Jesus" is the general designation used by the writer in the narrative itself, occurring around 250 times. However, there appears a variation from this usual narrative designation which is striking; that is, the use of "the Lord" in place of "Jesus" (4:1; 6:23; 11:2; 20:20; 21:12).

2. *Designations by the people.* Popular designations of the Lord as John rememberd them were: "the man called Jesus" (9:11), "Jesus the son of Joseph" (1:45; 6:42), "Jesus of Nazareth" (18:5, 7; 19:19), and "this man" (9:16, 24; 11:47; 18:17, 29).

3. *Designations by the disciples.* By His followers "teacher" and "rabbi" are used most frequently (1:38, 49; 3:2; 4:31; 6:25; 9:2; 11:8, 28; 20:16). "Lord" was also used with a

reverential recognition of His authority (13:13-14). Thomas uses it with clear implications of deity (20:28).

4. *Messianic designations.* However, the word *Christ* is infrequently used in the Gospel. This is in line with the purpose of John in contrast to the Synoptics. However, John pointed to Jesus as the Christ (1:20, 25; 3:28); the disciples recognized Him as Messiah (1:41; 11:27); He Himself announced it to the Samaritan woman (4:25-26); the people speculated about it (4:29; 7:26-42; 9:22; 10:24; 12:34); and He was called king (1:49; 12:13; 18:33, 37).

5. *Son of God.* This title definitely has Messianic implications (1:49; 11:27; 20:31). It speaks of the supernatural origin of Jesus (5:25; 9:35; 10:36; 11:4). It is connected with His miracles (5:25; 9:35; 11:4), and was clearly recognized by the people as a claim to deity (10:33, 36). The very use of this title forbids anyone saying that Jesus Himself did not claim to be God nor that it was not so understood by the people of His day.

6. *Son of man.* This seemed to be the Lord's favorite designation of Himself. The person so described is no mere earthly being (6:62), for He is the giver of eternal life (6:27; 3:14-15) and the judge of all men (5:27). As in the Synoptics this title has soterio-eschatological implications.

7. *Figurative designations.* In line with John's use of symbols we find certain figurative designations of the Lord in the Gospel. He is called the light of the world (8:12; 9:5; 12:35-36, 46); the light of men (1:4, 5, 7-9); the door (10:7, 9); the bread of life (6:33, 35, 41, 49); the good shepherd (10:11, 14); the bridegroom (3:29); and the paraclete (14:16).

Certain comparisons can be made between John's designations of the Lord and those of the other Gospel writers. There is less distinctively Messianic emphasis; rather there is more specific emphasis on the deity of Christ. The title *Son of man* everywhere appears to be the Lord's favorite self-designation, and John uses more figurative descriptions than the other writers.

B. *The Doctrine of the Logos*

1. *In Philo* (cir. 20 B.C.—cir. A.D. 54). No one can discuss the *Logos* without referring to Philo, who was the representative of the theosophy of Alexandrian Judaism. This was an attempt to combine elements of Judaism with elements of Platonic philosophy and Oriental mysticism. In summing up the Platonic idea of divine archetypes Philo used the term *Logos*. He substituted the word *Logos* for the Platonic word *idea,* and used the term to denote the intermediate agency by which God created material things and communicated with them. Whatever Philo did mean he certainly did not mean by *Logos* a personal redeemer from sin as John reveals the *Logos*:

> While, therefore, Philo thinks in a cultural perspective akin to that characteristic of the author of the Fourth Gospel, two vast differences sway his doctrine. On the one hand, it is speculative, not ethically personal. On the other hand, it fails completely to determine the nature of his mediator in itself, vacillating in a manner which shows how vague and fluid the conception really was.[2]

2. *In John.*

a. The meaning of *Logos.* The way John introduces the term *Logos* assumes that his readers would understand it. This would not naturally point to Alexandrian theosophy but to Judaism; therefore, one would suspect that the origin of the phrase is to be found in Judaism. In the Old Testament the Word or wisdom of God is often personified as an instrument for the execution of God's will as if it were distinct from that will (Ps. 33:6; 107:20; 119:89; 147:15; Prov.

[2]R. M. Wenley, "Philo," *International Standard Bible Encyclopaedia* (Grand Rapids: Eerdmans, 1943), IV, 2382.

8). In the Apocrypha that personification continues (Ecclus. 1:1-20; 24:1-22; Wisd. 6:22—9:18). In the Targums (the Aramaic paraphrases of the Old Testament) it is carried still further and while these Targums were not written at the time of Christ they were in use orally by Jews who had forgotten Hebrew. In them the Word of God takes on a distinct personification. This seems to be that on which John is building when he suddenly opens his Gospel with the word *Logos*.[3] As he uses it the concept narrows to a personal being who is the Son of God and the complete expression of the thought of God in communicating Himself to man. It is entirely stripped of any philosophical or mystical meaning by its identification with the person of Jesus Christ.

b. The relationships of the *Logos* (John 1:1-14). In the central passage on the *Logos,* John lists a number of relationships which the Son of God sustains. (1) His relation to time (v. 1a). Before "the beginning" the *Logos* was (*eimi*) already in existence.[4] Pre-existence to time or at least to recorded history is predicated of the *Logos.*

(2) His relation to God (vv. 1b-2). He is said to be distinct from and at the same time equal with God, for He was with (*pros*—implying two distinct persons) God and at the same time was God.

(3) His relation to creation (v. 3). He is the sufficient agent of creation, for *all* things were made by Him; He is the mediate agent, for creation was accomplished through Him; and He is the necessary agent, for without Him nothing was made.

(4) His relation to man (vv. 4-5, 9-13). To man the *Logos* brought life and light. John speaks of life thirty-six

[3] A. Plummer, *The Gospel According to St. John, Cambridge Greek Testament* (Cambridge: Cambridge University Press, 1891), pp. 62-64. In the past liberal scholars have commonly held that John's concept of the *Logos* was based on Hellenistic thought. As a result of studies in the Dead Sea Scrolls, however, there has been a great swing to the conclusion that the background of the Gospel of John is Judaic.

[4] Arndt and Gingrich, *A Greek-English Lexicon of the New Testament,* p. 222.

times in the Gospel—more than any other book in the New
Testament. Indeed, this is the purpose of his writing (20:
31), and the avowed purpose of the coming of the Son of
God (10:10; cf. I John 5:12). The *Logos* also brought light
to mankind. A universal enlightening is spoken of (v. 9)
which is probably the revelation of God in nature, and a
specific enlightening in the person of the Son has also shone
in the world. Though some deliberately rejected, those who
received Him became children (not sons, for this is exclusively a Pauline revelation) of God.

(5) His relation to flesh (v. 14). The *Logos* became flesh
so that the glory of God might be seen of men. Since the
glory of God is the manifestation of His attributes, the purpose of the Son taking upon Himself flesh may be said to be
to show God off to men.

Several philosophical ideas concerning *Logos* are contra-
dicted by what John wrote. (1) The *Logos* of John is very
God, not some lesser God, for He is God and He was the
Creator of all things. (2) The *Logos* of John is personal,
for He is face to face with God and He gives life to men.
(3) The *Logos* of John became flesh in a permanent relationship of incarnation. He is not merely an appearance of
God but is the God-man, Jesus Christ.

C. *The Deity of Christ*

1. *Affirmed by divine names given to Him.* The titles *Son
of God* and *Logos,* both of which attest to deity, have already
been discussed. To these may be added two names of Christ
in the Revelation: "the first and the last," and "the beginning and the end" (1:17; 22:13).

2. *Affirmed by attributes revealed of Him.* The Son is said
to be omniscient (John 1:48-50; 4:29; 20:24-28; Rev. 1:14;
2:18, 23; 19:12), omnipotent (Rev. 1:8), and omnipresent
(John 14:23; 1:48).

3. *Affirmed by works attributed to Him.* Among other

works which are assigned to Jesus which are unmistakably the works of God are the work of creation (1:3), the work of judging men (5:27), and the ability to give life (5:24; 10:17). If Jesus can do these things He must be God, for these are the works of deity alone.

4. *Affirmed by the worship given to Him.* The Son receives the worship of men (John 20:28; Rev. 5:8, 14) and of angels (Rev. 5:11-13; 7:11-12; 19:10; 22:9). That which is normally given to God is given to the Son.

5. *Affirmed by His miracles.* The sign-miracles recorded by John are one of the major and uniquely Johannine proofs of the deity of Jesus. Each one in some way points to the fact that He is God. The first at Cana of Galilee (John 2:1-12) was done purposely to show forth His glory. Since it was well known that miracles in the Old Testament were performed for the glory of God, and since this one was to show forth Jesus' glory, the conclusion was that Jesus was God. The nature of the miracle being an act of creation added to the proof. The second (4:43-54) showed the necessity of believing the Son in order to have life. The third (5:1-23) led to a discussion during the course of which the point was made very clear to the Jews that Jesus was claiming to be God (cf. v. 18). The fourth (6:1-14) was a sign to signify that Jesus claimed to be the sustainer of life, a thing which only God can do. The fifth (6:15-21) resulted in the disciples' worshiping Him (cf. Matt. 14:33). The sixth (9:1-41) demonstrated that He was the light of men and resulted in worship on the part of the one given sight. The seventh (11:1-44) was like the first; i.e., for the glory of God and for proof that Jesus is God. Each one in some particular way points to the fact that "Jesus is the Christ, the Son of God."

6. *Supported by His pre-existence.* While pre-existence does not actually prove deity, it is a strong support to the doctrine. Four passages in John are relevant: 1:1 (the Word

did not come into existence but was already in existence in the beginning) ; 6:62 (the Son was—*eimi*—in Heaven before He came into earthly existence) ; 8:58 (pre-Abrahamic existence was understood in this case to be a claim to deity as well as pre-existence, cf. v. 24) ; and 17:5 (Christ always had—the verb is imperfect—glory side by side with the Father before the world was in existence). Biblical theologians have offered several explanations of the meaning of these verses on pre-existence. Briefly, the explanations arrange themselves into those which finally affirm real historical pre-existence and those which affirm what is called ideal pre-existence (that is pre-existence only in the mind of God but not in reality of distinct persons in the Trinity.[5] Ideal pre-existence of course carries with it a denial of the deity of Christ, for in such a view He would be simply another man whose life purpose merely pre-existed in the mind of God but whose existence did not begin until He was born in Bethlehem. For further study the student is referred to Stevens' discussion and refutation of this idea.[6] His conclusion is worthy of repetition:

> At this point our inquiries bring us again face to face with the great problem of doctrinal theology respecting the person of Christ. That problem is, whether this altogether exceptional intimacy between the Father and the Son, taken in connection with the sinless perfection of Christ and his explicit assertions of an eternal fellowship with God, does not force us beyond the limits of humanity for the explanation of his person, and require us to posit an ontological relation as its only adequate ground. . . . Those who are convinced that the consciousness of Jesus was "purely human," would do far better to seek the confirmation of their conclusion in some other field than that of exegesis. As against this conclusion the apostolic Church and, for the most part,

[5] W. Beyschlag, *New Testament Theology* (Edinburgh: T. & T. Clark, 1899), I, 250-55.
[6] G. B. Stevens, *The Theology of the New Testament*, pp. 205-12.

the Church of all subsequent ages have held that the self-testimony of Jesus as presented in the New Testament compels the inference that he eternally partakes in the nature of Deity. I hold that this conclusion is correct.[7]

D. *The Humanity of Christ*

Confirmations of the customary proofs for the humanity of Jesus are also found in John's Gospel. He possessed a human body (John 19:31, 40), soul (12:27), and spirit (11:33; 13: 21). He experienced those things which can only come to human beings, for He was thirsty (19:28-30), tired (4:6), and emotionally disturbed (11:35; 12:27; 13:21). These prove beyond doubt that He was truly human as well as truly divine.

John's major contribution, however, to this doctrine is found in the ramifications of the phrase *and the Word became flesh* (1:14). Since the verse and context teach that the *Logos* became a human person, the word *flesh* in this instance stands not for the material flesh only but for the whole person, material and immaterial. That the *Logos-Word* became a person is what John is saying, and in the statement a number of characteristics of the person are implied.[8]

(1) The Lord's humanity was complete. The Word became flesh, not the Word became a body, for a person is more than body. This refutes the error of Apollinarianism which taught that the *Logos* supplied the place of the part which belongs to the perfection of manhood.

(2) The Lord's humanity was real and permanent. The Word became flesh, not the Word clothed itself with flesh. This refutes Gnosticism, which held that the *Logos* only assumed in appearance or for a time that flesh which was foreign to Himself.

(3) The Lord's human and divine natures remained with-

[7]*Ibid.,* p. 212.
[8]Cf. B. F. Westcott, *The Gospel According to St. John* (Grand Rapids: Eerdmans), I, 20-21.

out change, each fulfilling its part according to its proper laws. The Word became flesh and dwelt among us. Both terms, *Word* and *flesh,* are preserved side by side in the statement so that it is not merely the Word that dwelt among us or flesh among us but the Word become flesh that dwelt among us. This refutes Eutychianism, which taught that the result of the Incarnation was a third nature.

(4) The Lord's two natures were united in one person. The Word became flesh and tabernacled among us (1:14). There is no change of subject with the verb *tabernacled,* and yet it is in the singular; therefore, the Word become flesh is a union in one person. This refutes Nestorianism, which taught that the Lord had a separate human personality and a divine personality which were joined but not united. The person Jesus Christ was undiminished deity and perfect humanity united in one person forever. This is fully borne out by John's testimony.

III. The Doctrine of the Holy Spirit

Although John has more to say about the Holy Spirit than the Synoptists, his development of the doctrine is not systematic nor necessarily complete. Nevertheless, some of the most important revelations concerning the Spirit are found in Johannine theology.

A. *The Person of the Spirit*

Concerning the person of the Spirit John affirms three things.

1. *He is a person.* It is in John's writings that is found the ungrammatical use of the masculine pronoun standing in place of the neuter word for spirit (14:26; 15:26; 16:13-14). Indeed, the use of the masculine seems to be the writer's preference unless extremely pressed by grammatical propriety, and it can only be accounted for by realizing that John assigned personality to the Holy Spirit.

2. *He is a distinct person.* The Holy Spirit is not merely another form of Christ, for He is distinct from the Son, being another Comforter who bears witness to the Son (14:26; 16:13-14). He is distinct from the Father and yet is mentioned along with the Father and Son as part of the Trinity (Rev. 1:4-5; 4:5; 22:17).

3. *He proceeds from the Father and Son.* This is the word which is used to describe the Spirit's relationship to the other members of the Trinity (15:26). The present tense of the verb infers the eternal character of the procession

B. *The Work of the Spirit*

John's main contribution lies in this area, and what he says of the Spirit's work could almost be summarized in a single word: comforter, or advocate, or paraclete. This seems to be his favorite term for describing the counseling or legal work of the Spirit (14:16, 26; 15:26; 16:7; I John 2:1).

1. *He will pronounce the world guilty* (16:7-11). One of the principal duties of the Spirit today is to give demonstrable proof[9] to the world of sin, righteousness, and judgment. Although He had done convicting work before (Gen. 6:3), the Lord states that in a particular way this would be the Spirit's work after His departure. The distinctiveness of the work to this age is easily accounted for since each of the three counts in the Spirit's indictment of the world is based on the work of Christ. He convicts of sin because they reject Christ. He convicts of righteousness because only after Christ ascends to the Father will the world realize that they have misjudged Him. He enlightens concerning judgment which can only be done with full force after Satan is judged at the Cross. Therefore, this is a distinctive work of the Spirit today.

2. *He will remind the disciples.* One of the most important and immediate works of the Spirit was in relation to the

[9] Cf. Westcott, *op. cit.*, II, 219.

disciples to "teach you all things, and bring all things to your remembrance, whatsoever I have said unto you" (14: 26). This promise was twofold: (1) the disciples would be reminded of the facts so that their records would be inerrant, and (2) the disciples would be taught accurately the meaning of those facts so that their theology would be correct. The accuracy of the recording and interpreting is dependent on the work of the Spirit; to deny either is to defame His work.

3. *He will regenerate* (3:6). This aspect of the Spirit's ministry to men will be fully discussed under soteriology.

4. *He will foster the spiritual welfare of believers.*

a. By indwelling. Although indwelling was not unknown in the Old Testament it was not universal among all believers. Our Lord Himself draws the contrast when He summarized the Spirit's relation to men in the Old Testament as being with them (14:17). Now He is in believers, and that apparently is a different relationship. In the First Epistle John speaks of indwelling under the figure of anointing (2:20, 27).

b. By teaching. In the First Epistle the teaching ministry is based directly on the anointing or indwelling. Of course the presence of the Spirit does not in itself guarantee that the believer will be taught, but it makes it possible. The content of that teaching was forecast by the Lord (16:12-15) as including things which the disciples could not understand until after His resurrection and as pointing to Himself. Thus, the test of whether the Spirit is teaching is whether Christ is being glorified.

c. By filling. The Holy Spirit in fulfillment of the ceremony of the feast of tabernacles will satisfy the thirst and overflow the lives of those who believe in Jesus (7:37-39). Such filling results in service, for the rivers flow out of the believer to others.

Chapter 4

THE DOCTRINE OF SALVATION

I. THE DOCTRINE OF SIN

SALVATION IS FROM SIN; therefore, we would expect a Christological theology, as Johannine theology is, to contain a description of sin. What our author says concerning sin is primarily contained in the First Epistle rather than the Gospel.

A. *The Terminology of Sin*

The principal words for sin are all used in John's writings. Sin is therefore viewed as hitting the wrong mark (*hamartia,* John 1:29; 8:21, 24; I John 1:10), as that which is worthless (*ponēros,* John 3:19; 17:15; I John 2:13-14), as unrighteousness (*adikia,* John 7:18; I John 1:9), and as lawlessness (*anomia,* I John 3:4).

B. *The Definition of Sin*

"Sin is lawlessness" (I John 3:4) is both an exhaustive and definitive definition of sin. It is exhaustive because both words are preceded by the article, which means the phrase is convertible. Lawlessness is sin and sin is lawlessness. It is definitive because lawlessness is to be understood in the most absolute sense of the condition of being without law of any kind. It is contrariness to law, not simply violation of some specific in the Mosaic Law; therefore, it is the negation of that which is inherent in the very character of God Himself. Sin, then, is that which is contrary to God Himself.

C. *The Universality of Sin*

The universality of sin is proved by the state of condemnation in which rejectors of Christ are said to be (3:36; I John 3:14), by explicit statements that all have committed acts of sin (I John 1:10), and by the emphasis on the need for a Saviour (John 1:29; 3:17; 4:42; 5:34; 10:9; 12:47; I John 4:14).

D. *The Consequences of Sin*

The sin of the unbeliever incurs for him a debt (John 20: 23), a bondage to serve sin (John 8:32), an estrangement from God (John 3:36; 9:41), and death (5:24). Unbelievers who teach false doctrines promote community harm because of their sin (I John 2:18-19; II John 10-11). All of these consequences of sin add up to the fact that a man is unable to save himself (I John 3:8).

For the Christian, sin always brings loss of fellowship with God (I John 1:5—2:1), which can only be remedied by confession. If persisted in certain sins result in physical death (I John 5:16). Sinning always dulls a person's spiritual faculties, for the sinner cannot see God as He is or himself as he is. The more a man sins, the less he realizes about sin (I John 1:6, 8; 2:11). This is the deceitfulness of sin.

E. *The Cosmos*

Closely allied with the major themes of hamartiology is the Johannine doctrine of the cosmos. It is mainly a Johannine revelation, and the cosmos may be defined as all that acts as a rival to God. This includes its head, Satan; people who, though loved by God, are a part of it and therefore rivals of God; and the things, good or evil, which oppose God and His purposes.

1. *Satan's relation to the cosmos.* In John's writings Satan is called the Devil (John 8:44; 13:2), Satan (John 13:27), adversary (Rev. 12:10), and the evil one (John 17:15; I John 2:13; 3:12; 5:18). He is the ruler or prince of the cosmos (John 12:31; 14:30; 16:11) and as such exerts an influence over men who live in the world (John 8:44; 13:2, 27; I John 3:8; 5:19). In His own inscrutable counsels, God has seen fit to include this delegated authority of Satan over the world system.

2. *Christ's relation to the cosmos.* It was inevitable that our Lord, who always did those things which pleased the Father (John 8:29), should be hated by the cosmos, for they were rivals (John 15:18). His work on earth was to effect the basis of the judgment of the prince of the cosmos, which He did on the Cross (John 12:31; 14:30; 16:11). The ultimate fruits of that victory will not be finally and fully realized until the consummation of all things when the Devil will be cast into the lake of fire and brimstone forever (Rev. 20:10).

3. *The Christian's relation to the cosmos.* A number of things are said about the believer's relation to the world. He is not of it (John 15:19) though not yet removed from it (John 17:15). He is not known by the world and therefore hated by it (I John 3:13). Victory is assured for every Christian while he remains in the cosmos, for faith is that victory (I John 5:4), and there is sufficient resource available for all believers to be overcomers. The Lord has made it fully possible; it remains only for us to make it fully practical. That victorious life will be characterized by separation from the world (I John 2:15-17). This is not removal nor a hermit's kind of life, but it is siding with God and not with His rival, the cosmos. To side with the world is not to love God, for one cannot love the enemy of God and God at the same time (v. 15b). It is to be interested in things which do not find their origin in God (v. 16) and which are transitory (v. 17).

Simply and basically, separation from the world means doing the will of God (v. 17).

II. THE INCARNATION

One of the major emphases in Johannine theology is the doctrine of the Incarnation. This is partly due to the erroneous concepts John was combating in his own day either that Christ could not take a body or that He took temporarily an ordinary human body. That deity was permanently united to humanity is a basic tenet of John.

A. *The Importance of the Doctrine*

In Paul the Incarnation is principally related to the humiliation of Christ, but in John it is related to revelation. That is why we say that Johannine theology is theological or Christological. This revelation of God which came as a result of the Incarnation not only shows us God (John 1:14; 14:9), but it destroys Satan and his works (I John 3:8) and takes away our sins (I John 3:5). In other words, John is saying that were deity not united with humanity in one person, Jesus Christ, there would be no knowledge of God, no victory over Satan, and no salvation from sin. As we shall see shortly, the Incarnation is also the basis for Christian ethics. It is not that John is minimizing the work of the Cross (cf. I John 2:2; John 3:14; 10:17-18); he is merely emphasizing that the validity of the work on the Cross depends on the reality of the Incarnation. Those who deny the doctrine and its ramifications are antichrists (I John 2:22; 4:3; II John 7)—that is how important it is.

> As compared with the Pauline theology the Johannine does not so fully centre the attention upon the death of Christ. It is less emphatically a theology of the cross. The idea of revelation comes to the front ... It is manifest too that John was less inclined than Paul to dwell upon the judicial aspect of Christ's work. . . . Still, it needs to be acknowledged that in the background of the

Johannine representation there is a sufficiently distinct recognition of essentially the same objective phase of atonement as appears elsewhere in the New Testament. This is especially noticeable in the Epistle. Nothing in the Pauline writings more clearly implies that the universal dispensation of grace is based upon Christ's work than does the Johannine declaration that He is the propitiation . . . for the sins of the world.[1]

John's emphasis must be recognized, and at the same time the theological balance, which is John's own, must be preserved.

B. *The Proofs of the Incarnation*

Some of the proofs which John uses for the Incarnation are necessarily the same as those which prove the humanity of Jesus. The use of *sarx*, flesh, in John 1:14, and the meaning of the title *Son of man* are two such. In addition the many citations concerning the home and family life of the Lord prove the reality of the Incarnation (John 1:46-47; 2:1; 6:42; 7:3, 10, 41, 52; 19:25-26). Too, the opening testimony of the First Epistle is one of the strongest statements of the reality of the Incarnation (I John 1:1-3). The disciples had heard, seen, beheld personally, and handled Jesus Christ, and so certain were they of the reality of this divine-human person that they were staking their lives on that truth which they preached. It was no mere phantom or even theophany of which John testified in these verses. The Incarnation was real; revelation was its consequence; salvation its climax; and Christian ethics its outcome.

III. The Work of Christ

A. *In His Life*

The life of Christ was a revelation of God. Therefore, his life revealed grace (John 1:17-18) as He exegeted God. It revealed truth, for He is truth (John 14:6; I John 5:20), and

[1] H. C. Sheldon, *New Testament Theology* (New York: Macmillan, 1922), pp. 346-47.

He witnessed to the truth (John 18:37) which liberates the captive (John 8:32) and sanctifies the believer (John 15:3; 17:17). His life also revealed an example which the believer is exhorted to imitate (I John 2:3-11). That imitation is the proof of one's profession as a follower of the Master, and Plummer is probably right when he says that "in all cases it is His loving self-sacrifice that is to be imitated."[2]

B. *In His Death*

1. *The significance of His death.*

a. The death of Christ means deliverance. Personal deliverance from a lost state is one of the benefits of the death of Christ (John 3:17; 12:47). This is not a national Israelitish deliverance, and yet it was well known (cf. John 4:22). We may conclude from this that the deliverance expected in the time of Christ was not only national and from Rome but also individual and from death.

b. The death of Christ is a propitiation. Only John uses the noun *propitiation* in the New Testament (I John 2:2; 4:10). Propitiation is inseparably connected with the idea of divine wrath; therefore, propitiation affects God, for that is where the wrath is. Thus, propitiation may be said to be the satisfying of God through the working out of His plan whereby sin, the cause of God's wrath, is removed through the death of Christ.[3] It is, according to John's clear statement, for the whole world.

c. The death of Christ took away sin. The blood stands for violent death; therefore, to speak of the blood of Christ taking away sin means the death of Christ takes away sin, not a life liberated and offered as an offering to God.[4] The blood, that is His death, is the basis for eternal life (John 6:53-56),

[2] A. Plummer, *The Epistles of St. John*, p. 39.

[3] For a full treatment cf. Leon Morris, *The Apostolic Preaching of the Cross* (Grand Rapids: Eerdmans, 1955), pp. 125-85.

[4] Cf. Westcott, *The Epistles of St. John*, p. 35, for this double idea in blood, and see A. M. Stibbs, *The Meaning of the Word "Blood" in Scripture* (London: The Tyndale Press, 1947), pp. 1-35.

it continually effects cleansing from sin (I John 1:7), and it is the basis for victorious living (Rev. 12:11).

d. The death of Christ means possession of eternal life. This is a constantly reiterated theme of John (John 3:36; 5:24; 6:47, 54; 20:31; I John 5:12-13). Eternal life is not merely the endless duration of a being in relation to time measurement, but it is a quality of life which is inseparable from Christ Himself. Death has no effect on it (John 6:50-58; 8:51-52; 11:26), for bodily resurrection is in many ways a natural outcome of the possession of eternal life. While eternal life is always regarded as a present actuality, it is also viewed as something future as far as complete realization is concerned (John 4:14, 36; 6:27; 12:25; 14:19; I John 3:2). The full enjoyment of it awaits a future day.

2. *The meaning of the new birth.* No discussion of the death of Christ would be complete without reference to the classic discourse with Nicodemus on the new birth (John 3:1-12). The Lord spoke on this occasion of three characteristics of the new birth which is based on His death (3:14).

a. It is supernatural (3:4). Nicodemus' question, "How can a man be born when he is old?" was not a foolish one. Evidently he thought Jesus was speaking of physical birth when He said a man had to be born again, because he reasoned that the character of a person stemmed from his birth; therefore, he could see no way to begin again morally except to begin again physically, and this was the way he interpreted the Lord's words. Nicodemus thought it would be wonderful to start over with a clean slate but did not see how it was possible apart from a new physical birth. Therefore, Nicodemus did not understand that the new birth was supernatural. The mystery of religion is not punishment but forgiveness.

b. It is spiritual (3:5-6). The kingdom of God is spiritual; thus, the new birth, the means of entrance, must be spiritual also. It is being born of water and spirit. The mention of water was probably to turn Nicodemus' mind to John the Baptist's baptism unto repentance;[5] thus water and spirit picture the two sides of a spiritual birth—the water of the outward testimony of repentance and the spirit of the inward change of heart.

c. It is sovereign (3:7-12). As the wind blows where it wills, so God chooses whom He will; and as the effects of the wind are seen, so the results of the new birth are seen in a changed life. Nicodemus himself illustrates the fact that a man cannot understand or will it in his own strength. Intellectual struggle may only postpone the moment of salvation; obedience of faith can immediately effect it.

3. *The appropriation of salvation.* The very first statement in the Gospel concerning the new birth makes it dependent upon faith (John 1:12). The verse also mentions the object of faith, Christ. Thus it is throughout the Gospel —the Son as the bearer of salvation must be the object of faith (3:15-16, 18, 36; 4:29, 39; 7:38; 8:24; 20:29, 31; I John 3:23; 5:1, 12). Faith involves the most thorough kind of appropriation of the person and work of Christ as the basis for the believer's confident persuasion for salvation. The figure of eating His flesh and drinking His blood attests to that thoroughness (6:53-56). Faith in His person involves belief in His deity (John 3:13; 8:24; 9:22; 12:42; I John 2:23; 4:15), and faith in His work involves belief in the efficacy of His death to effect deliverance from sin (John 1:29; 3:14-17; 13:19). In John's thought faith that saves is joined directly to the person and work of Jesus Christ.

IV. THE LIFE OF FELLOWSHIP

Since faith is this personal appropriation of the most thorough kind, there arises from it a relationship between the believer and the one in whom he has placed his faith. This person-to-person fellowship also has a horizontal rami-

[5]Cf. B. F. Westcott, *The Gospel According to St. John*, I, 108-9. Possibly the *kai* is epexegetical—"of water, even the Spirit."

fication in the community relationship of all believers. In John's thought this life of fellowship—both on the vertical and horizontal plane—stems directly from the saving work of Christ; therefore, a discussion of it properly belongs under soteriology.

If John's emphasis on this theme were only slightly different, this section might be called his doctrine of the Church. But his emphasis is not such, for the word *church* is nowhere used in the Gospel or First Epistle.[6] With respect to the ordinances, there is complete silence concerning baptism and the Lord's Supper as church ordinances.[7] Therefore, we are bound to follow John's own emphasis and consider the relationships of the group under the doctrine of salvation, for salvation is the cause of which this, according to Johannine theology, is the effect.

A. *The Conditions for Fellowship*

Believers become brethren by virtue of being joint partakers of the new birth through faith in Christ. Brethren maintain fellowship with Christ and consequently with one another by meeting a certain condition. That condition is "walking in the light" (I John 1:7), or walking in obedience to a standard which is God Himself, who is light. It is practicing the truth (I John 1:6) or living in obedience to the standard of Him who is truth. Such a life brings fellowship with one another in the community relationship (I John 1:7). When sin is committed and the standard is not met fellowship is broken and confession is necessary (I John 1:9). Thus fellowship depends on our responding to the standard, which is God Himself and realizing our imperfect state by confession of known sin. The life of fellowship is a life of no unconfessed sins which is also a life of progressive growth, for confession involves repentance and forsaking of sin.

[6]The organized group is referred to in I John 2:19 and 3:14-18, and of course the word *church* appears in the Third Epistle and the Apocalypse, but we are here pointing out John's emphasis.

[7]The mention of the disciples of Jesus baptizing (3:22; 4:1-2) cannot be considered as referring to an ordinance of the church.

B. *The Characteristics of Fellowship*

Two words stand out in the First Epistle as the chief characteristics of individual and community fellowship—righteousness and love. Righteousness means that sin is not practiced as the prevailing habit of life (I John 3:4-9). It does
not mean perfectionism or freedom from committing all sin,
but it does mean that righteousness, not sin, is that which
habitually characterizes the life. The characteristics of love
are also described by John in detail (I John 3:10-18). It is
unlike the love Cain had; it will not be received by the
world; it is manifest in our love for the brethren, which
could involve being willing to lay down our lives for others
but which should involve for all the giving of ourselves and
our money for the benefit of our brethren. Not all will be
called upon to give up life for the brethren, but all are called
to give up personal abilities and resources in the service of
others. It is an easy thing to say "I love God" and even to
appear very pious when saying it. John says that real piety
is shown not by what we say about our love for God but by
what we do in showing our love for our brethren (I John 4:
11-21).

C. *The Conduct of Fellowship*

A life that is walking in the light and that is characterized
by righteousness and love must also conduct itself properly
in the various relationships of life. Of these John speaks too.

1. *In relation to the life of Christ* (I John 2:1-11). The
life of Christ serves as a pattern which the Christian is to
imitate. This includes two things: His word (vv. 3-5) and
His walk (v. 6). It is necessary to obey His commands in
order to perfect our love for God, and to imitate His actions
in order to prove our profession as followers of Him.

2. *In relation to the world* (I John 2:12-17). Mention has
previously been made of the Christian's responsibility to be

separate from the world, for the things of the world are not of God.

3. *In relation to antichrists* (I John 2:18-29; 4:1-6). Many antichrists were active when John wrote; therefore, it was necessary for believers to be on guard in their relationships. An antichrist is "one who assuming the guise of Christ opposes Christ,"[8] and some in John's day even belonged outwardly to the Christian community (I John 2:18-19). John believed that these persons were empowered by superhuman forces (I John 4:3) so that a believer needed supernatural discernment to recognize them. However, there are two tests which John mentions for discovering antichrists. The first is doctrinal (I John 4:2-3). Anyone who does not openly acknowledge the person of the incarnate Saviour is antichrist. This means more than simply acknowledging the fact of His coming, for it incorporates the idea of the permanence of flesh which the Incarnation effected. The second test is an audience test, for John suggests that an examination of those who listen to a prophet will determine what sort of prophet is speaking (I John 4:4-6). Christians should apply these tests in order to guard their own fellowship with Christ against antichrists.

Thus, in soteriology as in all of Johannine theology the development of the writer's thought centers in the person of Jesus Christ. Sin is understood for what it is only by seeing God as He has been revealed through Christ. The incarnation of Christ revealed God to man. Salvation, the work of this person, comes to man through faith in that One and what He did. The resultant life of fellowship continues that relationship with Christ and expresses it in the community relationships of all believers.

> These doctrines are the foundation pillars of apostolical teaching; and these are the very ideas which, with a decided reference to the superiority of the new covenant

Westcott, *The Epistles of St. John,* p. 70.

over the old dispensation, are fully realized in John's system by the grand view which he takes of Christ as the manifested Word of God, and of the faith which hath overcome the world.[9]

[9]C. F. Schmid, *Biblical Theology of the New Testament*, p. 548.

Chapter 5

ESCHATOLOGY

JOHANNINE ESCHATOLOGY is found mainly in the Apocalypse. Since this is the case, certain foundational matters concerning the Revelation need to be considered as a basis for the doctrinal investigations.

I. INTRODUCTORY MATTERS CONCERNING THE REVELATION

A. *Authorship*

Generally speaking there is not much agreement today concerning the authorship of the Apocalypse. Conservatives hold that the same person who wrote the Gospel and Epistles also wrote this book, and that that person was the apostle John. This is determined on the basis of the evidence already cited concerning John the apostle and John the presbyter. Others are equally certain that John could not have written the book chiefly because it is such a different work from the Gospel.[1] That is obviously true, but its very nature as an apocalypse demands that it move in a different world with dissimilar style and tone. More recently a documentary theory has arisen respecting the book; i.e., it was a compilation of a number of little apocalypses. Some add that John was the compiler; which accounts for the association of his name with the book.

[1] Cf. G. B. Stevens, *Theology of the New Testament*, p. 526.

345

B. *Date*

Traditionally a date of 95-96 has been assigned to the Revelation. It is based on the testimony of Irenaeus, who said, "The vision of the Apocalypse was seen no very long time since, but almost in our own days, towards the end of Domitian's reign" (i.e., 81-96).[2] More recently this late date has been given up for an earlier one which places the book toward the end of the reign of Nero (54-68). However, if Irenaeus' testimony be given any weight the later date is the only conclusion possible. His testimony also rules out any idea that the visions were given earlier and John or someone compiled them later, for he said that the vision was seen, not written, in Domitian's day. Actually, the trend of the most recent scholarship seems to be back toward the traditionally later date.

C. *Methods of Interpretation*

The basic method of interpretation divides all commentaries on the Revelation and casts the mold for the theology of the book. One must not straddle the fence at this point; otherwise there can be no theology. There are four viewpoints on this matter.[3] (1) The preterist view holds that the prophecies of the book were fulfilled in the early history of the Church. (2) The historicist view sees a continuous fulfillment throughout the entire Christian era. While it is true that there may be relevant applications of the book made for every generation, the problem under discussion is interpretation, not application. (3) The allegorical or spiritual view considers the book an allegory which pictures the constant conflict between light and darkness. (4) The futurist view regards the entire contents of the book, except for the first three chapters, as yet to be fulfilled. The first three

---

[2]*Against Heresies*, V, xxx, 3; cf. Eusebius, *Ecclesiastical History*, V, viii.
[3]An excellent critical discussion of the interpretation of the Revelation is found in W. Graham Scroggie's *The Book of the Revelation* (Cleveland, Ohio: Union Gospel Press, 1920), pp. 75-156.

viewpoints are based on the principle of allegorical interpretation while the futurist view is the result of the consistent use of the principles of literal interpretation. The book itself supports the futurist interpretation in 1:19 and 4:1, and it is in agreement with other prophetic Scriptures if they are plainly interpreted.[4]

In handling this particular portion of God's Word one should never forget that the book is not sealed (22:10) and that a special blessing is for those who read it (1:3). These two things ought to encourage every Christian's study of the Revelation.

II. DEATH

A. *Spiritual Death*

John conceives of spiritual death as a state of alienation from God. It is the lack of spiritual life which is in Christ; therefore, it is the state of not being in Christ (John 5:24; I John 3:14). He recognizes that there may be a profession of having life, but it is only a lifeless thing (Rev. 3:1). The remedy, of course, for spiritual death is spiritual life or salvation. This has its source in the Son (John 5:26; I John 5:12), it is secured by believing (John 1:12), and its surety is the resultant love for the brethren (I John 3:14). As has been pointed out from the First Epistle, a lack of love for the brethren is the sure sign of abiding in the state of spiritual death.

B. *Physical Death*

Physical death is the end of life in the earthly body or the separation of the life-giving spirit from the body so that as a result the body decays (John 11:39). During the life of Christ physical death was used as a means of demonstrating the power and glory of God (John 4:47; 11:4, 15). Sometimes death is seen as a release from suffering (Rev. 9:6).

[4]For further study see the author's *The Basis of the Premillennial Faith* (New York: Loizeaux, 1953).

On other occasions it is a means of judgment (I John 5:16). In the latter two instances it is definitely connected with sin and comes as a result of having committed sin.

The Lord plainly stated that the power of physical death would be broken for all men by resurrection (John 5:28-29; cf. 8:51). Resurrection reverses death, and Christ's own resurrection is the guarantee of that. For the unbeliever resurrection is unto condemnation in the eternal lake of fire (Rev. 20:12 ff.), and for the believer it is to an eternal glorified state (Rev. 21:4).

C. *Eternal Death*

This is the final state of the unbeliever. It is the permanent continuation of spiritual death unremedied, and finds its continuing consummation in the lake of fire (Rev. 20:14). God will evidently prove to the unbeliever that he deserves this punishment by his own works (Rev. 20:12-13; 21:8; John 5:29) as well as his rejection of the Son of God.

D. *The Intermediate State of the Soul After Death*

For the believer the state after death is one of conscious bliss while awaiting the resurrection. Consciousness is displayed in many ways in the Revelation (6:10; 7:9, 15; 14:3; 20:4), and the bliss is described in equal detail (5:9; 6:11; 7: 10, 16-17; 14:13; 19:8). It could not be otherwise, for the believer at death is ushered into the presence of God immediately (cf. Rev. 20:4—when John looked, the sitters on the thrones, saints of this age, were *already* there).

The unbeliever's intermediate state is hades. Just as soon as death claims the body hades claims the soul (cf. Rev. 6:8 where both follow the horseman in order to claim their victims immediately). Horrible as hades is, it is nonetheless only a temporary abode which delivers its captives to the lake of fire for eternal torment (Rev. 20:14).

The abyss is very closely identified with hades in John's

writings. Satanic hosts are more particularly connected with the abyss, while human beings are associated with hades. The abyss has a superhuman ruler over it (Rev. 9:11); the beast ascends from there during the tribulation (Rev. 11:7; 17:8); the locust-instruments of judgment came from there (Rev. 9:1-10); and the consummation of the abyss seems to be the same as hades, the lake of fire (cf. Matt. 25:41).[5]

III. JUDGMENT

Closely linked with the doctrine of death is that of judgment; indeed, the two are often spoken of in the same passages.

A. *Judgment in Relation to Christ*

Judgment is invariably linked with Christ the judge (John 5:22; Rev. 20:11-12, ASV). The reason for this is clearly stated (John 5:27)—Christ will judge men because He is a son of man.[6] In other words, a man will judge men. The purpose of this arrangement is also explained; it is so that the Son will be honored by men (John 5:23).

[5]An interesting note substantiating the possibility of eternal fire is found in F. C. Schwarze, "The Bible and Science on the Everlasting Fire," *Bibliotheca Sacra*, 95:105-12, January, 1938. The author suggests that the eternal lake of fire may be in liquid form and shows that such a phenomenon exists today in dwarf or midget or white stars. Here are excerpts from his discussion: "A midget star is one which, because of some things which have happened to it. . . should be roughly 55,000 or more *times* as big as it really is!" The stars have a temperature of 30,000,000 degrees Fahrenheit or more, and "at such high temperatures all matter would be in the form of gas. . . . in a white dwarf the pressure is so great that gases become compressed to the consistency of a liquid although they may still respond to the characteristics of a gas." How this could continue perpetually is explained: "Before such a star could cool off and gradually become dark it would have to expand to normal proportions. That is, it would have to get to be more than 5,000 times its present size. Here is the difficulty. Such expansion would cause enormous heat, which, in turn, would absolutely keep the star compressed, so that, *insofar as astronomers and physicists know, the midget stars can never cool off*. . . . The white dwarf, to all intents, can never burn out." This is not to suggest that God will use these stars to compose the lake of fire; this is quoted merely to show that the literal idea of a lake of fire is not fanciful, because a similar phenomenon already exists in the universe.

[6]The absence of the article before both nouns differentiates this phrase from the Messianic title *the Son of man*. The construction concentrates attention upon the nature of the person as being human.

B. *Judgment in Relation to Resurrection*

Actually judgment is a corollary of resurrection (John 5: 22-29). Those whom the Son does not will to make alive spiritually are by that very act judged and left in the death which, paradoxically, they themselves have chosen. They are spiritually dead; they will not be made alive; therefore, the only result is a resurrection unto judgment—a passing from the state of death into judgment. Although it is not especially a Johannine revelation (but cf. Rev. 4:4, 10) it is true that even the believer's resurrection is followed by judgment.

C. *Judgment in Relation to Living Persons*

The judgment of the Christian is Pauline; the judgment of the unbeliever Johannine (Rev. 20:12-15). The scene is before the throne, whose occupant is Christ (John 5:22). Heaven and earth are dissolved and the second resurrection takes place. Then with all unbelievers gathered before Him, the record books are opened and judgment is meted out on the basis of the record of each individual. The person is in that particular judgment because he is an unbeliever, but once there he is judged according to works. Perhaps this implies corresponding degrees of punishment in the lake of fire. When the book of life is opened not a single name of those standing before the throne will be found therein, for all of those who come into this judgment are condemned in the lake of fire. This judgment does not prove whether Heaven or Hell is to be the final destiny of those being judged; it is a judgment to prove that Hell is the deserved destiny.

IV. Antichrist

Though all do not agree on details it is universally acknowledged that antichrist is a major eschatological concept of Johannine theology.

A. *The Concept of Antichrist*

The concept basic to this doctrine is complex and needs to be given careful attention.

1. *The word antichrist.* The prefix *anti* can of course mean either *instead of* or *against*. Thus, antichrist could mean either one who is a substitute for Christ or one who is against Christ. When *anti* is used in the former sense in compound with other words (as *antibasileus*, vice-king) it does not have the sense of an unlawful substitute but of one who rightly acts in the place of another. In contrast, the scriptural picture of antichrist is of one who usurps authority. When this idea of usurping is included the Scripture uses the word *pseudochristos*, false Christ.

On the other hand, *anti* in compound means against, and antichrist in this sense would mean one who is against Christ. Thus, unadulterated opposition, not usurpation, is the principal emphasis in the word. This sense of *anti* appears to be more in line with the scriptural picture of antichrist. In John's day an antichrist denied that Jesus is Christ. In the final apostasy Antichrist sets up his own religion of worship of himself. This is not substitution which imitates or acts in place of Christ, but outright opposition. Thus, antichrist means one who is opposed to Christ openly, not a false Christ.

2. *The contemporary antichrists.* In John's own day antichrists were present (I John 2:18; II John 7) and were even associated with the church group. These were forerunners of a coming great Antichrist, and John does not deny that a future Antichrist is still to arise. Those of John's day were not just people who were unchristian but who were definitely antichristian. John associates them with the Antichrist to come in order to impress upon his readers the peril of their teaching.

3. *The coming Antichrist.* In the First Epistle John acknowledges the well-known character of the future Anti-

christ (2:18). He is described in detail in the Apocalypse (11:7; 13:1 ff.).

4. *The spirit of antichrist.* John in one place speaks of the spirit of antichrist (I John 4:3), which is evidently a super-human spirit working through the Antichrist. He is suggesting that those of his own day are demonically inspired men, and the future Antichrist is likewise. In the Revelation it sometimes appears as if the Antichrist were only a man and sometimes as if he were the Devil himself. Evidently this concept of the spirit of antichrist explains that seeming contradiction (11:7; 13:8; 17:11).

B. *The Characteristics of Antichrist*

Essentially, antichrist is one who opposes God. That opposition may be open attack as in the coming day or it may be more underhanded as in John's day. Antichrist may belong to the Christian group outwardly though not organically. The basic doctrinal heresy promoted by the antichrists of John's own time was the denial of the Incarnation. In the coming day Antichrist's attacks will cause people to be put to death (Rev. 11:7).

C. *The Culmination of Antichrist*

Even in John's time the Antichrist was expected and while there were forerunner antichrists, so to speak, in his day, they are always compared to the great single Antichrist to come, not vice versa. Therefore, this future personage is the outstanding one. A good deal of confusion has arisen over the use of the name *Antichrist* in relation to the two important characters of the last days, the first and second beasts of Revelation 13. Many attach the name *Antichrist* to the second person mentioned in that chapter; that is, to the one commonly spoken of as the religious leader of the end time. Others, and this author is one of them, feel that the first beast is the outstanding figure in those days and that the name *Antichrist* belongs to him. Both groups agree that the first beast is the man of sin, but some fail to see that he exercises both political and religious functions. On the basis of the concept of antichrist formed from the meaning of the word and from the outstanding character of the person, the name must be applied to the one who takes the leadership in the last days— general leadership in the world and specific leadership in opposing God. This can only be the first mentioned person in Revelation 13.

In John's description of him (Rev. 13:1-10; 17:8-13) certain things are clear. He is related to a confederation of ten nations and rules over it. He has characteristics like a leopard, bear, and lion. These take the reader back to Daniel's description of the world empires (Dan. 7) and thus liken the Antichrist to characteristics which were seen in those kingdoms. His empowering is of Satan as has already been mentioned.

His activity in the last days is also described. Though his power is limited and delegated, it is extensive while it lasts (cf. 13:4b, 5, 7, 10). He is able to kill and capture people (v. 10), to control buying and selling (v. 16), and to set up his own religious system which centers in worship of himself. He is aided in all this by a subordinate (the second mentioned person in Rev. 13), who performs miracles, directs worship to the first beast, and who supervises the marking of people with the mark of Antichrist. Antichrist's political duties will undoubtedly take him away from Palestine often so that a subordinate will be necessary to look after things there while he tends to his far-flung affairs.

Careful balance is needed in this doctrine. John's teaching concerning the Antichrist to come must never blind us to the danger of the presence of antichrists in any period of Church history, and the truth of contemporary antichrists must not tend to lessen our interest in every detail that can be learned about the Antichrist to come.

V. Eschatology of the Jews

The simplest way to consider what John says about the future for the Jews is by categories or groups of Jewish people.

For unredeemed Jews the future holds the same as it does for unredeemed Gentiles. Those who have to pass through the tribulation will of necessity experience the judgments of that period. During eternity their lot, as all unsaved people, is the lake of fire.

John introduces a special group of Jews in the Apocalypse, the 144,000 sealed witnesses (Rev. 7:4-8; 14:1-5). If the language of the text be taken at face value this is a group of that exact number who are particularly described as the servants of God. Their sealing guarantees special protection until their work of witness is finished. They are redeemed people and evidently remain a distinct group among all redeemed as "firstfruits unto God and to the Lamb" (Rev. 14: 4).

Among the witnesses to the grace of God during the tribulation, two are singularly outstanding (Rev. 11:1-14). Their unusual testimony, which includes the power to kill their enemies, to prevent rainfall, and to bring plagues on the earth, continues for forty-two months, or the first part of the tribulation. When their work is done God takes them through physical death. Then after men have made a spectacle of their dead bodies for three days they are raised and taken to Heaven where they dwell with the redeemed for eternity.

During the tribulation days there will be a faithful remnant of Jews who believe. For these there will be intense persecution by Satan and his followers. Protection will be divinely given in a wilderness place (Rev. 12:1-17). Some, however, may be martyred and be part of the group mentioned in Revelation 15:2-3.

The state of all redeemed Jews to whatever group or age

they may belong is one of eternal bliss. Although it is difficult to be definite about details of the eternal state, perhaps
it may be suggested that their special abode is the New Jerusalem (which will be discussed in detail later).

VI. ESCHATOLOGY OF THE CHURCH

The concepts involved in the use of the word *church* are
often overlapping. However, a distinction must be made
between the group that is constituted as belonging to an
organization and the group that is constituted as belonging
to the Saviour. The latter ought to belong to the former,
and the former ideally ought to be composed only of the
latter, but such is not always the case. Therefore, in the
outline to follow it is not suggested that these groups are
mutually exclusive; it is rather a matter of emphasis in distinction, not exclusiveness of distinction.

A. *The Future of the Organized Church*

The letters to the seven churches in Revelation 2—3 were
of course written to historic local congregations of John's
day. However, since not even all the churches in Asia Minor
received a letter (and such an important one as the one in
Colosse is left out) one would rightly suspect that the Holy
Spirit signified which ones should be chosen for specific reasons. Therefore, it would seem that these seven are also representative of the Church in all this age and characteristic of
conditions as they exist continually and in every place. Some
futurists also see these churches as prophetic churches; i.e.,
they trace the historical development of ecclesiasticism, each
church representing conditions in a specific period of Church
history. Undoubtedly this is the least important of the meanings of the letters. All of the conditions pictured in these
letters will be represented in the Church until its consummation. In the future, just as in the past, the Church, so long
as she is here on earth, will leave her first love, hold the doc-

trine of Balaam, permit Jezebels in the group, have imperfect works, and be lukewarm. There will also be those conditions which merit commendation for the true and professedly true elements will co-exist until the rapture.

When the believing element is removed at the rapture (John does not speak of this specifically in the Apocalypse, though in the chronology of the book it would come at the beginning of chapter 4), the Church does not cease to exist or function, but becomes a truly and completely apostate Church. The eschatology of this organization is recorded in Revelation 17 under the figure of Babylon the harlot. This is the Church organization which during the first part of the tribulation unites Church and State (v. 2), rules the beast (vv. 3, 11), displays herself with great grandeur and pomp (v. 4), is organized as a federation (v. 5), and reigns with cruel ruthlessness (v. 6). When the Antichrist shows his true colors by demanding the worship of himself he must destroy this rival. So complete is that destruction (v. 16) that it may be said that organized Christendom comes to an end at that time.

B. *The Future of the Universal Church*

In this section we consider the promises made to individuals who are true believers. All such individuals together form the universal Church, and, obviously, many of them are in local organizations and exhibit characteristics listed in the preceding section. However, we are considering now those things which pertain to all believers because they are joined to the mystical Body of Christ.

1. *The hope of the Church.* In the upper room the Lord told His disciples of that which would be the hope of the Church through all its history. The hope centers in His personal return for them—it is the hope of seeing Him (John 14:1-3). Secondarily, we have the hope of the mansions or abiding places in Heaven for eternity. Also our hope in-

cludes a change in our own nature to be like Him (I John 3: 1-3).

2. *The future occupation of the Church.* In the Apocalypse the redeemed are seen worshiping God and the Lamb (4:10-11; 5:8). This evidently will be one of the principal occupations of the Church throughout eternity. The Church is also seen on thrones judging (Rev. 20:4), though what this involves in particular John does not say.

3. *The marriage supper of the Lamb.* A Hebrew marriage has three stages: (1) the legal marriage consummated by the parents of the bride and groom; (2) the groom's going to take his bride from her parents' home; and (3) the wedding feast or supper. It is of this last stage that John speaks in Revelation 19:7, and this means that the Bride has already been taken from her home on earth.

VII. THE TRIBULATION

Most of the contents of the Apocalypse concern the future time of tribulation. While there is wide divergence of opinion concerning the interpretation of basic and detailed features of the material, to enter into discussion of these matters would be disproportionate to the plan of this book. Reasons have been given for preferring the futurist, literal view of the Revelation, and that view will be the working principle on which this section is based.

A. *The Duration of the Tribulation*

The total length of the period is given in chapter 11. The two witnesses are said to carry on their work for 1,260 days; then the beast who kills them is said to continue on for forty-two months; thus the total period is seven years. This of course is confirmed in other places in the Scripture (cf. Rev. 12:6, 14; 13:5; Dan. 9:27).

B. *The Distinctiveness of the Tribulation*

The Lord had declared that this time would be as no other

period in the history of the world (cf. Matt. 24:21), but it is a Johannine revelation as to what makes the time so singular. The tribulation has come not merely when times are bad but when the race realizes that it is threatened with extinction and acts accordingly (6:15-17). Men may speak of possible extinction as they do today, but it is when the realization of that becomes so vivid that the ordinary activities of life are disrupted completely that the tribulation has begun.

C. *The Description of the Tribulation*

This writer's conviction is that the chronological movement of the book follows the three successive series of judgments (chaps. 6, 8-9, 16), the last of which moves very rapidly to its conclusion. The intervening chapters reveal matters which fit into the basic chronology and pick up some of the details which of necessity are omitted in the description of the judgments. On the basis of such an understanding of the plan of the book, this is the general outline of events during the tribulation as John saw them.

1. *Events of the first half of the tribulation.*

a. The 144,000 Jewish witnesses are sealed near the beginning of the time (7:1-8).

b. The federation of churches comes into existence (17:1-6).

c. The ten-kingdom confederacy of nations begins its rise to power under the leadership of the Antichrist (17:12).

d. The seal judgments are poured out on the earth.

(1) Cold war (6:1-2). There is first conquest apart from war (cf. v. 4).

(2) Open war (6:3-4). Revolution and war follow.

(3) Famine (6:5-6). One day's wages will buy only one measure of wheat, whereas it would normally have bought eight measures.

(4) Destruction of one-fourth of the population of the earth (6:7-8).

(5) Martyrdom (6:9-11). Even this early some are killed for their faith.

(6) Physical disturbances in the universe (6:12-17). This is when the race shows by its actions that it realizes that extinction is imminent.

e. The two witnesses are carrying on their potent testimony all during this period (11:1-6).

2. *Events at the middle of the tribulation.*

a. The two witnesses are slain after their forty-two months of testimony (11:3, 7).

b. The Antichrist will show his true colors at this time. He has of course been on the stage of history before this, but it is not until now that he reveals his true character and demands to be worshiped (11:7; 13:1-10).

c. Satan, the accuser, is cast out of Heaven (12:7-12).

3. *Events of the last half of the tribulation.*

a. The persecution of Israel is intensified (12:13-17).

b. The trumpet judgments are poured out on the earth.

(1) Smiting of the earth (8:7). One-third of the vegetation is destroyed.

(2) Smiting of the salt waters (8:8-9). One-third of the sea turns to blood.

(3) Smiting of the fresh waters (8:10-11). One-third becomes bitter.

(4) Smiting of the heavens (8:12-13). The uniformity of nature is upset.

(5) Men plagued with scorpion-like stings for five months (9:1-12).

(6) One-third of the population destroyed (9:13-21). This destruction coupled with the one under the fourth seal leaves the earth with one-half or less people than entered the tribulation after the rapture of the Church. Yet in spite of all this display of the wrath of God, men will not repent of the evil of their hearts.

c. The mark of the beast is required for trade (13:16-18).

d. Toward the very end of the period and in rapid succession the bowl judgments are poured out on the earth.

(1) Judgment in the earth (16:1-2). This brings grievous sores which are still on people when the fifth bowl is poured out (cf. v. 11).

(2) Judgment in the sea (16:3). All the oceans (which cover 72 per cent of the earth's surface) becomes as blood so that all the fish die.

(3) Judgment in the rivers (16:4-7). The fresh waters also become as blood.

(4) Judgment in the sun (16:8-9). So intense becomes the heat of the sun that men are scorched, and yet they will not repent.

(5) Judgment in the throne of the beast (16:10-11). The capital of his kingdom is plagued with darkness.

(6) Judgment in the Euphrates (16:12-16). The blood-waters of the Euphrates will be dried up so that armies of the nations of the East can pass over quickly.

(7) Judgment in the air (16:17-21). This will cause widespread disturbances and destruction including hailstones weighing 125 pounds each.

e. The commercial system of the world is overthrown (18).

f. The armies of the world will be brought together to the great battle of Armageddon (14:20; 16:14; 19:19).

g. The Lord Jesus Christ will return in power and great glory (19:11-16).

In general, this is a brief sketch of the major events of that terrible period of the outpouring of the wrath of God. That God could do such things men do not deny; that God would do them some find difficult to believe. Two thousand years of relative silence and gracious dealings may have made us insensitive to the holiness, wrath, and justice of God. That God will do these things is the only possible way the plain sense of the text can be understood. One is forced to the conclusion of Seiss:

> . . . if it is not literal, then were not the plagues of Egypt literal, nor is any other sort of fulfilment possible; and thus the tremendous record is rendered meaningless. I take it as it reads; and if any dissent, on them is the burden of proving some other sense, and of reducing to agreement their mutually destructive notions as to what it does mean. Take it as God has caused it to be written, and there can be no disagreement; take it in any other way, and the uncertainty is endless.[7]

VIII. THE MILLENNIUM AND ETERNAL STATE

A. *The Position of Christ*

Of the position of Christ during the millennium and eternal state John has some specific things to say. He was shown that the Lord's rule during the millennium would be world wide in its extent and that it would be forever (the millennium merely being the first part of that, 11:15). It is implied in 20:9 that Jerusalem will be the capital of the millennial kingdom, since that city will be the center of Satan's attack at the end. The character of the King's rule is plainly stated:

> and out of his mouth goeth a sharp sword, that with it he should smite the nations: and he shall rule them with a rod of iron: and he treadeth the winepress of the fierceness and wrath of Almighty God (19:15).

In eternity the Lamb will be over all the universe including the lake of fire (14:10), and He will be the light of the heavenly city (21:23).

B. *The Position of Satan*

At the beginning of the millennium Satan will be bound (20:1-3) in the abyss (9:1-3; 17:8). This is a temporary abode where for a thousand years he will be confined alive

[7]J. A. Seiss, *The Apocalypse* (New York: Charles C. Cook, 1901), III, 72.

so as to be unable to deceive the nations of the earth. At the end of that time he will be loosed and will lead a revolt against God (20:7-9). After this brief release his final judgment will take place and he will be cast into the lake of fire forever in company with the beast, false prophet, and his angels (20:10).

C. *The Position of the Unbeliever*

Unbelievers who are dead have no part in the millennial state, for they will not be raised until after its conclusion (20:11-15). Then they will find their place in the lake of fire forever. Those who are alive and who refuse to accept the King during the millennium will follow Satan in his last revolt, but their eventual destiny is also the lake of fire.

D. *The Position of the Believer*

Believers will be the inhabitants of the New Jerusalem during these periods. Much discussion has been raised among premillennialists as to whether the New Jerusalem is millennial[8] or eternal.[9] In reality the city seems to belong to both periods.[10] John saw it as the dwelling place of the Bride (21:9) which relates it to the millennium. It is also clearly related to eternity as well (21:1-8). In both periods eternal, not temporal, conditions obtain in the city and for its inhabitants. Therefore, the New Jerusalem is millennial and eternal as to time and position, and it is always eternal as to conditions inside it. (Rev. 21:9 ff. seems to be describing the millennial time of the city and its eternal conditions which of course will characterize it even during this time.)

The delights of that city which will be enjoyed by the redeemed include fullness of fellowship with Him who is the fullness of life (22:4), rest (14:13), fullness of blessing (22:

[8]Cf. Scott, Seiss, Gaebelein, Ironside, and Grant.
[9]Cf. Newell, Larkin, and Ottman.
[10]Cf. J. Dwight Pentecost, *Things to Come* (Findlay, Ohio: Dunham Publishing Company, 1958), pp. 563-83.

2), joy (21:4), service (22:3), worship (7:9-12; 19:1), full enjoyment of paradise wherein is no sin or any of its consequences.

Johannine eschatology is in truth

> the crown of that stem whose foliage is spread forth before our eyes in the prophetic and Apostolic writings of the Old and the New Testament. As streams lose themselves in the ocean, so do all the expectations of blessedness opened to us in Scripture unite in the Apocalyptic perspective; and precisely to the latest book of the New Testament the investigation as to the higher unity of the different doctrinal systems attaches itself easily, and as it were, without any effort.[11]

In summing up Johannine theology, let it be repeated that his viewpoint is theological, which is to say Christological, and his principal thought categories are few. The doctrines of God, salvation, and future things encompass all of Johannine theology. His is the true capstone of the doctrinal development of the New Testament from the perspective of Biblical Theology, for the totality of Johannine thought centers in the person of Jesus the Son of God, the redeemer and judge of the world.

[11]J. J. Van Oosterzee, *The Theology of the New Testament* (New York: Dodd and Mead, 1871), p. 414.

Conclusion

OUR SURVEY OF NEW TESTAMENT THEOLOGY has now carried us through all the parts of the progress of revelation as deposited in the New Testament, from the Gospels to the Apocalypse, from Bethlehem to the new Jerusalem. Our task has been to systematize God's truth as it was unfolded through many successive acts and through the minds of the various writers of the New Testament. Our interest has been centered in the different emphases of the human instruments of revelation as seen in their writings. The main divisions of the progress of revelation are readily ascertained, and there can be little debate about them. The Synoptic theology, Pauline theology, and Johannine theology are the three major areas of doctrinal developments, but between the Synoptic and Pauline theologies comes the important contribution of the early Church as seen in Acts and James. Between the Pauline and Johannine theologies comes the later development as reflected in Hebrews and the Epistles of Peter and Jude. Thus, these seven divisions are the obvious categories of New Testament Biblical Theology.

Likewise, the emphasis within these sections have clearly emerged from our study. The Synoptic theology is primarily a theology of the King and His kingdom. This we discovered from Matthew, the theological Gospel, and it is the key which unlocks the theological meaning of the life and ministry of Christ. The theology of Acts is as a bridge between the Gospels and the teachings of Paul. The Acts continues the record of the work of Christ in His resurrected state and introduces the new entity, the Church, the doctrine of which is further developed by Paul. The theology of James shows that the close relationship between doctrine and life was heeded by some and needed by others in the early Church. The principal substructural doctrine of his theology is the Word, which begets us unto the new life and which governs it.

A pivotal point in the progress of revelation in the New Testament is introduced in Pauline theology. Here the new position of the redeemed in the sphere of resurrection life in Christ is revealed. Paul's doctrine is everywhere ethical, to the intent that members of the Body of Christ would practice in all aspects of life their exalted position in Him. Doctrinal consistency between Paul and Christ is apparent, for Pauline theology is largely an elaboration of the Saviour's promise that "at that day ye shall know that I am in my Father, and ye in me, and I in you" (John 14:20). The theologies of Hebrews and Peter and Jude are pointedly Christological, presenting the Lord as the cure for difficulties and aberrations in the life of the Church. The climax of New Testament Theology is reached in the Johannine writings. It is Christ the divine Saviour and Judge who is presented therein. Again continuity is evident, for the Apocalypse is a fulfillment of the Saviour's promise that He would send the Holy Spirit to "show you things to come" (John 16:13). Too, the eschatology of Paul, complete as it is, still needs the final word concerning the consummation as contained in the Revelation. The portents of doctrinal and ethical declension seen in Peter and Jude create a need for a further word from God as given in the last book of the Bible. Thus the development of the self-revelation of God in the New Testament is progressive both in its stages and emphases.

Progressive development and diversified emphasis does

not mean doctrinal disharmony. Everywhere in the historically conditioned progress of revelation there is manifest a

> higher unity . . . [so that] not simply in fundamental
> conception, but also in the presentation of the principal
> subjects, yea, even in a number of unimportant matters,
> there is to be observed an unsought and an unambiguous
> agreement between them [the different writers]. Upon
> no single question of life does the answer of the one
> contradict that of the other. . . .[1]

It was pointed out in the introduction that Biblical Theology is foundational to Systematic Theology. This higher
unity perceived by the method of Biblical Theology proves
the validity of the doctrines of Systematic Theology, for
if the teachings of the various writers of the New Testament only contained a conglomeration of human opinions
which were found often to be contradictory, there would
be no true dogmatics. The cardinal doctrines of God, Christ,
sin, salvation, the Church, and the future are consistently
and harmoniously presented by the writers. Though this
is a phenomenon so remarkable that there is no counterpart in the history of religions, the Christian realizes that
it could not be otherwise; for this unity is the work of
the Lord of Glory, who through the Holy Spirit guided
each human author in his own individual way so that all
contribute without blemish or blur to that perfect and harmonious picture which we call the New Testament Scriptures, supervised by the divine Author Himself. The study
of Biblical Theology gives us overwhelming confidence in the
authority of the Scriptures, for in the survey of the various
parts with their different functions, relations, and emphases
we see the diversities coalescing into a unified doctrinal
scheme. The parts become a whole; in the many writers, we
see the one Author; the books become one Book.

[1]J. J. Van Oosterzee, *The Theology of the New Testament* (New York:
Dodd & Mead, 1871), p. 416.

From the position of students, who address themselves
with critical interest to the works of Matthew, of Paul,
or of John, we have risen to the higher level of believers,
who open with holy joy "the New Testament of our
Lord and Saviour Jesus Christ." . . .[2]

This is the glorious goal toward which Biblical Theology
points.

[2]T. D. Bernard, *The Progress of Doctrine in the New Testament* (Grand
Rapids: Zondervan, n.d.), p. 215.

SELECTED LIST OF BIBLICAL THEOLOGIES

Adeney, W. F. *The Theology of the New Testament*. London: Hodder and Stoughton, 1894.

*Bernard, T. D. *The Progress of Doctrine in the New Testament*. Grand Rapids: Zondervan Publishing House, n. d.

Beyschlag, W. *New Testament Theology*. 2 vols. Edinburgh: T. & T. Clark, 1899.

Bruce, A. B. *St. Paul's Conception of Christianity*. Edinburgh: T. & T. Clark, 1894.

Bultmann, Rudolf. *Theology of the New Testament*. 2 vols. New York: Scribner's, 1951.

Gould, E. P. *The Biblical Theology of the New Testament*. New York: The Macmillan Co., 1900.

Kennedy, H. A. A. *St. Paul's Conceptions of the Last Things*. London: Hodder and Stoughton, 1904.

*———. *The Theology of the Epistles*. London: Duckworth, 1919.

King, J. M. *The Theology of Christ's Teaching*. London: Hodder and Stoughton, 1902.

McNeile, A. H. *St Paul, His Life, Letters, and Christian Doctrine*. Cambridge: Cambridge University Press, 1920.

Moffatt, J. *The Theology of the Gospels*. New York: Charles Scribner's Sons, 1913.

*Ramsay, W. M. *The Teaching of Paul in Terms of the Present Day*. London: Hodder and Stoughton, n. d.

Rostron, S. N. *The Christology of St. Paul*. London: Robert Scott, 1912.

*Schmid, C. F. *Biblical Theology of the New Testament*. Edinburgh: T. & T. Clark, 1877.

Sheldon, H. C. *New Testament Theology*. New York: The Macmillan Co., 1922.

Stauffer, E. *New Testament Theology*. New York: The Macmillan Co., 1955.

*Stevens, G. B. *The Johannine Theology*. London: Richard B. Dickinson, 1894.

*———. *The Pauline Theology*. London: Richard B. Dickinson, 1892.

*———. *The Theology of the New Testament*. Edinburgh: T. & T. Clark, 1899.

Stewart, J. S. *A Man in Christ*. London: Hodder and Stoughton, 1935.

*Van Oosterzee, J. J. *The Theology of the New Testament*. New York: Dodd & Mead Co., 1871.

*Vos, G. *Biblical Theology; Old and New Testaments*. Grand Rapids, Wm. B. Eerdmans Publishing Co., 1954.

*Weidner, R. F. *Biblical Theology of the New Testament*. 2 vols. New York: Fleming H. Revell Co., 1891.

*Weiss, B. *Biblical Theology of the New Testament*. 2 vols. Edinburgh: T. & T. Clark, 1882.

Wilder, A. N. *New Testament Faith for Today*. New York: Harper and Brothers Publishers, 1955.

*These books will be found to be the most helpful and/or to represent viewpoints similar to those taken in this book.

———

BASIC REFERENCE WORKS FOR THE STUDY OF NEW TESTAMENT BIBLICAL THEOLOGY

Alford, H. *The Greek Testament*. 4 vols. London: Rivingtons, 1859. Reprinted, Chicago: Moody Press, 1958.

Allis, O. T. *Prophecy and the Church*. Philadelphia: The Presbyterian and Reformed Publishing Co., 1945.

The Ante-Nicene Fathers. 9 vols. Grand Rapids: Wm. B. Eerdmans Publishing Co., 1951.

Arndt, W. F., and F. W. Gingrich. *A Greek-English Lexicon of the New Testament and Other Early Christian Literature*. Chicago: The University of Chicago Press, 1957.

The Cambridge Greek Testament.

Carnell, E. J. *An Introduction to Christian Apologetics*. Grand Rapids: Wm. B. Eerdmans Publishing Co., 1948.

Carrington, P. *The Early Christian Church.* Cambridge: Cambridge University Press, 1957.

Chafer, L. S. *Systematic Theology.* 8 vols. Dallas: Dallas Seminary Press, 1947.

Davidson, F. *Pauline Predestination.* London: Tyndale Press, 1945.

Edersheim, A. *The Life and Times of Jesus the Messiah.* 2 vols. Grand Rapids: Wm. B. Eerdmans Publishing Co., 1943.

Encyclopaedia Biblica. 4 vols. New York: The Macmillan Co., 1899.

Expositor's Greek Testament. 5 vols. Grand Rapids: Wm. B. Eerdmans Co.

Fairweather, W. *The Background of the Epistles.* 2 vols. Edinburgh: T. & T. Clark, 1908.

Hamilton, F. E. *The Basis of Millennial Faith.* Grand Rapids: Wm. B. Eerdmans Publishing Co., 1952.

Hastings, J. *A Dictionary of the Apostolic Church.* 2 vols. Edinburgh: T. & T. Clark, 1915.

——. *A Dictionary of the Bible.* 5 vols. New York: Charles Scribner's Sons, 1901.

——. *A Dictionary of Christ and the Gospels.* 2 vols. Edinburgh: T. & T. Clark, 1912.

The International Critical Commentary. Edinburgh: T. & T. Clark.

The International Standard Bible Encyclopaedia. 5 vols. Grand Rapids: Wm. B. Eerdmans Publishing Co., 1947.

Kennedy, H. A. A. *St. Paul and the Mystery-Religions.* New York: Hodder and Stoughton, n. d.

Ladd, G. E. *Crucial Questions About the Kingdom of God.* Grand Rapids: Wm. B. Eerdmans Publishing Co., 1952.

Machen, J. G. *Christianity and Liberalism.* New York: The Macmillan Co., 1923.

——. *The Origin of Paul's Religion.* New York: The Macmillan Co., 1921.

McNeile, A. H. *An Introduction to the Study of the New Testament.* Oxford: Oxford University Press, 1953.

Morris, L. *The Apostolic Preaching of the Cross.* Grand Rapids: Wm. B. Eerdmans Publishing Co., 1955.

Moulton, J. H., and Milligan, G. *The Vocabulary of the Greek Testament.* Grand Rapids: Wm. B. Eerdmans Publishing Co., 1952.

Pentecost, J. D. *Things to Come.* Findlay, Ohio: Dunham Publishing Co., 1958.

Peters, G. N. H. *The Theocratic Kingdom.* 3 vols. Grand Rapids: Kregel, 1952.

Ramm, B. *Protestant Christian Evidences.* Chicago: Moody Press, 1953.

Ramsay, W. M. *The Church in the Roman Empire Before A.D. 170.* London: Hodder and Stoughton, 1894. Reprinted, Grand Rapids: Baker Book House.

Robertson, A. T. *A Grammar of the Greek New Testament in the Light of Historical Research.* New York: Hodder and Stoughton, 1919.

————. *Luke the Historian in the Light of Research.* Edinburgh: T. & T. Clark, 1920.

Ryrie, C. C. *The Basis of the Premillennial Faith.* New York: Loizeaux Brothers, 1953.

Schaff, P. *History of the Christian Church.* 8 vols. Grand Rapids: Wm. B. Eerdmans Publishing Co., 1950.

Scroggie, W. G. *Guide to the Gospels.* London: Pickering and Inglis, 1948.

————. *Know Your Bible.* London: Pickering and Inglis, 1940.

Stibbs, A. M. *The Meaning of the Word "Blood" in Scripture.* London: Tyndale Press, 1947.

Tenney, M. C. *The New Testament, An Historical and Analytical Survey.* Grand Rapids: Wm. B. Eerdmans Publishing Co., 1953.

Warfield, B. B. *The Lord of Glory.* London: Hodder and Stoughton, 1907. Reprinted, Grand Rapids: Zondervan Publishing House.

Wright, G. E. *Biblical Archaeology.* Philadelphia: Westminster Press, 1957.

Zahn, T. *Introduction to the New Testament.* 3 vols. Grand Rapids: Kregel, 1953.

Commentaries on various New Testament books by J. B. Lightfoot, C. J. Ellicott, F. Godet, B. F. Westcott, A. Plummer, and K. Wuest.

WORKS CITED

Alexander, J. A. *The Acts of the Apostles*. New York: Charles Scribner's Sons, 1872. Reprinted, Grand Rapids, Zondervan Publishing House.

Alford, H. *The Greek Testament*. 4 vols. London: Rivingtons, 1859. Reprinted, Chicago: Moody Press, 1958.

Allen, W. C. *A Critical and Exegetical Commentary on the Gospel According to St. Matthew. International Critical Commentary*. Edinburgh: T. & T. Clark, 1907.

Allis, O. T. *Prophecy and the Church*. Philadelphia: The Presbyterian and Reformed Publishing Co., 1945.

Appleton, G. *John's Witness to Jesus*. New York: Association Press, 1955.

Baur, F. C. *Paul, His Life and Works*. London: Williams and Norgate, 1876.

Bernard, T. D. *The Progress of Doctrine in the New Testament*. Grand Rapids: Zondervan Publishing House, n. d.

Beyschlag, W. *New Testament Theology*. Edinburgh: T. & T. Clark, 1899.

Bigg, C. *A Critical and Exegetical Commentary on the Epistles of St. Peter and St. Jude. International Critical Commentary*. Edinburgh: T. & T. Clark, 1902.

Blenkin, G. W. *The First Epistle General of Peter. Cambridge Greek Testament*. Cambridge: Cambridge University Press, 1914.

Bruce, F. F. *The Acts of the Apostles*. Chicago: Inter-Varsity Christian Fellowship, 1952.

Brumback, C. *"What Meaneth This?"* Springfield, Mo.: Gospel Publishing House, 1947.

Brunner, E. *Man in Revolt*. Philadelphia: Westminster Press, 1947.

Buis, H. *The Doctrine of Eternal Punishment*. Philadelphia: Presbyterian and Reformed Publishing Co., 1957.

Calvin, J. *The Institutes of the Christian Religion*. Translated by Henry Beveridge. 2 vols. Grand Rapids: Wm. B. Eerdmans Publishing Co., 1953.

Carnell, E. J. *An Introduction to Christian Apologetics.* Grand Rapids: Wm. B. Eerdmans Publishing Co., 1948.

Carr, A. *The Gospel According to St. Matthew. Cambridge Bible for Schools and Colleges.* Cambridge: Cambridge University Press, 1896.

————. *St. James. Cambridge Greek Testament.* Cambridge: Cambridge University Press, 1896.

————. *St. Matthew. Cambridge Greek Testament.* Cambridge: Cambridge University Press, 1887.

Carrington, P. *The Early Christian Church.* Cambridge: Cambridge University Press, 1957.

Chafer, L. S. *Systematic Theology.* 8 vols. Dallas: Dallas Seminary Press, 1947.

Clarke, W. K. L. *New Testament Problems.* London: Society for Promoting Christian Knowledge, 1929.

Crichton, J. "Messiah," *International Standard Bible Encyclopaedia.* Grand Rapids: Wm. B. Eerdmans Publishing Co., 1943.

Dana, H. E., and Mantey, J. R. *A Manual Grammar of the Greek New Testament.* New York: The Macmillan Co., 1927.

Davidson, F. *Pauline Predestination.* London: Tyndale Press, 1945.

Deissmann, A. *Bible Studies.* Edinburgh: T. & T. Clark, 1901.

————. *Light from the Ancient East.* New York: Hodder and Stoughton, n. d.

Dix, Gregory. *The Apostolic Ministry.* K. E. Kirk, ed. London: Hodder and Stoughton, 1946.

Edersheim, A. *The Life and Times of Jesus the Messiah.* Grand Rapids: Wm. B. Eerdmans Publishing Co., 1943.

————. *The Temple, its Ministry and Services.* London: Religious Tract Society, 1908. Reprinted, Grand Rapids: Wm. B. Eerdmans Publishing Co.

Edwards, D. M. "Mystery," *International Standard Bible Encyclopaedia.* Grand Rapids: Wm. B. Eerdmans Publishing Co., 1943.

Ellicott, C. J. *A Critical and Grammatical Commentary on St. Paul's Epistles to the Philippians, Colossians, and to Philemon.* London: Longmans, Green, and Co., 1888.

English, E. S. *Re-thinking the Rapture*. Travelers Rest, S. C.: Southern Bible Book House, 1954.

Eusebius. *Ecclesiastical History*.

Filson, F. V. "The Epistle to the Hebrews," *Journal of Bible and Religion*. January, 1954.

Finney, C. G. *Lectures on Systematic Theology*. South Gate, Calif.: Colporter Kemp, 1944.

Gibbon, E. *The Decline and Fall of the Roman Empire*.

Godet, F. L. *A Commentary on St. Paul's Epistle to the Romans*. Edinburgh: T. & T. Clark, n. d. Reprinted, Grand Rapids: Zondervan Publishing House.

———. *A Commentary on the Gospel of St. Luke*. Edinburgh: T. & T. Clark, 1890.

Gore, C. *The Question of Divorce*. London: John Murray, 1911.

Gray, J. M. "Peter," *International Standard Bible Encyclopaedia*. Grand Rapids: Wm. B. Eerdmans Publishing Co., 1943.

Hamilton, F. E. *The Basis of Millennial Faith*. Grand Rapids: Wm. B. Eerdmans Publishing Co., 1952.

Harnack, A. *What is Christianity?* London: Williams and Norgate, 1904.

Harrison, P. N. *The Problem of the Pastoral Epistles*. London: Oxford, 1921.

Henry, C. F. H. *Christian Personal Ethics*. Grand Rapids: Wm. B. Eerdmans Publishing Co., 1957.

Hobart, W. K. *Medical Language of St. Luke*. London: Longmans, Green, and Co., 1882. Reprinted, Grand Rapids: Baker Book House.

Hogg, C. F., and Watson, J. B. *On the Sermon on the Mount*. London: Pickering and Inglis, 1933.

Irenaeus. *Against Heresies*.

James, M. R. *The Second Epistle General of Peter and the General Epistle of Jude*. Cambridge Greek Testament. Cambridge: Cambridge University Press, 1912.

Kelly, W. *Lectures on the Church of God*. London: Morrish, 1918.

———. *The Preaching to the Spirits in Prison*. London: F. C. Race, n. d.

Kennedy, H. A. A. *St. Paul and the Mystery-Religions.* New York: Hodder and Stoughton, n. d.

———. *St. Paul's Conceptions of the Last Things.* London: Hodder and Stoughton, 1904.

———. *The Theology of the Epistles.* London: Duckworth, 1919.

King, J. M. *The Theology of Christ's Teaching.* London: Hodder and Stoughton, 1902.

Kraeling, C. H. *John the Baptist.* New York: Charles Scribner's Sons, 1951.

Ladd, G. E. *Crucial Questions About the Kingdom of God.* Grand Rapids: Wm. B. Eerdmans Publishing Co., 1952.

Lenski, R. C. H. *The Interpretation of the Epistles of St. Peter, St. John, and St. Jude.* Columbus, Ohio: Lutheran Book Concern, 1938.

Liddon, H. P. *St. Paul's First Epistle to Timothy.* London: Oxford, 1897.

Lightfoot, J. B. *Biblical Essays.* London: The Macmillan Co., 1893.

———. *St. Paul's Epistle to the Philippians.* London: The Macmillan Co., 1885. Reprinted, Grand Rapids: Zondervan Publishing House.

Lillie, J. *Lectures on the First and Second Epistles of Peter.* London: Hodder and Stoughton, 1870.

Lindsay, J. "Biblical Theology," *International Standard Bible Encyclopaedia.* Grand Rapids: Wm. B. Eerdmans Publishing Co., 1943.

Lindsay, T. M. "Baptism," *International Standard Bible Encyclopaedia.* Grand Rapids: Wm. B. Eerdmans Publishing Co., 1943.

Lock, W. "Love-feasts," *A Dictionary of the Bible.* Ed. J. Hastings. Edinburgh: T. & T. Clark, 1899.

Machen, J. G. *Christianity and Liberalism.* New York: The Macmillan Co., 1923.

———. *The Origin of Paul's Religion.* New York: The Macmillan Co., 1921.

———. *The Virgin Birth of Christ.* New York: Harper and Brothers Publishers, 1930.

McNeile, A. H. *An Introduction to the Study of the New Testament.* Oxford: Oxford University Press, 1953.

——. *St. Paul. His Life, Letters, and Christian Doctrine.* Cambridge: Cambridge University Press, 1920.

Manson, W. *The Epistle to the Hebrews.* London: Hodder & Stoughton, 1941.

Major, H. D. A., Manson, T. W. and Wright, C. J. *The Mission and Message of Jesus.* London: Ivor Nicholson and Watson, 1937.

Mayor, J. B. *The Epistle of St. James.* London: The Macmillan Co., 1897. Reprinted, Grand Rapids: Zondervan Publishing House.

Miller, R. B. "Sermon on the Mount," *International Standard Bible Encyclopaedia.* Grand Rapids: Wm. B. Eerdmans Publishing Co., 1943.

Milligan, G. *The Theology of the Epistle to the Hebrews.* Edinburgh: T. & T. Clark, 1899.

Moffatt, J. *A Critical and Exegetical Commentary on the Epistle to the Hebrews. International Critical Commentary.* New York: Charles Scribner's Sons, 1924.

——. *The Theology of the Gospels.* New York: Charles Scribner's Sons, 1913.

Moorehead, W. G. "Jude, The Epistle of," *International Standard Bible Encyclopaedia.* Grand Rapids: Wm. B. Eerdmans Publishing Co., 1943.

Morris, L. *The Apostolic Preaching of the Cross.* Grand Rapids: Wm. B. Eerdmans Publishing Co., 1955.

Newell, W. R. *Hebrews Verse by Verse.* Chicago: Moody Press, 1947.

Nicole, R. "Old Testament Quotations in the New Testament." *The Gordon Review.* February, 1955.

O'Hair, J. C. *A Dispensational Study of the Bible.* Chicago: O'Hair, n. d.

Orr, J. "The Bible," *International Standard Bible Encyclopaedia.* Grand Rapids: Wm. B. Eerdmans Publishing Co., 1943.

Pentecost, J. D. *Things To Come.* Findlay, Ohio: Dunham Publishing Co., 1958.

Peters, G. N. H. *The Theocratic Kingdom.* 3 vols. Grand Rapids: Kregel, 1952.

Plummer, A. *The Epistles of John. Cambridge Greek Testament.* Cambridge: Cambridge University Press, 1886.

———. *A Critical and Exegetical Commentary on the Gospel According to St. Luke. International Critical Commentary.* Edinburgh: T. & T. Clark, 1910.

———. "The General Epistles of St. James and St. Jude." *Expositor's Bible.* Grand Rapids: Wm. B. Eerdmans Publishing Co., 1943.

———. *The Gospel According to St. John. Cambridge Greek Testament.* Cambridge: Cambridge University Press, 1891.

Plumptre, E. H. *The General Epistle of St. Peter and St. Jude. Cambridge Bible for Schools and Colleges.* Cambridge: Cambridge University Press, 1893.

Rackham, R. B. *The Acts of the Apostles.* London: Methuen and Co., 1951.

Ramsay, W. M. *The Church in the Roman Empire Before A.D. 170.* London: Hodder and Stoughton, 1894. Reprinted, Grand Rapids: Baker Book House.

———. *The Teaching of Paul in Terms of the Present Day.* London: Hodder and Stoughton, n. d.

———. *Was Christ Born at Bethlehem?* London: Hodder and Stoughton, 1898.

Renan, E. *The Apostles.* New York: Carleton, 1869.

Robertson, A., and Plummer, A. *A Critical and Exegetical Commentary on the First Epistle of St. Paul to the Corinthians. International Critical Commentary.* Edinburgh: T. & T. Clark, 1914.

Robertson, A. T. *A Grammar of the Greek New Testament in the Light of Historical Research.* New York: Hodder and Stoughton, 1919.

———. *Luke the Historian in the Light of Research.* Edinburgh: T. & T. Clark, 1920.

———. *Word Pictures in the New Testament.* New York: Harper and Brothers Publishers, 1930.

Robinson, J. A. "Deacon and Deaconess." *Encyclopaedia Biblica.* London: Oxford, 1897.

Rostron, S. N. *The Christology of St. Paul.* London: Robert
    Scott, 1912.

Ryle, J. C. *Expository Thoughts on the Gospels.* New York:
    Baker and Taylor, 1858. Reprinted, Grand Rapids: Zondervan.

Ryrie, C. C. *The Basis of the Premillennial Faith.* New York:
    Loizeaux Brothers, 1953.

———. *The Place of Women in the Church.* New York: The Mac-
    millan Co., 1958.

———. "The Significance of Pentecost," *Bibliotheca Sacra,* Octo-
    ber, 1955.

Salmon, G. *The Human Element in the Gospels.* London: John
    Murray, 1908.

Sanday, W., and Headlam, A. C. *A Critical and Exegetical Com-
    mentary on the Epistle to the Romans. International Critical
    Commentary.* New·York: Charles Scribner's Sons, 1895.

Schaff, P. *History of the Christian Church.* 8 vols. Grand Rapids:
    Wm. B. Eerdmans Publishing Co., 1950.

Schechter, S. *Some Aspects of Rabbinic Theology.* New York: The
    Macmillan Co., 1923.

Schmid, C. F. *Biblical Theology of the New Testament.* Edin-
    burgh: T. & T. Clark, 1877.

Schmiedel, P. W. "Resurrection and Ascension Narratives," *En-
    cyclopaedia Biblica.* New York: The Macmillan Co., 1914.

Schultz, H. *Old Testament Theology.* Edinburgh: T. & T. Clark,
    1895.

Schurer, E. *A History of the Jewish People in the Time of Jesus
    Christ.* Edinburgh: T. & T. Clark, 1890.

Schwarze, F. C. "The Bible and Science on the Everlasting Fire,"
    Bibliotheca Sacra. January, 1938.

Scroggie, W. G. *The Book of the Revelation.* Cleveland, Ohio:
    Union Gospel Press, 1920.

———. *Guide to the Gospels.* London: Pickering and Inglis, 1948.

———. *Know Your Bible.* London: Pickering and Inglis, 1940.

Seiss, J. A. *The Apocalypse.* New York: Charles C. Cook, 1901.
    Reprinted, Grand Rapids: Zondervan Publishing House.

Sheldon, H. C. *New Testament Theology.* New York: The Mac-
    millan Co., 1922.

Smith, W. R., and von Soden, H. "Hebrews," *Encyclopaedia Biblica.* New York: The Macmillan Co., 1914.

Stevens, G. B. *The Johannine Theology.* London: Richard B. Dickinson, 1894.

——. *The Pauline Theology.* London: Richard B. Dickinson, 1892.

——. *The Theology of the New Testament.* Edinburgh: T. & T. Clark, 1899.

Stewart, J. S. *A Man in Christ.* London: Hodder and Stoughton, 1935.

Stibbs, A. M. *The Meaning of the Word "Blood" in Scripture.* London: Tyndale Press, 1947.

Tenney, M. C. *The New Testament, An Historical and Analytical Survey.* Grand Rapids: Wm. B. Eerdmans Publishing Co., 1953.

Trench, R. C. *The Star of the Wise Men.* Philadelphia: H. Hooker, 1850.

——. *Synonyms of the New Testament.* Grand Rapids: Wm. B. Eerdmans Publishing Co., 1950.

Van Oosterzee, J. J. *The Theology of the New Testament.* New York: Dodd and Mead, 1871.

Vitringa. *De Synagoga Vetere.* Franequerae: Johannis Gyzelaar, 1696.

Vos, G. *Biblical Theology.* Grand Rapids: Wm. B. Eerdmans Publishing Co., 1954.

Warfield, B. B. *The Lord of Glory.* London: Hodder and Stoughton, 1907. Reprinted, Grand Rapids: Zondervan Publishing House.

——. "Predestination," *A Dictionary of the Bible.* Ed. J. Hastings. Edinburgh: T. & T. Clark, 1902.

Weidner, R. F. *Biblical Theology of the New Testament.* New York: Fleming H. Revell Co., 1891.

Weiss, B. *Biblical Theology of the New Testament.* Edinburgh: T. & T. Clark, 1882.

Wenley, R. M. "Philo," *International Standard Bible Encyclopaedia.* Grand Rapids: Wm. B. Eerdmans Publishing Co., 1943.

Westcott, B. F. *The Epistle to the Hebrews.* London: The Macmillan Co., 1892. Reprinted, Grand Rapids: Wm. B. Eerdmans Publishing Co.

———. *The Gospel of St. John.* London: John Murray, 1908. Reprinted, Grand Rapids: Wm. B. Eerdmans Publishing Co.

Wilder, A. N. *New Testament Faith for Today.* New York: Harper and Brothers Publishers, 1955.

Wuest, K. S. *First Peter in the Greek New Testament.* Grand Rapids: Wm. B. Eerdmans Publishing Co., 1945.

———. "The Rapture-Precisely When?" *Bibliotheca Sacra.* January, 1957.

Zahn, T. *Introduction to the New Testament.* 3 vols. Grand Rapids: Kregel, 1953.

Subject Index

Scripture Index

This is a selected list of references limited for the most part to passages on which interpretative comment is made in the text.